THE LEGACY OF JAMES COOK

The Story of the Bay of Islands

Brian J. S. Harley

Canadian Cataloguing in Publication Data

Harley, Brian J. S., 1924
THE LEGACY OF JAMES COOK
THE STORY OF THE BAY OF ISLANDS

ISBN 0-9684476-0-0

Published by:
Harkim Enterprises Limited
8 Stonehenge Place,
Corner Brook, NF A2H 3B4
Tel/Fax 709 634-1625

Original Illustrations and Cover Painting By:
Ed Hollett of Hollett Visual Communications

Printed and bound in Canada

Robinson Blackmore Publishing and Printing Limited
Grand Falls-Windsor, Nfld.

To my parents
who sacrificed for my education
and were so sad to see me emigrate to Canada

Acknowledgements

Many residents, and especially those of the faculty of Grenfell College have given me information, pictures and support. As I was denied funding from the Provincial Arts Council and did not qualify for funding from the Canada Council. I was fortunate to obtain the services of Ches Loughlin, who organized the production of this book, and the staff of Robinson Blackmore Printing and Publishing Limited, who printed it in a timely fashion.

I would like to thank my editor Heidi Cramm and Beverly Green and Janet Neville for their computer expertise. Also all the librarians who assisted me with research at libraries in U.K. and Newfoundland, especially Elizabeth Behrens and her staff at the Ferris Hodgett Library at Grenfell College. Professor Olaf Janzen gave me invaluable help and guidance with the historical sections and Bruce Stevenson made copies of old Western Star editions available to me.

Bob Verge, publisher of the Western Star and Rita Atkinson of the Humber Log were most helpful, as was constable Ken Dean, the curator of the R.N.C. Museum, Gordon Billard, the curator of the Anglican Synod records and Olga Eastman, an enthusiastic supporter of the Corner Brook Museum.

I feel that Ed Hollett's chapter icons and cover drawing enlivened this edition and I am grateful to Don Meiwald for photographing the Pilot Paintings and to Warwick Hewitt for drawing some charts and the pictures of Reverend Curling's two vessels.

CONTENTS

THE LEGACY OF JAMES COOK

A History of the Bay of Islands

FOREWORD

The west coast of Newfoundland still seems a remote area of the island to many Canadians and sometimes even to those living on the Avalon Peninsula of Newfoundland. It's development proceeded quite differently from the rest of Newfoundland for complex reasons detailed in this book. Permanent settlement only started in the 18th century. When James Cook produced the first accurate map of the area after his visit in 1767 he recorded no signs of settlement in the Bay of Islands. Our history of settlement on the West Coast is somewhat unique, as there is no evidence of displacement or destruction of an indigenous native people by settlers such as occurred with the Beothucks on the East Coast of Newfoundland and of other native peoples in North and South America.

I am not a professional historian but am inclined to agree somewhat with Thomas Carlyle's view that "The history of the world is but the biography of great men." In compiling this work I have therefore highlighted the contributions of great men such as Joseph Curling, Thomas Sears, Eric Bowater, and several other men and women, and especially that of James Cook. In Cook's case, I have recounted his biography up to his departure from Newfoundland in 1767. In view of the international significance of his later Pacific voyages of discovery, I have emphasized that the 5 summers he spent surveying in Newfoundland were instrumental in making his later voyages so successful.

I have also tried to picture for you how the early pioneers lived and remind you that the comparative prosperity of the Bay of Islands in today's Newfoundland is also due to the efforts of ordinary men and women. Some historians have assumed that prosperity in Corner Brook is primarily due to the construction and function of the paper mill. This belief stems from Sir Richard Squires' claim that the building of this paper mill would "put the Hum on the Humber." I will describe several other factors which I have termed magnets and which, like the paper mill, have contributed to making Corner Brook the focal settlement not only in the Bay but of the whole west coast and have indeed put a hum on the Humber.

In so doing, I have tried to be as accurate as possible. However it is more than likely that inaccurate dates and details are present and I can only hope that readers will excuse me; relying on oral histories and historical personal accounts has inherent problems. I have tried to indicate my sources wherever possible. I must also point out that some readers may disagree with me on some matters, especially my views on recent events and future prospects for this area. References to a person's opinion or statement usually refers to their comments recorded in the Bowater Oral History Project donated to the City of Corner Brook and now located in Grenfell College library, unless otherwise stated. Permission to use the story attached to the Crosbie Dehydrating Plant was given by Linda Harris and that of the fate of the Flirt by Robinson Blackmore.

Please note that the use of the term West Coast, refers to the west coast of Newfoundland and B. of I. refers to the Bay of Islands, Newfoundland (Cook named another Bay of Islands in New Zealand).

As this book was produced for entertaiment rather than reference I have omitted an index and have amplified the descriptions of the chapter headings.

The Canada Winter Games will be hosted by this part of the west coast of Newfoundland, centred in Corner Brook. Residents hope that this occasion will bring many visitors to this part of Canada and that this book may enable them to learn something of its unique history and friendly people.

James Cook

*From the painting by Nathaniel Price
(1776)*

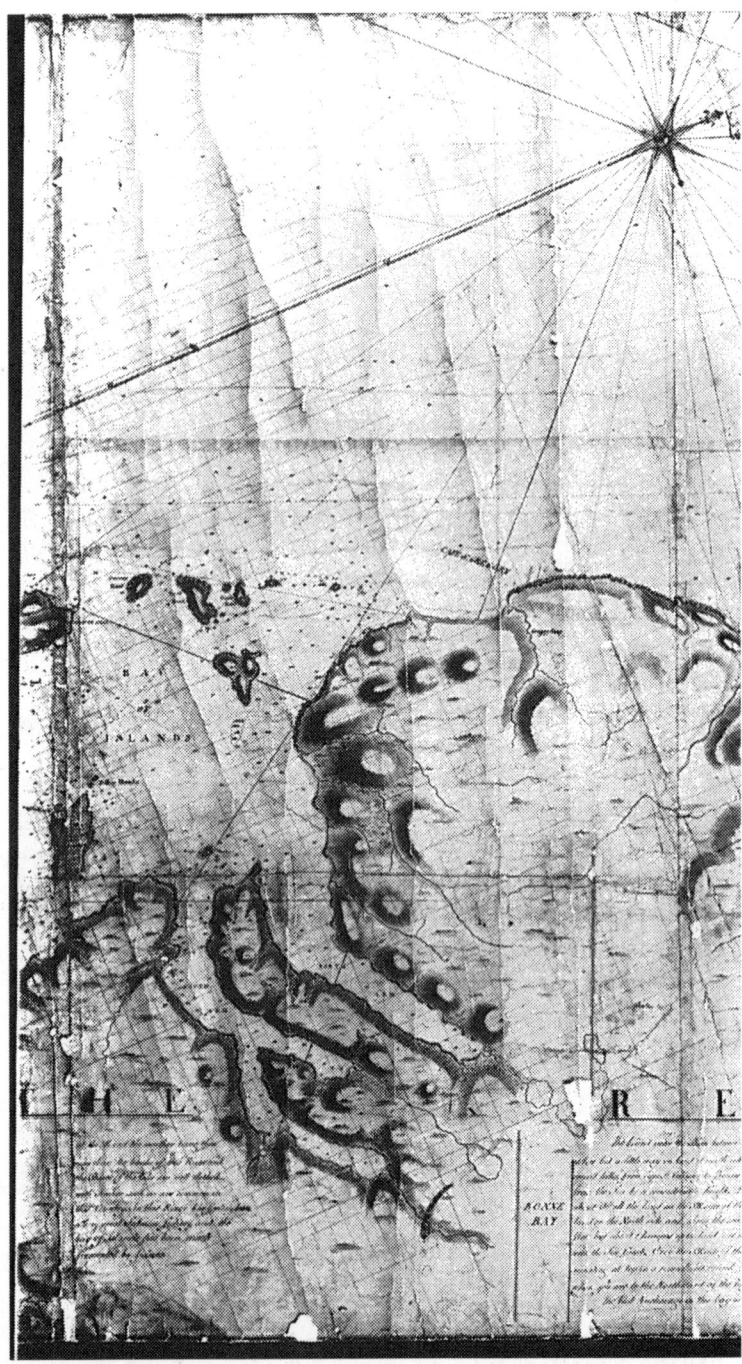

These facing pages show a microfilm copy of Cook's original charts produced in 1767. These charts are old and have not reproduced well.

Left, Bay of Islands. Above, Bonne Bay
—From a microfilm purchased from the Admiralty
Hydrographic Museum, Taunton, U.K.

The young Dr. Harley's first visit to Newfoundland

Outer Bay of Islands, Newfoundland — Photo courtesy of Douglas Cook

Introduction

My first visit to the Bay of Islands was in April 1956 when I responded to an advertisement in the <u>Canadian Medical Journal</u> and decided to fly from Ottawa to the west coast of Newfoundland, to check the potential for a private practice in Internal Medicine in the city of Corner Brook. I expected that there would be transportation by road for the 60-mile journey from what was then the only airport on the west coast, located close to the then active USAF base in Stephenville. I was surprised to learn on arrival that the woods road from Stephenville Crossing to Corner Brook was closed because of the spring breakup. This apparently happened every year at about the same time. The only method of transportation was the passenger train, popularly known as the "Newfie Bullet," that travelled daily in each direction from Port aux Basques to St. John's. I boarded it at Stephenville Crossing, a 10-mile taxi drive from the airport. The train was not full and I was so excited that I was on my feet for most of the journey, admiring the scenery as we slowly wended our way up Harry's River to George's Lake and down Cook's Brook, and I can still recall my amazement at the first sight of the Bay of Islands at Mount Moriah. The scene had a majestic quality about it, reminiscent of what I had previously seen in Scotland, with steep cliffs visible to the left and small settlements set on sloping hills to the right leading eventually to the town of Curling and then Corner Brook.

My visit was a successful one; I first experienced the friendly hospitality of the townspeople, especially the doctors and their families who welcomed me as the first potential medical specialist outside St. John's. So different from my experience in Ottawa where, as an immigrant, I was perceived as a potential competitor.

I decided to locate in Corner Brook, in spite of my chief's advice to me after I had returned to Ottawa to complete my year's residency. When I told him that I felt that my services were welcomed and needed in Newfoundland, he said "Newfoundland may need you, but you don't need Newfoundland." For some reason this had the opposite effect on me than he had intended and only confirmed my decision to move my family to Corner Brook. At the time my sole partners and possessions were a wife, a 3-year-old daughter, a beaten up second-hand car, and a cat. After my previous visit to west Newfoundland and the experience of the unpaved road system, I welcomed the chance of travelling by the M. V. Gulf Port, which was employed by Clarke Steamship Company to carry merchandise from Montreal to Corner Brook. This passenger service was discontinued after 1965, once the Trans Canada Highway had been completed and paved in Newfoundland.

The 5-day journey down the St. Lawrence to Corner Brook was another trip I will always remember. The weather was good, the cabin was comfortable and even the cat seemed happily looking forward to a new life in a part of the world that was clearly unappreciated by the rest of Canada and some may say still is. On the 5th day we saw three big islands at the mouth of the bay, Guernsey Island popularly known as Weeball with its awesome sheer cliff faces, Tweed Island with its historical significance to the Basque and French fishermen and Pearl Island, the Big Island, as well as several of the nine smaller islands, all of which lie at the entrance to the three major fjords. As we sailed up the Humber Arm on a beautiful June morning we passed small communities on both sides as well as a community still present on Woods Island. A dramatic entrance to Corner Brook indeed, situated as it is almost at the upper end of the arm and marked by the ever-present columns of smoke from the paper mill.

There are now only two main tourist routes to enter the Bay of Islands from the mainland, since the Trans Canada Highway was completed and paved in 1965. Premier Joseph Smallwood gave "thanks to Mr. Pearson" then the Prime Minister of the government in Ottawa, because 90% of the construction cost was given to the province by the federal government for completion of the project. The Newfoundland

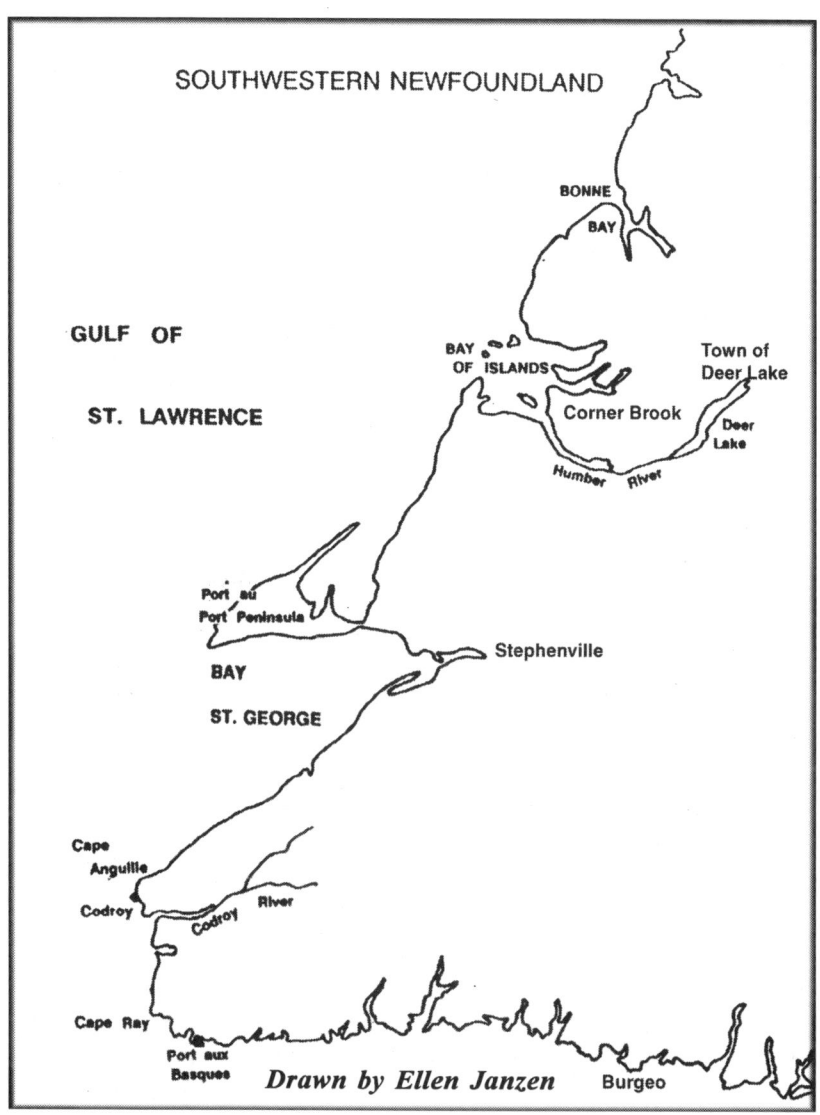

SOUTHWESTERN NEWFOUNDLAND

BONNE BAY

GULF OF

BAY OF ISLANDS

Town of Deer Lake

Corner Brook

Deer Lake

ST. LAWRENCE

Humber River

Port au Port Peninsula

Stephenville

BAY

ST. GEORGE

Cape Anguille

Codroy

Codroy River

Cape Ray

Port aux Basques

Drawn by Ellen Janzen

Burgeo

railway ceased operating in 1988, much to the sorrow of most Newfoundlanders. There is now no passenger steamship connecting with Montreal but occasional tourist liners still come into the Bay of Islands, mostly in the fall when the climate is usually benign and the colours in the woods are quite spectacular. Merchant ships still use the harbour at the oil terminals and at the terminal at Seal Cove in Corner Brook, and paper boats still carry pulp and paper from the mill to all ports of the world. Stephenville airport is now also used less frequently, as Air Canada and Canadian Airlines now fly into the new airport at Deer Lake. But a ferry service to the mainland is preserved by Marine Atlantic from North Sydney to Port aux Basques all the year round and to Argentia, on the Avalon peninsula, in summer. Travel from Channel/ Port aux Basques to the Bay of Islands continues along the Trans Canada Highway.

Perhaps it would now be appropriate to introduce the reader not acquainted with West Newfoundland and adjacent areas by briefly describing some points of interest on the journey to Corner Brook, the largest settlement in the Bay of Islands, first from Port aux Basques and then from Deer Lake. In this way we may perhaps understand the interdependence among communities developing in the west coast, now that there is a university campus in Corner Brook, and a Regional Health Board for the west coast from Port Saunders to Burgeo, a community on the south coast.

Unfortunately for the town of Port aux Basques, travellers usually arrive on the Marine Atlantic ferry from North Sydney somewhat tired by the journey, either early in the morning or late in the evening. Most tourists join the Trans Canada Highway and drive straight through the town passing between two mountains at the most southerly part of the Long Range Mountains, missing the old settlement of Cape Ray and a rather fine sandy beach. The road then passes through a notorious portion of the route known as "Wreckhouse," an open flat bog bounded by the sea on the left and the dark brooding mountains on the right. The area is notorious because of the exceptionally high winds which funnel across the road, making visibility impossibly difficult in the winter and occasionally blowing even large tractor trailers off the road in any season. W. E. Cormack in 1822 described the scenery amongst the mountains here as "sublime; the steep sides of the wedge shaped valleys appear smooth and striped at a distance, owing to the crumbled rocks and blocks detached by frost being hurled from the very summits to the bottom where they lie in heaps of ruins."

Soon we enter the Codroy Valley, the most fertile area of the west coast and indeed of the island. This area was settled by Gaelic-speaking Scots from Cape Breton in the 19th century and has the fine salmon river of the Codroy running placidly through meadows with the towering Long Range Mountains in the background. Turn off at Doyles to take a circuit through this picturesque valley. The name Codroy, by the way, is probably an Anglicised corruption of the Basque name Ca' de Ray becoming Cadray and eventually Codroy. The Basque fishermen used Codroy Island as an anchorage. It was the only one between Port aux Basques and St. George's Bay.

The next communities are known as the Highlands, settled at the mouths of the half dozen or so salmon rivers which run into the gulf from the Long Range Mountains. Unfortunately salmon are now scarce in these rivers due to a combination of circumstances including destruction of spawning grounds by timber cutting near river banks, the capture of salmon in cod traps and commercial fishing operations and of course, by poaching, which was considered an acceptable way of life in some coastal communities.

Before long excellent views can be had of St. George's Bay, the town of Stephenville, and the Port au Port Peninsula, an area of some excitement at this time because of a possible oil find. Later we cross the road to that peninsula, which is also well worth a side trip. The population here is different from other ports of the west coast, with some Acadians and French from St. Pierre settling on the isolated peninsula. The language is being preserved; some older residents speak only a dialect of French distinct from that of the Québécois. There are also a number of what English settlers call Jack O'Tars in the Bay St. George. These people are descendants of Mic Mac Indians who came from Nova Scotia and who often intermarried with the French. They speak English with a distinctive accent.

For 30 or 40 miles into Corner Brook the Trans Canada Highway has no large settlements but passes through moose hunting areas with pleasant wooded hills and valleys, descending Gallants Hill to cottage country on the shores of George's Lake and Pinchgut. Finally one passes through a short defile and suddenly the Bay of Islands comes into view. I still often catch my breath when I come through this area on a fine day in summer. Unfortunately, there is only a small parking space on the left side of the divided highway which has been designed as a viewing area, although there is a roadway on the top of the hill where one can take a photograph.

If you arrive by plane you will likely land in Deer Lake airport about 45 kilometres north of Corner Brook. This airport has a fine new airport terminal which opened in 1986 and has an unusually fine record of air worthiness. Heading south after leaving the airport, you pass the intersection with the Northern Peninsula Highway, designated as the Viking trail, which leads to St. Anthony. This trip is a must for anyone staying in the area for any length of time, though a full exploration of that trail needs several days as there are many interesting sites to visit. Major attractions include Gros Morne National Park with its peerless scenic drive through Bonne Bay, the trip to Trout River and its lake through the eerie Martian landscape of Table Mountain, and of course Gros Morne, one of the highest mountains in the Long Range and in the island of Newfoundland. If the weather is poor, a pleasant and informative time could be spent browsing in the Park Visitor Centre and swimming pool. In summer a boat trip up Western Brook fjord or Trout River is very rewarding.

Many people go no further on the highway but there are several places to explore on the route before one reaches L'Anse aux Meadows, the National Historic Site of the first Viking settlement, and St. Anthony with its museums dedicated to the Grenfell Mission which began its work on the Northern Peninsula and in Labrador late in the last century. It would be unfortunate not to visit Port aux Choix with its Maritime Archaic Indian Museum and settlement, just as it would be not to fish the fine salmon rivers along the coast. If you take the route from Plum Point to Roddicton, you will likely see several moose. The only way a tourist can reach the south shore of Labrador and visit the Basque Whaling Site at Red Bay is by ferry from St. Barbe to Blanc Sablon and it would also be a mistake not to make this trip, with perhaps the bonus of seeing a humpback whale or an iceberg en route.

But our main task is to describe the journey from Deer Lake south to the Bay of Islands and for our purposes we will pass up the trip down the Northern Peninsula and instead drive by the growing community of Deer Lake. The first settlers here were in Nicholsville at the mouth of the Upper Humber where it enters Deer Lake. This community was settled by one George Nichols from Nova Scotia in 1870. In 1923 Main Dam was constructed and the power station built in Deer Lake to supply the new paper mill in Corner Brook. The power lines will accompany the road on the left side most of the way to Corner Brook with Deer Lake visible on the right side. Gently sloping hills are seen on either side of this lake and a few woods roads are noticeable on the far side. At present the road passes through the enterprising community of St. Judes, another old established settlement. I call it enterprising because in season kids exhibit berries and bakeapples and even rabbits for sale in roadside stalls and of course worms for the anglers. Then comes Pynns Brook and here one begins to notice several farms and a forestry management area. A little farther on, in Pasadena, another pioneer settler, Leonard Earle, discovered that strawberries grew exceptionally well in a micro climate in that area. Today there are many farms growing strawberries and the community has a strawberry festival in July. Pasadena itself is mainly a dormitory community for people who work in Corner Brook and who take advantage of the lakeside beaches, snowmobile and cross country trails and other outdoor activities in their leisure time.

After Pasadena the lake narrows and we finally enter the defile of the Lower Humber with steep wooded slopes of the Long Range mountains, enclosing sandy pasture land by the banks of the river. We pass Humber Village, a planned residential area, and several large farms including Hammond Farm. This farm was started by Bowaters when it included a prize herd of dairy cattle, unfortunately destroyed by Brucellosis. Nearby, but hidden from the road, is Strawberry Hill, used as a residence by Sir Eric Bowater when he visited the paper mill. It is now a tourist home and definitely worth a visit. The defile down the Humber River becomes narrower and narrower and soon the manicured slopes of Marble Mountain are seen, rather grandly called "The Ski Capital of Newfoundland," and west Newfoundland's pride and joy. The little town of Steady Brook nestles on the right side of the road, which soon enters a steep-sided gorge. The river quickens and deepens, culminating in some rapids before entering the last few hundred yards of deep black water opening out into the Humber Arm with Brake's Cove on the left side and Hughes Brook on the right—both of these places played an important part in the early history of the Bay of Islands.

Just before the river enters the rapids we pass Shellbird Island; folklore has it that this island is the site of pirate treasure. Leaving the river we ascend a hill overlooking the Humber Arm where we have to turn off the highway to descend into the city of Corner Brook. A little more than 200 years ago the scene before you would have presented a very different appearance, for nobody lived there then, and tall pine trees lined the banks on both sides of the Humber Arm.

CHAPTER 1
Putting the Bay of Islands on the map

Before the Island of Newfoundland formed over 500,000,000 years ago, the fragile crust of the earth's continental surface covering what is now the North Atlantic Ocean split to form an ancient ocean known to geologists as Iapetus. This was the start of a concertina-like action of the Earth's crust in the area, officially known as the Wilson cycle, but more colourfully termed the "Harry Hibbs effect" after the well-remembered Newfoundland accordion player. As a result, the Iapetus Ocean closed to form the land mass of Pangea. The earth's crust and molten rock was pushed upwards to form a mountain range, higher than the Rockies, extending from what is now Scandinavia and Scotland and extending through Newfoundland down to North Carolina. Then, about 140,000,000 years ago, Pangea split to form our now recognizable Atlantic Ocean. Thus Europe was severed from North America, and the North Atlantic separated the two ends of this mountain range.

The Long Range Mountains, which cross the Humber Valley, are part of this Appalachian chain, which is one of the oldest remaining mountain ranges in North America. They are of Precambrian origin and therefore far older than the Rocky Mountains of western Canada, which they must have originally resembled. But over millions and millions of years, continuing through the time when the first plants and land animals appeared and through several ice ages, their sharp craggy peaks and pinnacles have been gradually eroded down to comparatively flat plateaus, riven by deep fjords and valleys carved out by glaciers. Nevertheless, conditions were at times warm enough to allow dinosaurs to roam a savannah-like terrain 100,000,000 years ago, although now no traces of their activity can now be found due to massive surface erosion.

Geologically, the Avalon Peninsula and east coast of Newfoundland land masses were contiguous in Pangea with what is now Spain and north Africa, whereas the land of western Newfoundland—the west coast—originated from the North American continent, the curious exception being the Bay of Islands and adjoining massifs. These are made of ancient ocean crusts similar to the rock formations that are found in Central Newfoundland.

The rocks of the north shore of the Bay of Islands are adjacent to and part of the unusual rock formations of the Trout River Table Mountains, which are part of Gros Morne National Park. They, like the Blomidon mountains and Lewis Hills on the south shore, are remnants of ocean crust which were heaved over the shallow rocks that had formed along the shoreline of ancient North America during the building of the Appalachians. Some people believe that oil deposits, now being searched for on the west coast, may lie below these hills.

The land area of the Blomidons and Lewis Hills include the Serpentine River and Lake, also interesting from a geological standpoint—this area was initially proposed as the site of the National Park. Approval was apparently withdrawn because of the possibility of future mineral discoveries in the area, but it still remains a magnificent potential trail and wilderness area. Incidentally, one of the Lewis hills is the highest mountain on the island of Newfoundland, according to Keith Nicol, professor of geography at the Sir Wilfred Grenfell College university campus in Corner Brook. He points out that the peak is 8 metres higher than Gros Morne in Bonne Bay, which has often been assumed to be the highest.

The climate of west Newfoundland is quite different from that of the east coast and Avalon. Fogs are infrequent. There is a cold northerly marine current offshore and the prevailing winds are westerly. Ice often rafts up in winter in the outer part of the bay, sometimes so thickly that it prevents even an ice breaker from maintaining a passage into the Bay. The three Arms of the Bay usually freeze in winter, as does most of the Gulf of St. Lawrence. But snowfall in the Humber Valley is heavier than most other regions in Newfoundland. The Canadian Geographic Society states that Corner Brook receives a heavier annual snowfall than any city in Canada, hence the good skiing conditions at Marble Mountain. Winters are prolonged and summers are short, with temperatures seldom above 30 degrees Celsius and low humidity, but the fall is pleasant and often lingers until mid-November, when snow begins to cover the ground. Unfortunately for outdoor sports activities, quite mild spells occur during most winters.

Twelve islands dot the entrance to the Bay of Islands, three larger than the rest and named Tweed, Pearl, and Guernsey. Two other large islands lie further inland, called Woods Island and Governors Island. The three arms of the Bay are called North Arm, Middle Arm (which divides into Goose Arm and Penguin Arm), and Humber Arm, into which flows the Humber River. All these arms were gouged out by glaciers in the ice ages and depths range from 500 feet, to 900 feet just outside Middle Arm. The shores of these arms were thickly wooded before human settlement, with white pine, hemlock, spruce and birch trees predominating.

Many settlements still flourish on both shores of the Humber Arm, on Cox's Cove on the Middle Arm (settled in 1840) and one or two settlers at the head of Goose Arm. As far as I know, North Arm is now uninhabited, though a few fishermen have built summer cabins.

The present settlements on the Humber Arm are, starting from the north side, McIvers, Gillams, Apsey Beach (now uninhabited), Meadows, Summerside (and Petipas Cove), Irishtown, and Hughes Brook. On the south shore of the Humber River is Brakes Cove, then Humbermouth, Corner Brook, Curling (formerly Birchy Cove and renamed by Archbishop Howley), Petries, Poverty Cove, Mount Moriah, Halfway Point, Benoits Cove, John's Beach, Frenchmans Cove, York Harbour, and Lark Harbour (first settled in 1840). Woods Island inhabitants were resettled 30 years ago to the main island but a few houses are still inhabited. Little Port and Bottle Cove are two small settlements outside South Head.

The present population of these settlements, though increasing, contrasts with the population recorded in the census of 1911, when inhabitants of the three arms exceeded the combined population of Humbermouth , Curling and Corner Brook But as will be described later, isolated families started settling in small sheltered coves in the inner Bay of Islands in the early part of the 19th century, giving family or descriptive names to these coves which often changed over the years.

After the last Ice Age began to recede some 20,000 years ago, Maritime Archaic Indians, possibly originating in Asia and crossing to North America by the Alaskan land bridge, began to exploit the rich fishing and hunting available on the Island of Newfoundland. Their arrival date is uncertain, probably around 4500 B.C. or even earlier. They fabricated bone, stone, and wood into implements, adornments, and religious symbols of considerable refinement. Apparently nomadic, they formed seasonal settlements to take advantage of fish and animal migrations. A settlement and cemetery of theirs at Port aux Choix has been well researched. These early settlers were followed by the Paleo Eskimos who lived only on the coast. The disappearance of Maritime Archaic settlement is as enigmatic as the disappearance of the Dorset Eskimos, who fished and hunted in a similar fashion on the west coast from about 600 B.C. to 600 A.D. These people appear to have been more proficient than the Indians in using dogs and sleighs for hunting and using even more imagination and skill in their use of stone and flint tools and ornaments. Following the Dorset were the Thule or recent Eskimos who brought all the well known elements of Inuit culture such as kayaks, large skin boats, and technology for hunting whales. But there is still no hard evidence that any of these early tribes populated the Bay of Islands on a permanent basis, although artifacts have been found at Bottle Cove in the Outer Bay and at Prince Edward Park near the Humber River, as well as at a campsite a short distance from Brakes Cove on Middle Arm.

The Norse sagas describe an encounter with natives they called Skraelings. It is now believed that those encounters took place on the northern tip of the island around the temporary Norse settlement at L'Anse aux Meadows around 986 A.D. Most authorities think that these Skraelings, likely Montaignais Indians, populated Labrador at the time.

Another settlement has been found at Cape Ray, on the west coast near Port Aux Basques. This is believed to be Dorset Eskimo and some of the artifacts found there suggest that seals were a staple food of these people. In those days seals appear to have been much more numerous and may have been harvested year round. Nowadays, seal herds are smaller. Some still drift southwards in the spring on the icefloes from the Arctic, travelling down the Labrador coast, through the Straits of Belle Isle and then giving birth to their pups, known as white coats.

The Newfoundland native islanders, whose origins are unknown, were known as the Beothuck Indians. They were a nomadic people dwelling in birch bark structures and following the seasonal migrations of the caribou herds back and forth the Northern Peninsula to the Buchans Plateau. They also fished salmon, mainly in the Exploits and other eastern Newfoundland rivers. There is no evidence that they hunted in the Bay of Islands, but they appear to have been active in the upper Humber and Deer Lake areas. In 1870 a Bonne Bay fisherman discovered a flint arrowhead which he gave to Rev. U. Z. Rule on his next visit, who in turn donated it to the St. John's museum in 1923. The curator at that time, Mr. Shortis, concluded that it must have been of Beothuck workmanship, as the Mic Mac Indians made their weapons of bone. Tall and athletic, the Beothuck Indians were both feared and hunted by white settlers and by the immigrant bands of Mic Mac Indians from Nova Scotia and the Montaignais Indians from Labrador. Because of this feuding and because of their apparent lack of immunity to European imported diseases, especially tuberculosis, the Beothuck race ceased to exist, as far as we know, around the middle of the 19th century.

The land of Terra Nova, said to have been discovered by the Vikings at L'Anse Aux Meadows after 986 A.D. and rediscovered by John Cabot in 1497, was confirmed as an island by Jacques Cartier in 1534. In the next year he entered the Bay of Islands, and later described the fishery off Cape St. George as "the best in the world, in less than an hour we caught more than a hundred cod fish."[1] He made the important discovery of a southerly route to the west coast and Gulf of St. Lawrence by the Cabot Strait, which was ice free much earlier than the other route through the Straits of Belle Isle. Although that great explorer Samuel de Champlain surveyed the west coast of Newfoundland in the next century, the map he produced in 1612 was poor and did not identify the Bay of Islands. Fabian O'Dea has reproduced some early maps of Newfoundland; these maps record many names for the area. For example, Gabriel Tatton's 1602 map of "Nova Francia" refers to the general location of the Bay of Islands as "B. Musico"; another early name was "Baie St. Julienne." The French later used to refer to it as "La Baie des Trois Isles." No map showed the distinctive arms of the Bay and the three large islands until Sieur De Courcelle's map of 1676. Neither was the even more distinctive Port aux Port Peninsula shown until Nicholas Comberford's map in 1646. This chart, now in the Bibliotheca Nazionale in Florence, remained the best map of the west coast until James Cook's map drawn up in 1767. Basques and French captains may have had better maps which they kept to themselves, although most fishermen did not rely on charts.

Between 1560 and 1590 Basque fishermen from southern France and northern Spain pursued a vigorous whale hunt based on Red Bay, on the Labrador Coast in the Straits of Belle Isle. They would harpoon the baleen whales as they migrated through the Straits in springtime and also took other whales such as the humpback and right whales, and flensed them for their blubber. They then boiled the blubber and exported the oil back to Europe to be used as fuel in lamps. They prosecuted this lucrative commercial activity with so much success that the whales became quite scarce. They also took and eliminated the walrus from the west coast. Then they turned to the cod fishery in the Straits of Belle Isle and the west coast and found that by sailing through the Cabot Strait they could commence fishing earlier in the year, as the southwest coast of Newfoundland is comparatively ice free. In their maps, the west coast appears to be an extension of the Straits of Belle Isle.

Basque fishing operations were based on a large mothership of 100 or 200 tons capable of making the outgoing transatlantic journey with crew and provisions and returning with crew and barrels containing blubber oil or dried fish. Smaller boats and shallops known as "grats" were sent out from the mother ship to fish for cod with bait, using herring, mackerel or squid, and employing long lines with bait hooks. They operated from a land base with a beach, where they could set up their stages to dry fish, which they were able to preserve with salt brought

<hr>

[1] From *The Voyages of J. Cartier* by Jacques Cartier, Montreal.

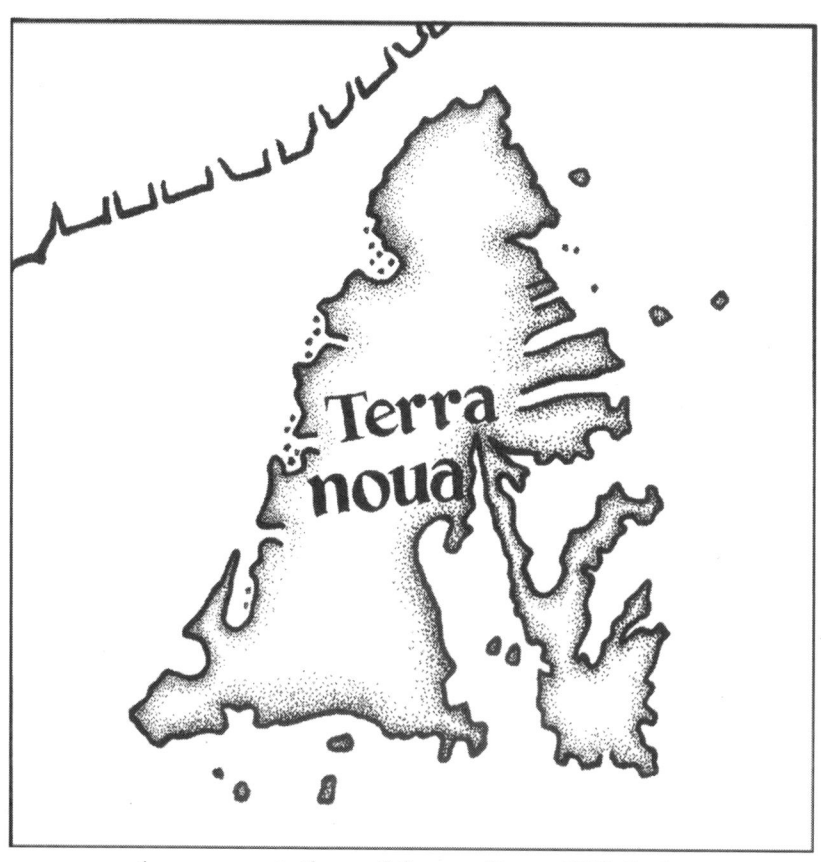

A representation of the outline of Nicholas Comberford's map of 1646

over from Europe. Sheltered land bases were scarce along the west coast but Codroy and Red Island, and Bernie and St. John Island near Port aux Choix were important sites. In the Bay of Islands, Sword Point on Governors Island, a flat island near York Harbour, was used, as well as Woods Island and Seal Island, the latter name reminding us that seals were still numerous in the Bay of Islands; according to a Captain Duhaldy writing in 1714, seals were also harvested. In the 16th century those fisheries along the west coast and the Gulf of St. Lawrence were favoured because of the relative absence of pirates, who were active on the other coasts of Newfoundland at that time. Later on, the legendary pirate Eric Cobham and his wife Maria Lindsay were said to have used Sandy Point as a base from 1740 to 1760 to prey upon French ships trading with New France.

There is no evidence that the Cobhams used the Bay of Islands for any purposes, but some residents quote a legend that these pirates were chased into the Humber Arm by a man o' war. The mate and a sailor were sent up the Humber River to hide three chests of valuables. They are said to have buried these chests on tiny Shellbird Island, after which the sailor was executed. The mate was, of course, killed by the Cobhams on his return to the pirate ship. The legend continues that Cobham returned later but could not find the location of the third chest. People have explored Shellbird Island for treasure in the past but have found nothing. It is a romantic story, which may have been made up to go along with the outline of the head of the Man in the Mountain, seen in the cliff overlooking Shellbird Island which looks like a pirate's head. There is also a recorded wreck which used to be located at Brake's Cove, said to have been a pirate vessel or an American privateer chased up the Arm during the War of 1812 and driven ashore. But Jerome Ollerhead's researches conclude that this vessel was only an unglamorous barge! Some still insist that treasure was found on Shellbird Island years ago and say that the island was a good deal larger in those days than it is now. A man named Hughes, a seaman captured by pirates, so the legend goes, was said either to have escaped from his captors or to have been set free. He settled in Hughes Brook, and today this settlement bears his name.

All these west coast fishing sites are mentioned in the book of sailing instructions written for Basque fishermen by Pierres Detcheverry, alias Donne of St. Jean de Luz, and published in 1677 in Bayonne. The instructions for navigation on the west coast on Newfoundland are original and indicate a fairly detailed knowledge of the coast. In addition to the islands previously mentioned, Detcheverry describes two other harbours just outside the Bay of Islands which were used by the smaller boats or shallops. These are now known as Little Port and Bottle Cove, and Little Port is named as Grat Lecque in his sailing instructions. This name means "Grat Place" in English and refers to their fishing practice of using these small boats called Grats, with provisions for a few days. But most fishing took place in the Gulf of St. Lawrence; the inner Bay of Islands and Humber Valley remained unexplored. Further information on the Basque fishery can be found in Selma Huxley Barkham's excellent little booklet entitled The Basque Coast of Newfoundland. In 1698 an order of the British Privy Council forbade Spanish and Portuguese ships to trade or fish between Cape Bonavista and Cape Race; despite this, records indicate that a group of Inuit canoes attacked a Basque ship in 1719 at New Ferrole.

After the Treaty of Versailles in 1783 when the French gained the west coast fishing rights, fishermen mainly from Brittany began to occupy the same fishing grounds as the Basques used to frequent. They initially employed the same fishing methods, though they introduced seine fishing later on at the end of the 19th century. They arrived each year by way of the Cabot Strait and picked up bait from St. Pierre or from settlements along the southern shore of Newfoundland. They fished codfish which they dried or salted on stages on a convenient shoreline. This fishing fleet was accompanied by warships to enforce the treaty, with a medical doctor on board. The ships officers provided rough justice. After 1713 the French shore was visited annually by the French Governor of Grand Bay and Nova Francia, but British warships had a right to visit the west coast and it is recorded that the first one entered St. George's Bay in 1594. Captain Tavernor had surveyed the south coast from Placentia to Grand Bank from 1713-15, and later petitioned to survey the west coast, a request denied in 1726.

The French and English had fought each other on the Avalon and east coast of Newfoundland for years and settlements were started there by both nations. The Treaty of Utrecht gave the fishing rights from Cape Bonavista to Point Riche to the French government in 1713. This infamous treaty, imprecisely written, was to be the origin of many of the future problems facing settlers on the west coast. It allowed seasonal fishing rights to the French without permitting them to winter, erect permanent dwellings or fortifications or permanent settlements. In the meantime the Bay of Islands also remained without permanent settlers of any nationality.

After another war with France, which Winston Churchill has called "the first world war,"[2] the French lost all their colonies in New France and most of them in India and West Indies. But the Treaty of Paris in 1763 returned the islands of St. Pierre and Miquelon to the French and confirmed French fishing rights on the French shore. This treaty was strongly opposed by William Pitt the Elder, Earl of Chatham, former Prime Minister of Great Britain, who was no longer in power. It must have been similarly opposed by the Admiralty, as by signing the treaty Great Britain lost it's last chance to hamstring the French Navy, who used the fishery for training purposes. And the British must also have worried that the concessions might enable France to set up bases on the French shore when war broke out again, which both sides knew was inevitable. The Treaty had specified Point Riche as the westerly limit of

[2] From Winston Churchill's *History of the English Speaking Peoples, Vol. III, Ch. V.*

the French shore, located just south of Old Port au Choix and at the northern limit of Ingornachoix Bay. On their maps, however, the French slyly substituted Cape Ray, near Port aux Basques, for Point Riche. In so doing, they asserted fishing rights to all the west coast, including Bay of Islands.

Now alerted to the potential threat of the French, Thomas Graves, Governor of Newfoundland, suggested that James Cook be commissioned to survey certain features on the coast of Newfoundland and in June 1763 he surveyed the islands of St. Pierre and Miquelon before they were handed back to France. In the same year Captain Samuel Thompson visited Bay of Islands in the 32-gun warship HMS Lark and gave Lark and possibly York Harbour their name. Later, the "Historical Chronicle" of the Gentleman's Magazine carried a letter by Captain Thompson, giving this account of the west coast of Newfoundland:

"That there are deer in great plenty, all sorts of furrs, excellent harbours, vast quantities of cod, fine rivers abounding with salmon and trout, and only one settler in 50 leagues of the coast, that there are no foggs, very little bad weather, a trade wind all the summer, and excellent conveniences for drying fish, that 4 French ships caught and cured their cargoes in ten weeks, one mile only within the limits prescribed by the late treaty; and that the reason the settlers are so few is, the resort of the Indians thither in the winter, where they come to furr and kill deer, and succeed so well that one man may make 60 L of his winter hunting and return to the continent early in the Spring." [3]

In 1764 Hugh Palliser became Governor of Newfoundland. He had known Cook in the past when they had served together on the HMS Eagle. In the same year he visited the Bay of Islands with his whole squadron under a direction from the British government "to visit all the coasts and harbours of the said islands and territories" (Janzen, letter to Western Star). He was the first governor to do so. He or his sailing master Joseph Gilbert may have named Guernsey Island (formerly known as Ouibal and now called Weeball), Tweed, Pearl, and Eagle, some of the largest of the 12 islands in the bay as well as Governors Island. Probably the Humber River was named by Captain Thompson the previous year as he also misnamed North Arm and Middle Arm as Medway and Thames, also after English rivers; they were not explored or recognized as fjords. Rough dwellings of both English and French origin as well as fur traps were noted, but no settlers were actually seen by Captain Thompson, Palliser, or later by Cook himself. Hugh Palliser's visit to the west coast has recently been commemorated by naming the North

---

[3] *From "A Letter of this Day's Dates from an Officer on Board the Lark." (Nov. 17, 1763). Gentleman's Magazine (Dec. 1763). Vol. 33, p. 612.*

Shore Road from Corner Brook to Cox's Cove "The Palliser Trail."

Three years after Governor Palliser's visit, James Cook sheltered from a storm in the Bay of Islands from the 20th to 25th of June 1767 and again from June 28th to July 8th. His survey work in Newfoundland was almost done by then, and on 31st of August in the same year he was back in the Bay of Islands where he spent 23 days surveying and making soundings in the bay and the arms, including 5 days exploring the Humber River and Deer Lake. He made no mention of any inhabitants there either.

Cook spent 4 summers between 1764 and 1767 surveying the southern coast of Labrador, the southern shore, and the western shore of Newfoundland, as well as the Northern Peninsula. On his final return to England he was able to get charts produced in 1768 which have stood the test of time for their accuracy. Some books give scanty references to these years of his career, and indeed a recent miniseries on A & E television did not mention his work in Newfoundland at all. Yet I believe that his accomplishments in this part of the world were important and even essential in ensuring the success of his Pacific voyages, and so, to set the record straight, the next two chapters will be a short account of Cook's early life up to his final return from Newfoundland in 1767, and North America's contribution to his subsequent Pacific voyages. As far as we in the Bay of Islands are concerned, we remember James Cook as the man who, quite literally, put us on the map.

CHAPTER 2

Captain James Cook

James Cook was born in Morton in Cleveland, North Yorkshire, England on October 27, 1728, the son of a migrant Lowland Scottish farm labourer and a North Yorkshire village woman. He had some schooling and was reputed to be good at Maths, but started work as a shopboy to a grocer. He then became apprenticed to John Walker, a Whitby shipmaster and owner and a coal shipper for the important east coast coal trade. Walker clearly took an interest in the lad and encouraged him to study navigation during the periods of shore leave during his 3-year apprenticeship on the colliers. He continued to take an interest in Cook's career all through his life.

After Cook's apprenticeship was over he continued his career as a merchant seaman and served on ships travelling the trade routes to Norway and the Baltic. He quickly rose to be a mate and was offered a mastership by Walker, but volunteered for service in the Royal Navy June 17, 1755. This was a strange choice for a merchant seaman, as the Navy was then a service "manned by violence and maintained by cruelty."[4] Minor offenses could result in 100 or more lashes with the cat o' nine tails. Although Cook was reputedly a humane person, he did not hesitate to use flogging as a punishment on his voyages when he was in authority, though he seldom sentenced more than 12 lashes.

After signing up he was sent to join HMS Eagle, being fitted for sea at Spithead, and in October Captain Hugh Palliser, the future Governor of Newfoundland, was assigned to the vessel. When war again broke out against the French, he saw his first action when HMS Eagle and HMS Medway captured the French Duc d'Aquitaine in the Bay of Biscay after a fierce battle. Palliser must have been impressed with his services but he refused a petition from Cook's Member of Parliament, supported by John Walker, that he be appointed to a commission, on the grounds that he had only completed 2 out of the required 6 years service as mate. But he did approve a recommendation for his promotion to master, which was a rank similar to a senior NCO or Warrant Officer in the Army. The master of a naval vessel was responsible for stores and equipment and for navigating the vessel under an officer's orders. He passed the examination in June 1757 and joined the frigate Solebay, later transferring to the 64 gun warship Pembroke blockading the French coast. Again he was fortunate because his captain was John Simcoe, an able officer interested in the science of navigation.

The next year Cook was present at the siege and surrender of Louisbourg and it was there that he met Samuel Holland, a military surveyor serving under Brigadier General James Wolfe. Holland intro-

---

[4] *This quotation from J. C. Beaglehole's account is ascribed to Admiral Vernon.*

duced him to the methods of a land surveyor and the use of the plane table and theodolite and the principles of triangulation. It was the knowledge of these methods more than anything else that made Cook such an accurate surveyor in Newfoundland in the years ahead, because until that time naval surveyors had worked from boats, an unstable and inaccurate platform. In his early surveys, Cook always tried to make his observations from the shore, using instruments, flags and cairns to fix his positions accurately and we find him increasingly using these methods later when he mapped the west coast of Newfoundland, leaving his mate to make the depth soundings from the Brig Grenville. In 1758 he made his first chart of Gaspé Bay and, in company with Holland, compiled a chart of the Gulf of St. Lawrence using plans previously drawn.

The next year he accompanied the British fleet on its dangerous passage up the St. Lawrence with Wolfe's army. The French did not believe that large ships could be brought up the St. Lawrence as far as the town of Quebec. There was a notorious unmapped area of the river known as "the Traverse," but sailing carefully and using soundings the fleet managed to navigate the river and appeared before Quebec. Cook has been given credit for this feat but he was not the only one involved. After the capture of Quebec the fleet returned to winter in Halifax where he spent his time studying astronomy and Euclid's trigonometry, encouraged by his commander Lord Colville, and drafted a chart of the St. Lawrence River in 1760.

He was transferred to HMS Northumberland and in 1762 he made his first visit to Newfoundland when that ship entered the harbour of St. John's after its recapture from the French by Lt. Col. William Amherst. Captain Des Barres, like Holland, was a talented military engineer who was in Amherst's force. Cook accompanied him to visit and make surveys of Carbonear and Harbour Grace. Cook made soundings in both harbours and concluded that ships of any size could lie therein. He noted that "a good survey of this coast is much wanting." But the war was now coming to an end and the Northumberland returned with the other British ships to Spithead, England, where he was paid off on December 8th after the end of hostilities.

Lord Colville had on occasions noted his appreciation of Cook's services in the 3 years he had served with his squadron and wrote a letter to the secretary of the Admiralty on December 30, 1762 indicating to their Lordships the value of his work and the charts he had made, and made this perceptive comment: "On this occasion, I beg leave to inform their Lordships, that from my experience of Mr. Cook's Genius and

Capacity, I think him well qualified for the work he has performed and for greater undertakings of the same kind."[5]

Cook was paid off with the handsome sum (in those days) of £291:19:3d and within 6 weeks of his arrival he married Elizabeth Batts, a 21-year-old woman of a respectable Barking family. We know little about their courtship other than that they were married by a license from the Archbishop of Canterbury without the calling of banns, which was the usual preliminary to marriage in the Church of England.

It was not long before he was called back to sea again by the navy, this time as a surveyor. The acquisition of new territory from the French in the last war had called for a great effort to chart North America. Des Barres was working for the Admiralty on a survey of the coast of Nova Scotia, and Holland was Surveyor General for North America. Cook was to be employed to complete the project with the survey of St. Pierre and Miquelon, due to be handed back to the French, and then to carry out a survey of the south and west coasts of the island of Newfoundland and the straits of Belle Isle. The French fishing rights of the 1713 Treaty were to be restored and it was necessary to fix the position of Point Riche, the westernmost limit of that shore. The French had been trying to confuse Point Riche with Cape Ray, so that they could fish along the whole of the west coast, including the Bay of Islands.

The Governor of Newfoundland for the previous 2 years had been Captain Thomas Graves, who had met Cook in St. John's after its recapture and had clearly been impressed with him, and he asked the Admiralty for his services to survey the south and west coasts of the island. The Admiralty eventually agreed, and also agreed to pay for the instruments that Cook needed and to provide a draftsman from the Ordnance Department, a Mr. William Test. But when Cook was ready to depart for Newfoundland in the Antelope under Captain Graves there was no sign of Mr. Test. The Admiralty eventually found another ordnance draftsman, Mr. Smart, but he sailed later and so Cook was forced to make the survey of St. Pierre and Miquelon without his services.

Cook spent 5 summers surveying and charting in Newfoundland from 1763 to 1767. Cook's genius lay in his ability to use cross references from a land base using the theodolite and a brass telescopic quadrant to fix latitudes, employing the skills he had learned from Holland and Des Barres. Until the invention of an accurate chronometer, no one could yet determine longitude accurately. The hydrographic work, taking bearings and soundings, was carried out by his mate on the Brig Grenville. He would return to St. John's in September and there he was

[5] Colville to Cleveland (Secretary to the Admiralty), 30/12/72, ADM 1/482.

probably able to study the charts made by the other ships in the squadron, who had stations on the Labrador coast, Anticosti, and the Magdalen islands, with the HMS Lark on station on the west coast.He would then draw in the details and take all his calculations back to England.

These charts were delivered to the Admiralty after his arrival in London, where, incredible though it may sound, they were filed and put into a drawer. The truth was that the Admiralty had no hydrographic department, whereas other countries, especially the French and Dutch, already had large departments producing modern, if not always accurate, charts. The next year his friend and patron, Captain Palliser, wrote on his behalf to the Admiralty asking permission for Cook to publish these charts on his own account, and when this permission was granted Cook had the financial resources to obtain the services of a well known engraver J. Larkin, who engraved and published his charts from 1766 until 1768.

In that first summer Cook was given the use of HMS Tweed to survey St. Pierre, serving under Captain Douglas. This survey had to be carried out rapidly, as the future French governor had already come to take over his duties when Cook arrived, and was indignant and irritated to be told that he could not land and take command of the islands until the survey was completed. Fortunately the weather was good, and Captain Douglas was able to keep the French governor placated. After Miquelon had been surveyed, the Tweed visited Ferryland and then St. John's. In conformity with the Admiralty's orders, Graves had already purchased a 68-ton schooner called Sally, built in Massachusetts and renamed Grenville, presumably to honour the current British Prime Minister.[6] This was to be Cook's own survey vessel and was later to be rerigged as a brig at his request.

After the Grenville had been made ready he visited and mapped Quirpon, Noddy Harbour, and York Harbour in Labrador. This gave him an opportunity to visit the French shore for the first time and that winter he and Palliser exchanged views about the increasing English settlement on the east coast, the violations of the Treaty by the French, and the absence of any mention of Point Riche in some of the current maps of the west coast. Palliser wrote to the Admiralty suggesting that Cook, though a Master and not an officer, be given command of the Grenville and also be given the services of an assistant surveyor. By being in command of the vessel he would be able to sail and revictual in London and thereby be able to arrive on station earlier in the season, instead of leaving the Grenville in St. John's over the winter. Their Lord-

[6] It is unclear to me whether Cook commanded the Grenville on its first voyage to Labrador. The ship was probably still under Capt. Douglas's command at that time.

ships agreed.

Hugh Palliser now took over the governorship of Newfoundland from Graves, who had been instrumental in obtaining Cook's services in the first place. Palliser had proved himself a brave captain and an excellent seaman and was to prove to be a fine Governor. Some Newfoundland historians blame him for lack of support for the settlement of the colony, but he was a stickler for orders and regulations, as shown by his inability to support Cook's promotion to an officer, previously mentioned. Indeed, Britain did not regard Newfoundland then as a colony, but as a base for a European centred seasonal fishery. But Palliser appreciated Cook's genius and supported him throughout his career, especially during Cook's last three voyages of exploration, and he later became one of the Lords of Admiralty.

Palliser's orders to Cook in 1764 were to continue the survey around the Northern Peninsula from Cape Bauld to the west coast. Cook started work moving from harbour to harbour, using a theodolite on shore as much as possible, fixing flags, measuring, and sighting. His mate William Parker, who had been chosen because of his drafting ability on the death of Smart, would draw carefully from offshore and the ship's boat would carry out soundings. But on August 6, the famous accident occurred when a powder horn blew up in Cook's hand, splitting through thumb and forefinger of the right hand and necessitating the services of a nearby French ship's surgeon, as the Grenville did not have one. The scar from this injury on his right hand enabled positive identification after Cook had been brutally killed 15 years later in Hawaii, with only his bones and the skin over his two hands recovered from the Islanders.

That winter he asked permission to change the rigging of the Grenville from a schooner to a brig so that he would be able to lay offshore more easily; their Lordships agreed. He was also given an increased complement of 20 seamen and as he was now acting independently, he was given 6 swivel guns and 12 muskets as armament.

In the summer of 1765 he surveyed the south coast from St. Lawrence to Bay d'Espoir. This was very difficult work with all the south coast islands and indentations. Two incidents are worth mentioning, one where he picked up two starving men in the woods between Burin and St. Lawrence and the other where the brig ran on a rock at Long Harbour but was refloated at high tide. That winter he requested and obtained a tent for use when surveying onshore, indicating the increased use he was making of land observations.

Next summer he began his observations where he had left off the previous year and continued around Cape Ray to Codroy. The year is noteworthy because he was able to make observations of an eclipse of the sun at Eclipse Island, off Burgeo. He was fortunate because it was one of the few days without fog. The observation seems to have been a spontaneous effort on his part and was not part of his orders; nonetheless, it later lead to important results. A similar observation of the time of the eclipse had been made in Oxford, England. This then enabled an expert mathematician, George Witchell, to use both observations to enable him to fix longitude from London with surprising accuracy. Cook's work was recounted to the Royal Society, of which he later was elected a fellow, and initiated Cook's national reputation.

The remainder of the west coast was surveyed in the summer of 1767, from Codroy to Point Riche. As in the previous summer he employed some inhabitants who knew the shore—from which community he obtained them remains unknown. The season was one of storms. One of the only settlements he mentioned was in St. George's Bay, where he noted a community of Mic Mac Indians.

Cook had to interrupt his survey of the shoals off Shag Island in Port au Port Bay because of a southwest gale which forced him to shelter in York Harbour in the Bay of Islands, as he called it. He stayed there from June 20th to 25th surveying the harbour and obtaining a latitude bearing on Guernsey Island. James Surridge, one of his crew members, died on June 24th but his journal does not record whether he was buried at sea or at York Harbour.

He returned to complete his survey of Port au Port Bay, but on June 28th another southwest gale forced him to shelter once more in the Bay of Islands. This time he could not work the vessel into York Harbour as he had intended to do and had to shelter in a small cove at the southern entrance to the "River Medway" (now North Arm). The next few days were employed in sounding "the rivers" including the River Thames which he renamed South Arm and now known as Middle Arm, fixing the position of Eagle Island, and later North Head and Shag Rock, and leaving the Bay on July 8th to complete the survey of what he termed Good Bay (Bonne Bay) and the remainder of the northwest coast of the Northern Peninsula as far as Point Riche.

On August 31st he again anchored in York Harbour and continued the survey of the Bay. The journal does not remark on any inhabitants but does mention the visit of a New England fishing schooner on September 5th which stayed until the 10th. On the 8th Cook took the ship's boat up Humber Arm and Humber River, returning on the 12th. He appears to have only gone as far as Deer Pond (Deer Lake). The surveying work continued and on the 22nd HM schooner Hope sailed into York Harbour. On the 25th Cook entered Lark Harbour and surveyed that bay, but on leaving the outer bay area 2 days later the fore top mast was carried away and the main top mast brought down. But the next day repairs were completed and the Grenville started on its voyage back to St. John's and from there to England.

Cook was supposed to have returned for another summer of exploration in 1768 but the Admiralty decided that he would be the right man to make observations on the transit of Venus across the sun in Tahiti as part of the British contribution to that event. He had accomplished a great deal in his 5 summers charting Newfoundland. In his absence his former mate Martin Lane completed the survey successfully in the Grenville. Cook then made his three famous voyages of discovery from 1768 to 1779, mapping New Zealand and the east coast of Australia in his first voyage, debunking the theory of a large southern continent in his second, and proving that there was no navigable western entrance to a North West Passage in the third. In the course of these travels, he discovered several islands, including the Hawaii group, where he was killed on February 14, 1779.

Cook thus passed out of Newfoundland history. He continued, however, to play a role in the history of Canadian exploration. On his third exploratory voyage, Cook took refuge in Nootka Sound in 1778 during the search for a western entrance to a North West Passage, which was expected to be a shortcut from Europe to the riches of the Orient. Nootka Sound is on the west coast of Vancouver Island in what is now British Columbia; he remained there for four weeks while his crew repaired the masts and rigging of his ship, the Resolution, and traded with the local Indian tribe. Apparently he did not appreciate that the land mass was in fact a large island; this voyage was one of exploration and not survey.

What sort of man was Cook? We have two portraits of him, one by Nathaniel Dance and the other by John Webber, both painted in 1776. The Dance portrait seems to me the best, though Elizabeth Cook disliked it, as she thought it made him look too severe. He was tall and well built and kept in good health until his last voyage, when he was evidently a tired man, increasingly prone to severe temper tantrums and subject to bouts of constipation. Some authorities feel that he must have had a chronic illness during his last voyage.

To his wife and family he appeared kind and loving, though he was at sea most of his life. His shipmates varied in their comments. In one of his later voyages a seamen called him a "despot"—if true, he was a benevolent one and was always concerned for his crew's welfare. He insisted on cleanliness for his crew and ship and made them eat as much fresh food as could be obtained, as well as sauerkraut and raisins. Spruce beer would be brewed whenever possible and he was remarkably tolerant of the regular use of rations of wine and spirits, though not of drunkenness. During the time of forced inactivity after his accident with the powder horn he punished some men for drunkenness (no flogging) and flogged a man with 12 lashes for not obeying his dietary instructions to prevent scurvy. On his later voyages he exhibited violent bouts of rage when his orders were not obeyed.

He himself was temperate and sober, somewhat moralistic but not religious. His character was humane and somewhat severe and lacking in humour. He was capable of meticulous attentions to detail and considerable powers of observation and never expected any one to do what he could not do himself. He was ambitious but modest, and considered himself "a plain man, zealously exerting himself in the service of his country."

If genius constitutes "an unlimited capacity for taking pains," he was indeed a genius. Palliser, ever an admirer, erected a monument to him at his home in Chalfont, England. The inscription starts "To the memory of Captain James Cook, the ablest and most renowned navigator this or any other country hath produced..."

We who live here are proud that this great navigator visited our shores and literally put the Bay of Islands on the map. We have been somewhat tardy in recognising him. Besides his peerless map he left no signs of his visit, save the names of some of the features, such as Cook's Brook. Some people remember a cairn he is thought to have erected near Cook's Brook which has long since disappeared. The South Shore Road has now been named after him—Captain Cook's Trail—and a plaque has been constructed by the Canadian government on a hill overlooking Corner Brook, another likely site of his survey work. Incidentally, the route to this site, inaccessible in winter, is poorly signposted. The access is by Poplar Road, a right turn along Atlantic Avenue, and then by an unmarked dirt road to the hillsite. It would be suitable if a portion of the proposed Bay of Islands museum could be used for some memorabilia which would further recognize his visit to this part of the world. There is no known drawing or painting of <u>Grenville</u>, but pictures of similar New England schooners exist. Surely some local craftsman could build a copy, rerigged as a brig, of course. But we also have to remember that it was not Captain Cook that surveyed Newfoundland. It was Master Cook; he was not promoted to an officer until his first exploration voyage on the <u>Endeavour</u>. The success of his three Pacific voyages was ensured by his experience in North America and especially Newfoundland—the knowledge of accurate charting, the control and accurate navigation of both ship and crew and, last but certainly not least, the control of scurvy. I intend to produce evidence for this opinion in the next chapter.

CHAPTER 3

Newfoundland's Contribution to Cook's Pacific Voyages

Many books describing James Cook's career and Pacific voyages gloss over the 5 summers he spent on his survey of Newfoundland, and some do not even mention it. A recent A & E television series in 1997 describing Cook's voyages never makes reference to Newfoundland. Even J.C. Beaglehole, Cook's accurate and painstaking historian, makes three errors in his description of the survey he made of the Bay of Islands in 1767. Beaglehole mentions only one forced visit to the Bay of Islands because of storms. In fact, Cook's own journal indicates two visits because of storms, on the first occasion from June 20th to 25th and on the second from June 28th to July 8th. He also implies that the seaman James Surridge died in Port au Port Bay on June 23rd, whereas the journal indicates that he died on June 24th while Grenville was still in the Bay of Islands. Another error implies that Cook named the three Arms Medway, Thames, and Humber, whereas Cook's published chart clearly names them as North Arm, South Arm, and Humber River. Olaf Janzen (Western Star, letter) has already indicated that it was likely that Captain Thompson named them as rivers in 1764. In Beaglehole's 714-page book he only gives 38 pages to the survey of Newfoundland.

However, Beaglehole and all other authors agree that Cook's three Pacific voyages of discovery owe a great deal to the hydrographic and cartographic skills which Cook acquired from men like Simcoe, Holland, and De Barré, putting these skills to effective use on his survey of Newfoundland. Rear Admiral Wharton, writing a century later after working in the same areas of Newfoundland and himself an eminent hydrographer, stated "The charts he (Cook) made in the Grenville were admirable—their accuracy is truly astonishing."[7]

There were other important contributions made to his future voyages of discovery during the 5 summers he spent in Newfoundland. He would never have been given the chance to command the Endeavour had he not shown exceptional seamanship and leadership when commanding the Grenville. The man originally selected for the first Pacific voyage to observe the transit of Venus across the sun in Tahiti was Alexander Dalrymple, but the Royal Navy refused to allow him to command one of their vessels because he was not a naval person. James Cook was suggested, probably by his patron Hugh Palliser, now at the Admiralty, as being a better choice. The Royal Society of London agreed on Cook for its mission. Their agreement was undoubtedly assisted by the knowledge of Cook's careful observations of an eclipse of the sun at Eclipse Island, off Burgeo on the south coast of Newfoundland on August 5, 1766. So we can, I think, safely say that his famous voyages of discov-

[7] *William Wharton "James Cook's Journals" 1893*

ery would never have occurred had he not been so successful in his Newfoundland surveys. On a more gruesome topic, his remains would not have been identified after his murder in the Hawaiian islands had he not had that scar on his right hand, produced by the powder horn explosion in 1764.

As a matter of speculation I have wondered about Cook's last 5 days of his survey in the Bay of Islands, which he spent navigating the Lower Humber River to what he called Deer Pond or Lake and which was not part of his official orders. This was the first time any European had ventured into the interior of Newfoundland; George Cartwright's journey up the Exploit's River occurred a year later in 1768. Did this short trip stimulate his appetite for adventure and encourage him to accept the opportunity of adventure on his first voyage of discovery on the Endeavour? For it became a voyage of discovery, not just a scientific expedition to observe the transit of Venus across the sun, when he opened the Admiralty's secret instruction at Tahiti. These instructed him to continue the voyage to search for Terra Australis Incognita, in the course of which search he discovered the islands of New Zealand as well as the east coast of Australia.

James Cook's Pacific voyages were so successful because of his concern for the health and fitness of his crews and in particular his accomplishment in preventing any severe cases of scurvy amongst the men under his command.[8] He succeeded by using empirical methods, though he did not know which of these were important. (We now know that an absence of Vitamin C in the diet causes scurvy.) He may have actually delayed the introduction of effective measures for preventing scurvy in other ships of the Royal Navy because, as was indicated in Cook's address to the Royal Society of London on March 7, 1776, when he received the Copley Medal, he advocated so many improvements in hygiene and diet that he could not be sure which of them were effective. We know now that his insistence on the use of fresh fruit and herbs and grasses for salads, and the brewing of spruce beer whenever possible while the ship was at anchorage, were the chief reasons for success against scurvy. However, his use of sauerkraut or pickled cabbage during the voyage was also very helpful, although he had to use his powers of leadership to persuade his crews to eat it, serving it to his officers first, knowing that his men would eventually agree to eat it if they saw it was enjoyed by the officers. Cook remarked, "the moment they see their superior setting a value upon it, it becomes the finest stuff in the world, and the inventor a damned honest fellow."

[8] K. J. Carpenter. (1986). The History of Scurvy and Vitamin C. Cambridge UP.

He may have noted the use of sauerkraut by the Dutch years ago when he was serving on the Whitby Colliers. The Dutch used sauerkraut in their navy to prevent scurvy. The Vitamin C content is about 10 to 15 milligrams per pound, and Cook thought that it would keep for 2 years.

Plants, vegetables, fruits, and especially citrus, and the inner bark and young shoots of trees, especially those of the black spruce, synthesize large amounts of Vitamin C, or Ascorbic Acid. Vitamins were only recognised as an essential component in human diets within the last century; Vitamin C was isolated in 1929 and synthesized a few years later. It is so important for human health because we are one of the few animal species unable to synthesize Vitamin C and must therefore obtain it from our diet, requiring 40-60 milligrams per day. Without it, our soft tissues begin to break down, and we literally fall apart.

James Lind carried out a classical experiment in 1747 while serving on HMS Salisbury. He had many scurvy cases and gave a different item of diet to each of six pairs of patients. Only the lucky two who were given 2 oranges and a lemon daily recovered and were able to return to duty within a week. He published his findings as well as an extensive historical account of scurvy in Edinburgh in 1753, but it appears to have had little impression on the powers that be in London, and the introduction of citrus fruits to the Royal Navy was not implemented until 1795 due to the political influence (we would now call it lobbying) of the Admiralty by two of Lind's followers, Sir Gilbert Blaine and Thomas Trotter. Contrary to some beliefs, Lind was not the first to discover the value of citrus juices. Lemon juice was first advocated as a cure in 1510 by Gilbertus Angelicus, and Sir James Lancaster used it in 1601 on a voyage around the Cape of Good Hope and advocated its adoption by the Royal Navy to prevent scurvy.

The French had also used citrus juices effectively, according to François Pyrard, who reported on the 1602-3 French expedition to the East Indies. He noted that the French called scurvy "Le mal de Terre"; this is now thought to be a corruption of "Le mal de Terre-Neuve" because it was first experienced by early French sea-based fishermen in Newfoundland. But the French introduced the use of citrus fruits to their navy even later than the British.

We do not know whether Cook was aware of Lind's work on the prevention and treatment of scurvy when he started his first Pacific voyage in 1768, but it appears that he followed the Admiralty's instructions to observe the effects of certain foods with which they provided him to try to prevent scurvy. These included wort, which was made by dissolving a cake of malt in boiling water (Vitamin C content less than 0.1 mg per 100 ml) and what was termed a "rob" of orange juice prepared by boiling the flesh of the orange, filtering it, and storing the filtrate as an essence. (The end result was a much reduced content of Vitamin C probably less than 0.5 mg per 100 ml.) He had little regard for "rob," but although he asserted in his journal in 1773 that "we have proof that wort will neither prevent or cure the sea scurvy" he seemed to change his mind later, supporting Sir John Pringle, the President of the Royal Society, in his opinion that wort was effective. Sir John seems to have distorted Cook's practical experience to fit his own theory of fermentation as the cause of scurvy.

Cook had first experienced the dreadful effects of scurvy when he was serving on Eagle and again on Pembroke when 23 men died and the rest of the crew were so incapacitated that they could not join the rest of the fleet on the initial assault on Louisbourg. It takes about 6 weeks to develop scurvy, perhaps a week or two sooner if a seaman's shore diet was deficient in the vitamin. So the disease only began to show itself in the long sea voyages that began in the 15th century. The first symptoms were infection and loosening around the teeth, skin and internal haemorrhages and a gradually increasing weakness leading to a pathetic bedridden state with emaciation and muscle contractures.

Lord Colville, who had commanded Cook's squadron based on Halifax, noted that scurvy was more prevalent in the fleet in springtime and claimed that the supply of frozen beef from Boston had been useful in prevention. In 1775, Admiral Samuel Graves wrote to the Admiralty from Boston deploring the physical effects of rum on his seamen and extolling the value of spruce beer in keeping them active and healthy. However, it would not appear that Colville's squadron were using spruce beer at that time, and it seems likely that Cook discovered its uses when surveying Newfoundland. We do know that spruce beer was commonly used by the settlers on the east coast from the diary of Joseph Banks, who carried out a botanical survey of that part of the island, and recorded the recipe after his visit in 1766. Cook's journal indicates many occasions when spruce beer was brewed during his own survey of Newfoundland. Although it is known as spruce beer, it can be brewed from the young shoots and branches of white pine and balsam fir, but black spruce seems to be more commonly used.

In Beaglehole's account Cook brewed spruce beer in Ship Cove, New Zealand on April 1, 1777, "according to the Newfoundland recipe".

Charles and Neil Begg's book gives the recipe as follows, in Cook's own words from his journal:

"We first made a decoction of the leaves or small branches of the 'spruce' tree (rimu) and the tea shrub (manuka) by boiling them 3-4 hours or until the bark will strip with ease from the branches, then take the leaves and branches out of the copper and mix with the liquor the proper quantity of molasses and inspissated juice, one gallon of the former and three of the latter is sufficient to make a puncheon or 80 gallons of beer, let this mixture just boil, and then put it into the cask and to it add an equal quantity of cold water more or less according to your taste and the strength of the decoction, when the whole is but milk warm put in a little grounds of beer or yeast, if you have any, or anything else that will cause fermentation and in a few days the beer will be fit to drink..."

Cook goes on to claim that when manuka was added the "beer was exceeding palatable and esteemed by everyone on board" but when rimu alone was used it was too astringent. He had first chosen rimu, according to Beaglehole, because it resembled the American black spruce.

The National Library of Canada holds a publication in which the inventor of a patented essence of spruce beer, Thomas Bridge of London, together with his partner Henry Taylor of Quebec City, petition the Admiralty to purchase their remedy for scurvy. The petition is worth recording verbatim:

"Humble Memorial of Thomas Bridge of Bread Street, London, Merchant.
To Right Honourable the Lords Commissioners of the Admiralty.

Sheweth

That your memorialist, and Dr. Henry Taylor of the city of Quebec in North America, having taken into consideration the surprising effects the Spruce Beer of that country had on the soldiers and seamen, when they came there almost emaciated with the scurvy, and also, the effect it has always had in keeping the seamen in health when on the Newfoundland station.

And taking also the opinion of Dr. John Fothergill.... that if an essence of the spruce could be made to contain all its virtues, and that could be made into well fermented beer, that it would be the best and most efficacious preventative, and most sovereign remedy for the scurvy.

That your memorialist in consideration of such opinions did join the said Dr. Taylor, and after great expense and pains, did make an essence so perfect that one pound and a quarter will make 63 gallons of double spruce beer, and yet it retains all the native virtues and flavour of the fresh cut spruce; and His Majesty was pleased to grant them his Royal Letters Patent for the same."

He then goes on to relate that in 1772 he offered a small quantity of his spruce essence to the Admiralty, where it was tried on HMS Rainbow going to the coast of Guinea under Captain Collingwood, whose surgeon stated:

"I am convinced from experience that spruce beer is a very great antiscorbutic, for during two voyages I have been at Newfoundland, where His Majesty's ships are supplied with spruce beer, I never saw one scorbutic patient. I therefore have no doubt, but that the Essence of Spruce prepared by the Patentee....will prove to be no less an antiscorbutic...."

The Admiralty declined to buy his essence!

Bridge then offered his essence to the East India Company, a privately owned company and repeated his request to the Admiralty in 1779, when he was asked to collect certificates from ships' surgeons to prove its efficacy. About half a dozen ships' surgeons and masters testified to its efficacy and that it had kept well on the long voyages to India.

The Commissioners of Sick and Wounded reported to Philip Stephens, Secretary to the Admiralty, that they had examined the certificates, had brewed beer from the essence under their supervision, that it appeared to be easy to brew and stable in any climate, and that the price of molasses and the essence seemed to be reasonable.

The Commissioners of Victualling did not agree and thought that the Essence of Wort was a more simple process, taking up less stowage and "is productive of more salutary ends" (whatever that means).

The Admiralty did not bother to reply to poor Thomas Bridge who wrote again a rather pathetic letter claiming that he had manufactured a lot of essence in anticipation of the Admiralty's acceptance of his remedy and offering some of his essence to the Admiralty without cost for the purposed of another trial. Again, no success.

This was the time when the Admiralty were still impressed with wort, promoted by Sir John Pringle and Dr. David MacBride. Sir John Pringle had a great reputation as an Army physician and had revolution-ised Army medicine by introducing principles of hygiene to combat dysentery. Cook had also agreed that wort was useful. I have no infor-mation as to whether the East India Company continued to use spruce beer in their vessels. It was not until the middle of the 19th century that citrus fruits became standard antiscorbutics in the Merchant Navy.

Scurvy killed more people than all those killed in wars from 1500 to 1800. The lack of a remedy for scurvy in the French Navy was chiefly responsible for the Royal Navy's successes at Quiberon Bay and Trafal-gar in the Napoleonic war. Unfortunately in the late 19th century confu-sion regarding remedies for scurvy again appeared, and it is regrettable that Scott's Antarctic expeditions failed to bring with them adequate sources of Vitamin C—the deficiency of this vitamin probably hastened the death of the Polar party. Amundsen used dogs and killed and ate them on their return journey.

The history of the prevention and cure of scurvy in North America and Newfoundland is interesting. The North American Indians have an extensive history of folk medicine. Some of the remedies are strikingly effective. The first contact Europeans had with Indian folk medicine occurred when Jacques Cartier's vessel became frozen in the St. Law-rence River in 1536. All but four of his men developed scurvy but he noticed an Indian chief who appeared to have cured himself of the scurvy, and asked him for the remedy. The Indian showed him a tree which they called Ameeda (probably a white pine) and told him to boil the branches and sprigs of this tree in water. When the liquor was drunk by his crew, all who were still alive improved dramatically. The remedy was not recorded for 40 years and seems to have been forgotten, for Champlain's seamen suffered from scurvy in his first voyage down the west coast of Newfoundland.

The Inuit and Innu used to eat their meat raw or frozen, which pre-served much of the Vitamin C. Some Indian tribes that hunted moose made a point of eating the contents of the animal's second stomach, which contained partially digested grasses. Some extracted the suprar-enal glands from the carcass and divided them between the party. We now know that these glands contain extremely high concentrations of Vitamin C. It would be interesting to know how the Norse settlers at

L'Anse aux Meadows in 981 A.D. avoided scurvy during the winter. Perhaps they brewed spruce beer; Scandinavian countries were familiar with it and called it Sprossenbier. The second Europeans settled at John Guy's colony at Cupids and, according to Henry Crout, many of them suffered from scurvy during their first winter and eight died before they started digging and eating the raw turnips that they had planted, which cured them, as turnips contain as much as 130 mg of Vitamin C per 100 gms. In the 1630 The Newfoundlanders Cure, Sir William Vaughn writes of Lord Baltimore's Ferryland Colony: "....to prevent the scurvy, we have tried in Newfoundland, that the tops and leaves of turnips or radish being boyled, is a sovereigne help."[9]

In 1766 Banks recorded that spruce beer was "the common liquor of the country" on his visit to Newfoundland. But some strange remedies were still in use, and one is recorded in Lind's Treatise on Scurvy. He described that this "cure" was common amongst buccaneers and reports a friend's encounter. While hunting in Newfoundland, he came upon what appeared to him to be a number of graves, with a mans head fixed to each. Struck with the novelty of the sight he went to the place, where he was further surprised to find the men alive; they informed him that they belong to a ship which lay in the road, and that having been reduced to unspeakable misery by the scurvy, they were thus interred in order to obtain a cure.

Even as late as 1852 we still find that Charles Nordhoff is advocating a cure for scurvy by interring the body in sand!

When in later years potatoes and onions and turnips and other root crops were harvested and could be kept through the winter in a root cellar, the use of spruce beer in Newfoundland became that of a tonic, often brewed in springtime. It is of course at this time of the year that the Vitamin C concentration in the human body is at its lowest level. This was shown as recently as 1942-43 in a survey carried out on the west coast at Norris Point in Bonne Bay by McDevitt, Dove, and Wright. They found that Vitamin C levels in the blood of most of the persons tested were well below normal values for 10 months of the year and especially low in early spring.

Spruce beer was still enjoyed in the early part of this century but nowadays people brew Home Brew from commercial kits, yeast and sugar. I recently asked an 85-year-old lady, born in Cox's Cove in Bay of Islands, whether her family ever brewed spruce beer. Her eyes lit up and she said that although she had lived in Toronto all her life she always asked her sister to brew spruce beer for her when she came "home."

[9] P. 73.

"Mind you," she said "you could get a little tiddly if you drank too much of it!"

The history of the treatment and prevention of scurvy is a sad one. The scientific community were slow to appreciate the possibility that it was a deficiency disease and were still under the influence of Galen's theories of the causation of disease and the belief that contagion and lack of cleanliness was an important factor. This belief may have been influenced by the fact that this was a disease of seamen, and not officers. The same class distinction in the disease was seen in the Army. It seems incredible to us now that citrus juices took nearly 200 years to be recognised by the naval authorities as effective and that Bridge's spruce beer essence was never given a chance. But some dietetic experts assert that when spruce beer is boiled and fermented in the way described by Cook, the Vitamin C level is reduced to less than 0.5 mg per 100 ml, which is apparently not a preventative and much less than a curative dose. Fresh unfermented spruce drinks contain from 15-100 mg per 100 ml. Some navigators claimed that spruce beer would not prevent scurvy: for instance, La Pérouse, after circumnavigating the globe felt that it would merely retard the appearance of scurvy.

In recent years the medical profession has been increasingly conscious of the value of alternative medicine or folk medicine. It seems reasonably certain that spruce beer, taken regularly in amounts up to 2 quarts per day, was an effective agent in preventing scurvy in spite of the low Vitamin C content. It is therefore possible that it may contain other chemicals in its bark or shoots which are not destroyed by heat and which enable the human body to synthesize its own Vitamin C or which supply another antiscorbutic, as yet undiscovered.[10] Perhaps Newfoundland's contribution of the recipe for spruce beer to the success of James Cook's Pacific explorations is far greater than has been previously imagined or described.

Many books describing Cook's life do not put sufficient emphasis

---

[10] In the pursuit of this theory I recently came across an article which could provide a possible explanation and may interest some scientists to follow up. Three Japanese biochemists published their isolation of an enzyme in yeast called L-Galactonolactose oxidase which they found was functionally similar to the key enzyme L-Gulonolactone Oxidase responsible for Ascorbic Acid (Vitamin C) biosynthesis in most animals, but which is lacking in humans and the guinea pig. It has been reported that injection of the missing enzyme L-Gulonolactone Oxidase to a guinea pig on a Vitamin C deficient diet will prevent the onset of scurvy. Could it be possible for a sufficient quantity of the yeast enzyme L-Galactonolactose oxidase in spruce beer to be be ingested and metabolised by man to synthesize enough Vitamin C to prevent scurvy?

on his work in Newfoundland, work which I feel was crucial to his last three Pacific voyages. There are several reasons for my opinion. Most importantly, he had commanded a naval vessel for the first time with safety and success. He had gained the confidence of his officers and men and rarely had the need to resort to flogging. Some of his crew volunteered to sail with him on his later voyages. Even more importantly, he had found methods of avoiding scurvy, the curse of long sea voyages. Begg claims that his defeat of scurvy gave Cook more satisfaction than all his discoveries.

The Humber River was the only river that Cook explored in Newfoundland and at the end of this 1767 summer he only had 5 days to spare for this trip, which was not really part of his commission. Logically one would have expected him to complete his survey of the Bay of Islands on July 8th before he surveyed Bonne Bay and points north, but he chose to return to York Harbour, when he might have more time for exploration. This last Bay of Islands survey and the Humber River trip are other reasons why his Newfoundland survey is important, as I believe that it whetted his curiosity for exploration, and influenced him to accept the subsequent chances of exploration in Australia, New Zealand, and the Pacific Islands.

Moreover, in his surveys of Newfoundland he succeeded in producing maps, charts and sailing instructions which were of a unique quality. Cook himself described his last chart of western Newfoundland as "his best trigonometrical chart." After it was engraved and published it measured 10 feet long at a scale of one inch to a mile.

CHAPTER 4

The French Shore Problem and Trouble with America

The Basque—from what is now Spain and adjacent France— were the first European fishermen on the west coast. The French also fished in Newfoundland coastal waters and had founded a settlement in Plaisance, now known as Placentia. But both Spain and France had been defeated in the war of the Spanish Succession, though a peace party headed by Robert Harley, Earl of Oxford, wasted the advantage gained by the allied armies under Marlborough by pulling out of the alliance just as the French were on the point of being totally defeated.

Article 13 of the subsequent Treaty of Utrecht in 1713, a source of controversy both then and in the next 191 years, is worth quoting:

"Article 13. The Island called Newfoundland with the adjacent islands, shall, from this time forward, belong of right wholly to Great Britain; and to that and the town and fortress of Placentia and whatever other places in the said island are in possession of the French, shall be yielded and given up. Nor shall the Most Christian King, his Heirs and successors or any of their subjects, at any time hereafter lay claim to any right to the said islands, or to any part of it, or them. Moreover, it shall not be lawful for the subjects of France to fortify any place in the said island of Newfoundland, or to erect any buildings there, besides stages made of boards, and huts necessary for the drying of fish. But it shall be allowed to the subjects of France, to catch fish, and to dry them on land, in that part only, and in no other bodies besides that, of the said island of Newfoundland, which stretches from the place call Cape Bonavista, to the northern point of the said island, from thence running down by the western side, reaches as far as the place called Point Riche....[11]

A large number of British residents strongly opposed Article 13. In fact, Robert Harley, a close friend and adviser to Queen Anne and the leader of the peace party, had an article of impeachment taken out against him by his opponents stating, amongst other things, "that he has treacherously advised the 9th article of the treaty of commerce with France, and the giving to the French the liberty of fishing and drying fish in Newfoundland."[12] He was successfully impeached and sent to the Tower but managed to secure his acquittal 2 years later. The articles of the Treaty of Utrecht also caused a riot in London, where the merchants and the general public were against the Treaty. The London merchants were now entering the Newfoundland fish trade and were in competition with the Bristol merchants. The North Britain published an antigovernment

[11] From the 1927 In the matter of the boundary between the Dominion of Canada and the Colony of Newfoundland in the Labrador Peninsula. London: William Clowes & Sons. [12] Cited in the 1763 Gentleman's Magazine, 33, 614.

pamphlet on the Treaty question and was ordered to be publicly burned in the City of London under the supervision of the Lord High Sherriff, whose surname was also Harley, and, I am glad to say, is also no relation of mine. This incited another riot, and the Sherriff barely escaped with his life.

The French were allowed to fish in Newfoundland waters because they could provide evidence of a previous settlement in Newfoundland in Plaisance. Although Spain accepted the Treaty, their government was unable to prove prior settlement of Newfoundland. Their boats were therefore driven out when they tried to start fishing again. European considerations were foremost in this treaty, as the English did not regularly fish on the Banks until after 1713. Nobody except the Basques were before that time interested in the wild and rocky west coast, and after the treaty their fishing stations on the French shore were gradually taken over by Frenchmen from Normandy and Britanny, predominantly from the ports of Granville, St. Malo, and St. Brieue.

There was no conflict over the interpretation of Article 13 of the Treaty of Utrecht until after the Treaty of Paris in 1763, which restored St. Pierre and Miquelon to France. But the French had tried to put Point Riche south of its location, at Cape Ray, and the British settlers had occupied Bonavista, Fogo, and then Twillingate, which were both part of the original French shore. When the Treaty of Versailles in 1783 fixed the shore southwards from Cape St. John to Cape Ray, the Bay of Islands legally became part of the French shore, and it was just about this time that Ralph Brake settled at the mouth of the River Humber, the first European to do so. It seems that the French were quite prepared to go to war again if they lost their rights to fish the French shore. Until 1763 the French government had only been interested in collecting custom duties on fish landed at the French fishing ports and in collecting various taxes, including one levied on salt.After 1763 the French government became "dirigiste"and gradually began to control, protect, and later to subsidise the Newfoundland fishery. Indeed, the French government had begun to appreciate that this fishery was vital to the functioning of the French Navy in wartime, as more than 1500 potential naval seamen were introduced to the fisheries annually.

Jean-François Brière, in his account of the French Newfoundland fishery in the 18th century, quotes Le Duc de Praslin, the French Secretary of State for Foreign Affairs, in a message to Le Comte de Guerchy on May 3, 1764: [13 & 14]

"I have finished talking to the Duke of Bedford [the head of the

British peace delegation]. I will not set any obstacle to you revealing our policy. We have set as our first condition for peace the conservation of our cod fishery, that is a sine qua non. If this had been refused by your Court, the war might break out again. I have made the English

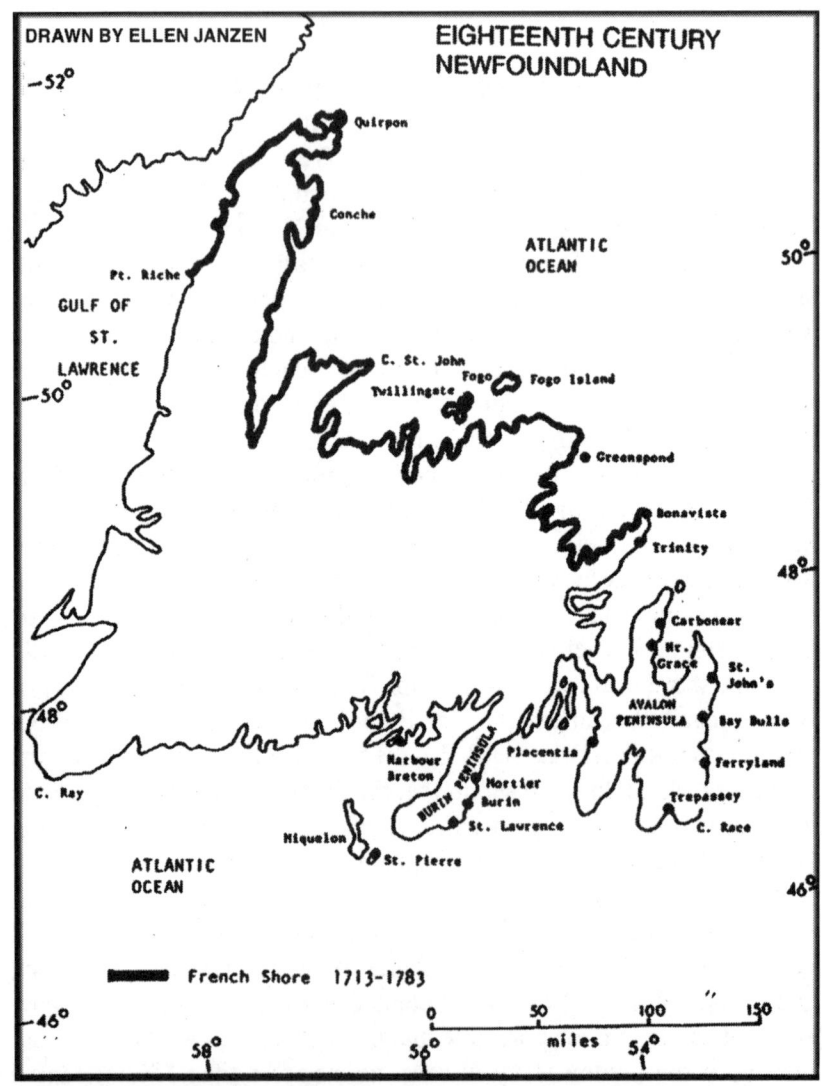

DRAWN BY ELLEN JANZEN

EIGHTEENTH CENTURY
NEWFOUNDLAND

-52°

Quirpon

Conche

ATLANTIC
OCEAN

50°

Pt. Riche

GULF OF

ST.

LAWRENCE

-50°

C. St. John

Fogo   Fogo Island
Twillingate

Greenspond

Bonavista

Trinity

48°

Carbonear

Hr.
Grace   St.
John's

AVALON
PENINSULA   Bay Bulls

Harbour
Breton

BURIN PENINSULA

Placentia

Mortier
Burin

St. Lawrence

Ferryland

Trepassey

C. Race

48°

C. Ray

Miquelon
St. Pierre

ATLANTIC
OCEAN

46°

■■■■ French Shore 1713-1783

-46°

58°

56°

0   50   100   150

miles   54°

---

[13] Le pêche française en Amerique du Nord au XVIIIe siècle. p. 232.

[14] J'ai fini per dire au duc de Bedford; je ne ferai aucune difficulté de vous devoiler notre politique. Nous avons mis pour première condition de la paix la conservation de la pêche de la mourue, c'était une condition sine qua non. Si elle avait été refusée par votre Cour, la guerre durevoit peut-être encore....(j'ai fait) entendre au ministre anglais que le maintien de la paix dependoit de la conservation de notre pêche et que si nous le perdions, nous serions obligés de recommencer la guerre.

minister understand that the preservation of peace depends on the preservation of our fishery and if we were to lose that, we would be obliged to go to war again."

John Mannion states that there is some evidence that the French tried to evict some families from the Bay St George area after the 1783 treaty but after 1793 the French Revolutionary wars, followed by the Napoleonic wars, meant that the French did not start fishing again until after 1815. Relations between the French and the settlers on the West coast ,who were by now well entrenched, seem to have been fairly amicable until the middle of that century.

The energetic Louis Bretel, a native of Granville, actively promoted the interests of the French Channel ports chiefly concerned with the Newfoundland fishery. He became Minister of Marine in 1784 and immediately instituted the bounty award of 100 livres per man, gradually reducing the taxes on salt and fish. The French accepted the right of concurrent fisheries at that time, provided that they were European and carried out on an annual basis. After the war from 1812 to 1815 both French and British governments resisted the claim of the United States to continue fishing in Newfoundland waters. At the same time, the French began to realize that the British subjects who had settled on the French shore were an increasing problem, occupying the best harbours and controlling the wood supply, though many were employed as "gardiens" of their fishing stages during the winter months. The French shore question would impact future settlement of the Bay of Islands and the development of the west coast.

Up to 1855, when Newfoundland was granted Responsible government, the French shore had remained an area of the island warily patrolled by both navies, with little quarrelling. From 1846 to 1886, at least eight conventions were held between Britain and France. When an agreement seemed to have been reached between the two parties in 1857, Newfoundland strongly protested; the agreement was not signed because it was so clearly biased in favour of the French. For instance, among other proposed British concessions, exclusive fishing rights were to be granted to the French on the Treaty shore from Cape St. John to Cape Norman and to four west coast harbours, including Little Port.

From then on the Newfoundland government became a third party in the controversy. The French government never accepted this, claiming that the matter was solely an international agreement between Britain and France. The British government appeared weak and unassertive in Newfoundland's best interests, but found itself in a difficult situation in attempting to satisfy the other two parties. Ultimately, Britain was reluctantly forced into the final solution whereby an amount of British taxpayers' money and a portion of the Empire was exchanged for those fishing rights.

The Newfoundland House of Assembly was excitable and strongly partisan in those days. At times the Colonial government appeared to the French and British governments as anything but Responsible or representative—an MHA for the Electoral District of St. George's, which then included Bay of Islands, was not elected until 1882. Because all the elected MHA's up to the end of the World War I lived in St. John's with one exception, James P. Howley, the difference of opinion between the settlers on the French shore and those on the east coast was never fully expressed in the House of Assembly. The west coast settlers depended on trade with the United States and Nova Scotia for the sale of their herring, and with the United States and France for the sale of bait. In 1888, the Colonial government implemented the Bait Act solely for the benefit of St. John's merchants who were desperately trying to make the French discontinue their bounties, amounting to 72% of the value of the French fish catch in 1877, and which had undercut the merchants' price for fish in the European market. The Bait Act was intended to put pressure on the French government by preventing settlers on the south and west coasts from selling bait to the French fishing fleet.

There are said to have been several petitions from west coast fishermen protesting the Newfoundland government's Bait Act, as this was really their only resort. One such petition, sent from St. George's by Father Howley, later Bishop Howley, even requested secession of the west coast to Canada! This division of the island was actually considered, but rejected by the Imperial government.

Father Howley appears to have been outspoken in his criticism of Colonial government in St. John's, although George Allen and others criticised his attempts to speak for the whole of the west coast. Howley had first supported the St. John's Patriotic Association, which was opposing a bill introduced by the Imperial government intended to preserve the status quo with France and to deny the Bait Act. At the end of 1890 he began to realize that the Colonial government in St. John's were only interested in their own local economy, and had no real interest in his St. George's diocese. He wrote to Lord Knutsford, the Colonial Secretary, and later to Sir John Thompson, Minister of Justice in the Canadian government that "there is really no French shore difficulty except what is made by the narrow minded and incapable government of St. John's."[15] Interestingly, this pro-Canadian sentiment on the west coast was chiefly responsible for deciding the issue for Confederation with Canada many years later.

Another very interesting petition has only recently been found and translated into English. This petition was sent to the Governor of St. Pierre by settlers from St. George's Bay in 1871, most likely from those on the Port au Port Peninsula; the names attached to the petition are all French. Claiming French citizenship, this petition protested the harassment of the settlers by the English and the customs officials and asked for the St. Pierre Governor's support. We now know that many living on the tip of the Port au Port Peninsula had migrated from St. Pierre.

St. John Chadwick in his book describes the inhabitants of the island of Newfoundland at the close of the century. Because of their isolation, he describes them as inward looking except for the wealthy, mostly of whom lived in St. John's and sent their children to schools abroad, often to the British Isles. There was fairly heavy emigration to the United States, but despite this the population was slowly increasing. There was no radio and no foreign newspapers. Those newspapers published in St. John's were extremely partisan—often scurrilous—and tended to exaggerate the importance of the island on the international stage. There was intense interdenominational feeling and marked differences between the wealthy merchants and the poor fishermen. Many of the Irish immigrants in St. John's nursed old grievances with the British government and resented the influence of the British-born governor.

These were the background factors that led to the passing of the Bait Act and the Bond-Blair Convention, both attempts by the Colonial government to settle differences with the French and the Americans by unilateral action. The British government, on the other hand, saw the maintenance of the treaties with France as a point of honour, vitally important to the preservation of the balance of power in Europe and the maintenance of peace with France. But Britain failed fully to appreciate that the nature of settlement on the west coast in the previous hundred years had completely changed the situation, and was putting increasing strain on the archaic treaties of 1713 and 1783.

One of the first serious incidents occurred in 1872 in Quirpon when French warship <u>Diamont</u> cut and destroyed the nets of fishermen on that coast. The French, who had just been humiliated by the Prussians in the Franco-Prussian War, were sent a diplomatic protest by Great Britain. The fishermen and the Colonial government, however, were furious and felt that this did not go far enough, and from that time began to seek

[15] Prowse, D. W. <u>A History of Newfoundland 1874-1901.</u> p. 225.

ways of resolving the situation by unilateral action.

One might question why the French were so reluctant to give up their fishing rights on the coast. This was not only a matter of Gallic pride, though this certainly was a factor. And it was not solely because of the value of the fishery, as this had been in decline and was still heavily subsidised. Even the French admitted that less than 500 fishermen visited the west coast in 1903, compared with 4,500 in 1850 and only 291 in 1899. The reason always given was the need of the French navy to use the Newfoundland fishery as a reserve of experienced sailors. The masters of their fishing schooners were required to serve in the French Navy for a period of time. But now the age of sail was giving way to the age of steam, and ironclads were replacing wooden vessels, necessitating a different type of training for naval operations.

The British were seemingly anxious to settle the French shore question but were unable to come up with answers satisfactory to all sides. The main objective of British Foreign Policy was to preserve the balance of power in Europe. After the defeat of Napoleon this meant containing Russia, hence the Crimean war where France was an ally. After the increasing threat from Germany in the latter half of the century, an alliance with France was still needed to try to preserve this balance of power. The French navy was now an ally, not an enemy. And so the needs of the west coast of Newfoundland were sacrificed to European Realpolitik, although discussion and diplomatic exchanges continued between the two powers.

Eventually in 1904 an agreement was finally reached whereby the French gave up all fishing rights on the west coast of Newfoundland in exchange for the cession of a small territory in west Africa and 55,000 pounds sterling as compensation by the British government. As a result, land could at last be sold and title established by west coast settlers, and there is little doubt that these land sales recouped a large sum for the government.

There are some who suggest that unilateral harassment of the French by the Colonial government was chiefly responsible for the French change of mind. Certainly the notorious Bait Act, passed by the Newfoundland House of Assembly in 1886 and implemented 2 years later, made life much more difficult for the French fishing fleet who were accustomed to buy bait from fishermen at settlements such as Fortune Bay along the southwest and west coasts. The difficulty was admitted by the French and resulted in a dramatic decline in the value of the fishery.

The Bait Act was passed partly in response to the French refusal to consider a west coast terminal for the railway and forced the French to obtain their bait officially from St. Pierre over the protests of the west and south coast settlers. These fishermen were quite happy to supply bait to foreigners and showed their displeasure by sailing to St. Pierre with bait to sell to the French. Perhaps more importantly, the Bait Act was intended to try to limit the French activities in the Banks fishery, which was far more important commercially than that of the west coast. The St. John's merchants, who comprised the Conservative Party, bitterly resented the French subsidies, which undercut the price of their fish in the European markets. And in spite of French protests the government completed the extension of the Newfoundland railway to Port aux Basques in 1896, inside a half mile of the shoreline.

But the lobster controversy may have been equally important to a final solution, as another important result of the 1904 agreement was that the French gave up their lobster canning factories which they had established along the west coast in competition—often in conflict—with those established by merchants and settlers. At one time they had 15 canneries to Newfoundland's 49; six lobster canneries were in Bay of Islands. The Newfoundland government had continued to protest strongly, and demanded the removal of the French factories, contending that the lobster was a crustacean, not a fish. Despite the obvious zoological truth of this argument, the British government proposed yet another conference with the French. As a result of these negotiations the existing canneries of both parties were recognised and allowed to continue operations and an agreement to this effect was signed on March 13, 1890.

When the terms of this agreement became known in Newfoundland it caused widespread indignation and meetings to protest "the Infamous Contract," and led to the formation of the St. John's Patriotic Association. The agreement between the two countries had been drawn up without directly consulting the Colonial government, now headed by Sir William Whiteway. The attitude of the French government seemed sufficient to inspire indignation and their Secretary of State actually admitted that the object of France was to discourage any human settlement of the French shore. But the great fire in St. John's in 1892 and the disastrous fishery of 1893, which caused the bank failure in 1894, drew the Colonial government's attention away from the issue until the next century. Destruction of lobster canneries on the west coast continued to be carried out by both sides and this dispute also contributed to the presentation of those west coast petitions to the House of Assembly to leave

Newfoundland and join Canada.

Captain Charles Campbell R.N. of HMS <u>Wiley</u> carried out a survey of the lobster fishery on the west coast in 1888 as the Imperial government was considering pulling down the settlers canneries to placate the French and to enforce the terms of the Treaty strictly. The captain described the lobster fishery at that time. He noted that there were three methods employed in catching lobsters on the French shore. Probably the oldest methods were by "claw nipping" in shallow water and by spearing. The second was by hand traps, a circular hoop of iron with a net stretched across it and two or three herring attached thereon. The last and by then the most common, and with variations still in use today, was by buoyed lines of cages—but these interfered with the fishing rights of the French. Apparently lobsters were "caught" differently on the east coast as W. F. Coaker complained, in a letter to the <u>Evening Telegram</u> on July 10, 1899, that the practice of hooking lobsters with bait interfered with the better practice of using traps.

Captain Campbell stated that as many as a thousand lobsters, worth 70 to 80¢ per hundred to the fishermen, had been taken in a boat in one day. The lobsters would be unloaded at the wharf of their particular factory. Boiled for half an hour, they then went to a smasher who broke the claws and took out the meat, which was then washed and packed in tins by a set of young girls. Another set dried the tin edges for soldering and cooling. The tins were packed, mostly unlabelled, and shipped to St. John's or Halifax.

He goes on to state that the lobster factories had become the mainstay of employment on the west coast, though in many areas the people were starving. Over a thousand men, women, and children were employed along the French shore. In the Bay of Islands there were two factories on Woods Island, one in Lark Harbour, Crabb's Brook, and Liverpool Cove, and one outside at North Head. The work was regular and paid better than the cod fishery, and the workers lived in separate bunkhouses adjoining the factory, with cookhouse, a packing room, and boiling and bath room in the factory area.

Captain Campbell reported that there was only one place on the west coast at Port Saunders where a factory had interfered with the French fishing for bait. This was because the manager had set his traps during the French fishing season and had fouled the French seine nets. In conclusion he stated that "if this industry was suppressed, or even curtailed, it would send the population of the whole coast back to ruin and starvation."[16]

[16] See Appendix to Ch. 17. "The Lobster Factories on the West Coast." Oct. 10, 1888, Enclosure 8 in No. 126.Prowse D.W. "A History of Newfoundland"

The British government had been inclined to allow the French to build factories to the same number as the settlers, but this proposal also caused a predictable outcry in St. John's, and in 1890 the British and French governments agreed to a "modus vivendi" proposal whereby only lobster factories of both sides constructed and in operation before July 1, 1889, were to be allowed. Any future factories were not allowed unless approved by both Naval Commanders; disputes would also be settled by them. This was a provisional recommendation for the following year, to enable a final agreement to be reached by both sides, but the final agreement was never reached and the "modus vivendi" continued year after year.

In 1890 there was a notorious incident whereby the French captain Reculoux, finding that a factory at Fishels was owned by James Baird, a St. John's fish merchant and supporter of the Bait Act, requested the British Commander, Sir Baldwin Walker, to remove it. This Sir Baldwin did, acting against his will on the direct orders of the Admiral. Mr. Baird immediately sued Sir Baldwin and won his case in the Supreme Court of Newfoundland and on appeal to the Privy Council. This was an important decision, as it declared that naval officers had no right to evict a private person without legislation from the responsible authorities, which in this case was the Newfoundland government.

After the final settlement of the French shore question in 1904, fishermen began to trap and can their own lobsters, selling to merchants at $10 per case, but their quality was poor and the market shrank. They had to obtain a licence and an Act of 1892 made it illegal to spear lobsters or to catch lobsters for canning between August 20th to April 1st. Since the late 1920s live lobsters have replaced the canned product. There was a total ban on the industry from 1924 to 1927 and obviously lobsters are far less plentiful these days than they were 100 years ago, but at the present time they fetch a far better price, around $4.50 per pound.

But another fishing dispute was still not settled. This was with the United States and had resulted from the concessions that were made to the former colonies after the War of Independence; the fishing rights that these colonies had previously enjoyed in North America were allowed to continue. These rights were conceded in the Treaty of Paris in 1783. After the War of 1812 between the United States and Great Britain, the Convention of 1818 revived some of these rights including the right to fish along the whole of the west coast of Newfoundland. The Americans claimed to be also allowed to enter bays and harbours in Newfoundland for shelter or repairs and to obtain wood, water, and presumably bait.

Exports of fish from the east coast were hampered by US customs duties from competing with American products in New England and in 1854 a Reciprocity Treaty was concluded with the United States to allow free entry for Newfoundland products to that country in return for the fishing concessions previously mentioned. As a result of lobbying by New England statesmen this treaty was abrogated by the United States in 1866, revived again in the Treaty of Washington in 1871, but again abrogated in 1885. Naturally this upset the Newfoundland government, which introduced the Bait Bill in the House of Assembly in 1886 to prevent US fishermen, as well as the French, from buying bait in Newfoundland without direct permission from the Governor. The British government rejected this Act after strong representations from the French government, but after discussions the Bill was reintroduced and passed, although implementation was delayed until 1888. In retaliation the US threatened an embargo on Newfoundland fish products resulting in the Newfoundland government commencing separate negotiations with the Americans.

In 1890, as the result of further negotiations the so called "Bond-Blair Convention," named after the chief negotiators on both sides, was refused approval by the British government after the Canadian government had protested this bilateral agreement that would undercut their fish exports to the US. The British government's refusal was deeply resented in St. John's but relationships between the Americans and the west coast fishermen were good in contrast to those with the French. American schooners paid higher prices for their fish than Nova Scotian competitors and often paid in gold. In addition many of their crew members were Newfoundlanders. Photographs taken in the Bay of Islands at the end of the century show large numbers of foreign schooners, up to 80 to 120 in the peak years from 1880 until 1890 still trading and fishing in Newfoundland waters. The Colonial government later passed legislation prohibiting the employment of Newfoundland settlers in American vessels, but many defied the regulation. They would row to the American vessel outside the 3-mile limit and sign on outside Newfoundland territorial waters for the duration of the fishing season, or would return home to fish inshore as assigned American crew members.

The Bond-Blair agreement had failed chiefly because of opposition from Canada. Ten years later Canada had still not finalised its own agreements with the US and Newfoundland was facing economic disaster with shrinking markets for the east coast fishery. Confederation with

Canada was suggested but Canada proposed terms of little benefit to the colony. In 1900 Sir Robert Bond received permission from the Imperial and the Canadian governments to resume talks with the US and in 1902 the Bond-Hay convention ended with a declaration that enabled the Americans to fish, buy bait, and recruit crews in Newfoundland in return for the free export of Newfoundland fish and mineral products to the US. Unfortunately this treaty was opposed by Senator Henry Cabot Lodge and the New England fishing interests and eventually rejected by the US Senate in 1904.

Finally the British government proposed that the whole question be referred to the Hague Tribunal. The governments of US and Newfoundland agreed. This body produced a report in 1910 that basically gave the Newfoundland government what it wanted in regard to their rights and privileges with regard to the American fishing fleet. In return the Americans were allowed access to all bays and harbours (including Bay of Islands). But from the beginning of the century trade with the New England schooners was becoming less important as the railway had enabled frozen herring to be exported to the mainland.

So the differences with the American and French governments was finally settled and the French had left nothing behind except a few French place names and a small isolated French-speaking community on the Port au Port peninsula. Fishing stations on islands like Codroy Island and Red Island were abandoned and the west coast was ready for further development. It proved a long time coming, and for the next 20 years after 1904 there was virtually no growth in the population or economy of the Bay of Islands.

CHAPTER 5

Early Settlement

There was no clear evidence of permanent settlement in the Bay of Islands up to the time of Cook's visit in 1767. He remarked on a settlement of Mic Mac Indians in St. George's Bay. Preceding this settlement French and Indian parties had sailed in summertime from Cape Breton to carry on hunting and fishing in southwest Newfoundland during the 17th and 18th centuries. In fact, some French immigrants from Ile Royale, near Louisbourg, had started a small settlement near Cape Ray in 1720s but were expelled by the British.

After 1783 the French were fully entitled to fish in the Bay of Islands, as the Treaty of Versailles put the west coast from Point Riche to Cape Ray legally in the French shore. Two years later, the French declared an extra bounty to all their crews fishing near the Bay of Islands, amounting to 75 livres per man, "on account of its being a rocky and dangerous coast."[17] However, permanent settlement within half a mile of the shoreline by the French or by anyone else was forbidden. Nevertheless future settlement began in the arms of the Bay of Islands, as the French fished in the outer part of the bay, using Little Port and Bottle Cove as their chief shore bases. Bottle Cove was called Batteau Cove and the French later permitted three families to settle there as "gardiens."

But yet another war was to break out. In 1793 France, now headed by a revolutionary government, declared war on Great Britain. This intermittent war was to last 22 years and had important effects on the west coast of Newfoundland because during this time no French vessels came to fish, and enterprising Newfoundlanders and their families started settling on the French shore. The French could not bother them because of Britain's dominance at sea, but times changed during 1812 to 1815 in the war between the US and Britain, when there are accounts of severe harassment of these settlers by privateers, especially Americans, who had been allowed fishing rights on the west coast since the 1783 Treaty.

The first permanent British settler in the Bay of Islands is generally believed to have been Ralph Brake. His descendants still live in many areas of the west coast including Bonne Bay, Trout River, and the Bay of Islands, with nearly 200 families of Brakes now listed in the west coast telephone directory. I am grateful to Neala Senior, a distant descendant, for research on this Brake family which, she established, came from Yetminster in Dorset, England. The name Brake is a surname from Guernsey in the Channel Islands and as well as from England, from the Old English word Brac—dweller by the copse or thicket.

Ralph Brake was the youngest of three sons. His father was probably a thatcher employed by the Parish of Yetminster, who paid for his

---

[17] Innis, H. A. (1954). The Cod Fisheries. Toronto: U of Toronto P. P. 216.

medical expenses and funeral when he died after a short illness in 1761. The three young boys became charges on the parish, and in 1772 the parish vestry meeting (what we would call now the town council) decided to send the boys to sea and apprentice them to a merchant. Many English merchants then sent ships in the summer to Newfoundland to engage in the fish trade. Ralph was only 13 when he was first apprenticed and we do not know where he served his apprenticeship. We do know that he settled in Bay of Islands at the mouth of the Humber River around 1780, because J.B. Jukes met him in 1840 on the first geological survey of the west coast and he was told then by the aged Brake that he had settled there 60 years before. Bishop Feild was told the same story by one of Ralph's sons on his visit in 1849. Ralph's wife Jane had died in 1818 at the age of 46. She left him with at least seven sons and several daughters.

In 1787 an Englishman is said to have netted the Humber River and to have brought 76 tierces (a cask measure containing 42 gallons) of salmon, as well as some £265 worth of furs to St. John's, a considerable sum in those days. Could this man have been Ralph Brake? If so, he would appear to have been then acting on his own account. We know that when Ralph died in 1842 he was believed to be a wealthy man; his family members were aware that he had money but each believed that the other had stolen it, resulting in a serious quarrel. One son John moved to Meadows. Others stayed at Riverhead, including the eldest, Edward, who was the only son to have been educated in England. Months after the old man's death the money was found in a can, hidden under a heap of salt in an old store.

Ralph Brake's two brothers had also settled in Newfoundland, one in Twillingate and another on the Burin peninsula. As permanent settlement on the island was still discouraged until the early 19th century, their dispersed settlement may have been the result of securing some sort of permission through their merchant masters to fish on their behalf, or by simply jumping ship. But jumping ship and settling alone in an uninhabited and remote part of the island are not sound procedures likely to result in survival; it is probable that Ralph began fishing as a merchant's representative or as an independent entrepreneur and found it so successful that he decided to make his home at Riverhead. The Brake boys are known to have traded with the Bird Company at Woody Point in the early 1800s so it seems quite possible that Ralph Brake retained some means of contact with the Old Country. After selling his fish in St. John's, he may have returned to England in 1787 and met and married his wife Jane in that country, as she is thought to be from England, although some of his relatives still believe that she was a local Mic Mac woman. He may even have persuaded the Bird Company to set up a trading post on the west coast. We know for a fact that this industrious pioneer and his family built a large vessel of 43 tons displacement named Hope which was later sold to a Canadian firm, sinking afterwards in the Gulf of St. Lawrence.

At approximately the same time, John Blanchard, who reputedly deserted a French vessel, settled at Meadows Point, on the north side of the Humber Arm where the headstones of the burial stones of his descendants have been found. At Brake's Cove, a headstone records the death of a John Brake in 1855, believed to be the son of the original Brake, and at Aspen Beach a William Blanchard was buried in 1865, the son of John. Another defaced headstone can still be seen at Petries Point, inside the Esso Terminal. It is believed to be that of Joseph Brake but the date is indecipherable. Other familiar names of some of the early settlers include a William Wheeler, who lived at Barber's Cove, now Meadows, also Mary Brooks and her three children and two families either named Pool or from Poole, England.

Captain Joseph Hackett notes that a Jean Prosper Compagnon, or Companion, was the only person said to have been living in Little Harbour in 1839. Compagnon is believed to have been an unordained deacon and is said to have performed layman duties in baptisms, funerals, and weddings in the area under the supervision of a Roman Catholic priest, M. Belanger, who first visited Bay of Islands in 1863. Jean was said to have been born in St. Malo, France, and legend asserts that he jumped ship and changed his name to Prosper for a time to avoid the French authorities. He apparently survived his three Mic Mac wives who he successively married, and with whom he had 21 children. His eldest son, William, died in Truro, Nova Scotia at the alleged age of 101, and claimed that he was born in the Bay of Islands in 1822. However, it is more likely that Jean Prosper Compagnon arrived in the Bay in 1839, as Captain Joseph Hackett asserts, and that William was born around 1845.

John Mannion writes in his book The Peopling of Newfoundland that in the early 19th century seven heads of household were present in the Bay of Islands, four of whom originally came from southwest England and three from the Burin Peninsula. By 1808, near the end of the war with France ongoing since 1793, 36 people were resident. At the end of this war, the French conceded salmon netting rights to the settlers, as long as these nets were placed only in rivers. These concessions were not legal contracts but were usually passed along through family inheritance. By 1840, netting of the Humber River had become so intense that the salmon catch had markedly declined, although the resident population in 1838 was still only 86 people. These early residents paid little attention to the cod fishery or sealing, discovering that herring were plentiful in the Bay. They began to carry on an increasingly profitable fishery in spring and fall in subsequent years, as well as fishing for herring through the ice. They also grew a few crops and trapped extensively in the winter.

Around 1800 the Bird Company, a trading company based in Poole, England, set up a summer station on Woody Point, Bonne Bay, employing up to 300 settlers, mostly from England, on the west coast from Bay of Islands to Forteau in Labrador, carrying out barter commerce with the settlers and at one time owning five vessels. The firm had to close operations in 1850 when competition with traders from Halifax and New England had made the operation less profitable. French fishermen also traded with settlers on a barter basis, obtaining herring bait in exchange for food, wine, brandy, rum, and tobacco and also employed some of them as "gardiens" to look after their stages in winter.

There were no resident clergymen; the first visit of an Anglican priest is recorded in 1829 when the Rev. William Bullock visited the bay with the Governor Sir Thomas Cochrane. As a result, there were no consecrated baptisms, marriages or funerals in those early days. There were no magistrates, although summary justice was administered by the captains of visiting warships. There were no doctors or apothecaries and no teachers or schools. The British government was only interested in policing the area by warship to make sure that the French kept the terms of the treaties. The French were only interested in seasonal fishing outside the Bay and tolerated the dwellings of the "livyers" as long as they didn't interfere with their fishery. In fact relations with the French at first seem to have been quite good, although later on in 1871 a Captain Brown listened to a Lark Harbour settler's complaint when he visited the Bay of Islands. Apparently, a Frenchman had threatened to enter this man's house and pull down the beams if he needed wood to repair his fish stage and nothing else happened to be handy.

So how did these early settlers live? We have to rely mainly on descriptions by visiting clergymen and one must remember that some of those were Englishmen living in the Victorian era, an era of evangelism and propriety—some might call it prudery. They were truly appalled at the lack of baptisms and consecrated marriages, the coarse language, the drunkenness, and the poor living conditions. One clergyman remarked on a dwelling or tilt that he saw which measured 12 by 15 feet and housed 15 children and adults! Maybe this tilt was like one of the sod huts seen in Ireland, but with wood supports. The chimney would be made of upright studs stuffed with moss. Snow or water was available to quench the fires but smoke would be everywhere, making the dwelling extremely unhealthy to live in, to say the least.

Edward Wix was one of these visiting clergymen—an Anglican—and he arrived in the Bay of Islands on May 23, 1835, on a brig travelling to Forteau. He only stayed in the Bay of Islands for a few days. This was the farthest point of his remarkable journey from St. John's to the west coast, visiting settlements in Conception Bay and Placentia and travelling by boat or on foot along the southern shore and west coast.

Edward Wix must have been totally discouraged by what he found in the Bay of Islands compared with what he had come across elsewhere in his travels. He appears to have given up on all hope of reforming the inhabitants, remaining on the brig on the last day of his visit and not bothering to go on shore. He comments that " none can imagine the difficulty of awakening, or of fixing the thoughts of persons thus utterly unused to any sacred appeals or sanctions. Schools in such places must at least accompany, if they do not precede, the missionary unless the same person be fitted to undertake the joint duties of the schoolmaster and that of the ordained spiritual guide."[18]

He went on to say that combining the two posts would leave less time for either one, and pointed out the impossibility of raising enough money in the area to provide a stipend. On Sunday, May 24th he managed to hold two full services and baptized 14 children, and later spent a few days in the outer Bay of Islands where he was entertained by the masters of six French ships who were harbouring in Little Port. He remarked on their good manners but deplored their Sunday fishing; Newfoundlanders on the east coast did not fish on Sundays. He then returned to St. John's via Port aux Basques and the south coast. He had clearly received quite a shock from conditions in the Bay, as recorded in his own journal:

"I was frequently during my journey, struck with surprise, but nowhere more then here, at the very marked difference that might be observed between the inhabitants of places only separated by a few leagues from each other. One who shall take the tour which I have recently taken might say, on reviewing the manners and customs of the people,

[18] From <u>Six months of a Newfoundland Missionary's Journal.</u> London: 1836.

through whose settlements he had passed, that he had seen no one peo-ple-Mores Multorum Hominum Vidit, Et Artes.

The difference of extractions has occasioned, as may be supposed, a marked dissimilarity between the descendants of Jerseymen, French-men, Irish, Scotch and English people. The people, too with whom the first settlers and their immediate descendants may have had contact or intercourse, have attributed much of the formation of the dialect, char-acter and habits of the present settlers. The inhabitants of Conception Bay, although a neck of land of only a few miles extent separated them from Trinity, may differ from the inhabitants of the latter, as much as if they were of a distant nation. The same may be said of the difference between those who live in Placentia and those who live on Fortune Bay. But a single league may often carry the traveller upon the same shore, from a people whose habits are extremely coarse and revolting, to a population which has suffered nothing—perhaps has gained—from its being far removed from the seat of advanced civilization and refine-ment. Much of the character of a settlement must, of course, depend, for several generation, on the character of its original settlers. The descendants of some profane, run-a-way man-of-wars man, or of some other character as regardless or ignorant of decorum and delicacy, are likely to show to a third and fourth generation a general licentiousness of conversation and conduct, which portray the foul origin of their stock. Between the people of the Bay of Islands, and those of Bay St. George, there was a difference as wide, as between the untutored Indian and the more favourite child of refinement. There were acts of profligacy, prac-tised indeed, in this Bay, at which the Mic Mac Indians expressed to me their horror and disgust. The arrival of a trading schooner among the people, afford an invariable occasion for all parties (with only one or two exceptions, and those, I regret to say, not among the females) to get into a helpless state of intoxication. Women, and among them possibly girls of fourteen, may be seen, under the plea of its helping them in their work, habitually taking their "morning" of raw spirits before break-fast. I have seen this dram repeated a second time before a seven o'clock breakfast. The same, the girls among the rest, are also smoking to-bacco in short pipes, blackened with constant use, like what the Irish here call "Dudees," all day long. The instant they drop into a neigh-bour's house and are seated by the fire, there is a shuffling of the clothes, and the pipe, already partly filled, is drawn from the side pocket, and applied to the ashes for lighting.

One woman who was pointed out to me here, who, in her haste to attack a quantity of rum, which she had brought on shore with her from a trading vessel, and under the influence at the time of a certain quantity which she had drank on board, left an infant of 6 months old on the land wash and forgot this her suckling child, until the body of it was discovered the next morning, drowned by the returning tide. The father, immediately after the discovery of the awful disaster, went on board, unwarned, and apparently unaffected, for another gallon of poison for the wake, or wicked drinking revel, which the custom on the Island has too commonly made an appendage to a funeral. The same person, for I can scarcely call the monster Woman, has overlayed another child of two years old, when she had retired to bed once in 1822, in a state of intoxication. She is now shamelessly cohabitating with her own nephew, and there are other instances on this Bay of adulterous and incestuous connections with which I am unwilling to pollute my journal—"for it is a shame even to speak of those things which are done of them"—unblushingly—it can be said—"in secret."

The habitual conversation of the people is of the most disgusting character, profanity is a dialect, common decency and delicacy are the rare exceptions, children swear at their parents, and frequently strike them."[19]

On his arrival in St. John's he was generally applauded and he wrote: *"Many have compared my visitation to the excursion of Mr. Cormack. It has not, I should imagine been very dissimilar and it would indeed be a matter of regret if the zeal of a missionary could not induce harm to make as much exertion, and to endure as much privation as others would have in the pursuit of philosophical research or the gratification of mere curiosity."* Zeal indeed! His subsequent report to Bishop Feild must have been both useful and provocative for on July 31, 1849, the Bishop sailed into the Bay of Islands on the mission ship, Hawk, making his first Episcopal visit to the west coast to get a first-hand look at the situation in the Bay of Islands. He saw the need for priests and teachers but agreed with Wix that funding would have to be almost wholly provided by the Mission. It was not until 1864 that he found a suitable individual for the job.

Other visitors were not so harsh in their comments. In August, 1840, J. B. Jukes, a geological surveyor appointed by the Colonial government, entered the Bay of Islands and noted several families including an Englishman, his wife, and two children living "in rather a poor state" at Frenchmans Cove.[20] Some of the three or four settlements on either side of the Bay had small gardens attached. At the mouth of the Humber

[19] From Six Months of a Newfoundland Missionary's Journal. [20] Jukes, J. B. (1842). Excursions in and about Newfoundland during the years 1839 to 1840. London.

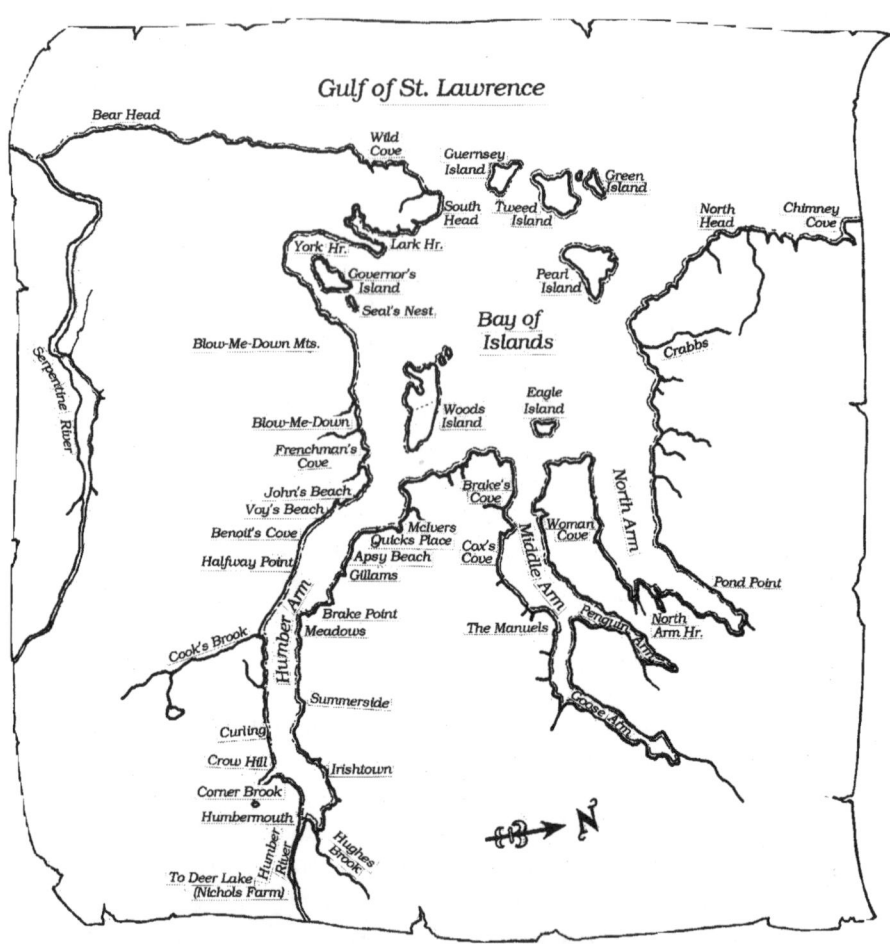

Bay of Islands, with some early place names —
By Warwick Hewitt

River he found an old man residing with his seven sons, six of whom were away hunting and trapping. One Ralph Brake said that he had been living there for 60 years, putting his settlement at around 1780. On the opposite side of the river he found an old Mic Mac woman living in a tent with her two daughters—she had a third daughter who was living with one of the Brake boys on the opposite shore. Although this old woman could not speak English, one of her daughters could. They were sitting cross legged on mats in a large wigwam made of a frame of poles and covered with large birch bark strips. The top of the wigwam was open to let out smoke and a curtain of deerskin served as a door. They were busy making baskets and moccasins and the tent appeared neat and

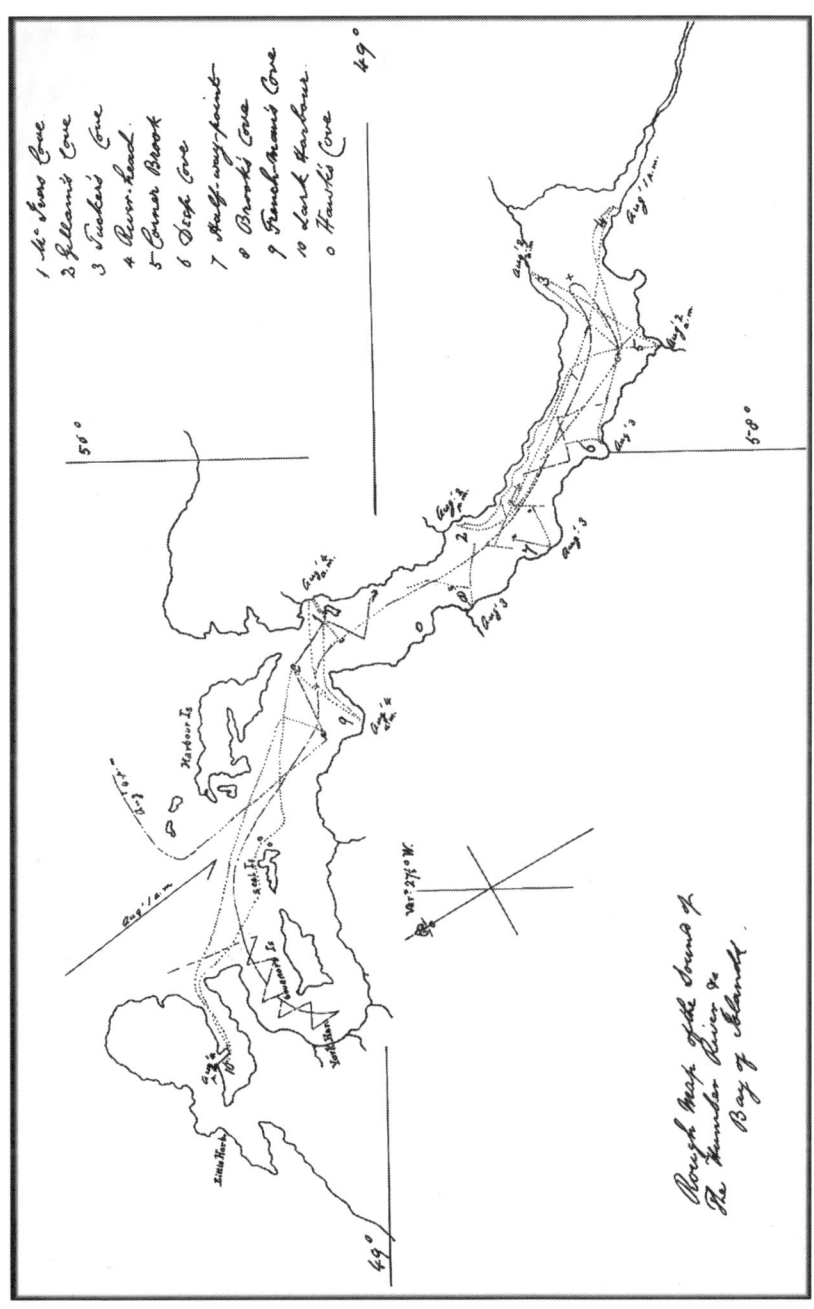

The visit of Bishop Field July 1849 in the mission ship "Hawk"—
Courtesy of West Newfoundland Anglican Synod

tidy. Juke's ship, the <u>Beauford</u>, anchored in York Harbour where he reported no sign of habitation.

In 1832 the island of Newfoundland received Representative government. Jukes' visit had been authorized by this government, which still had no effective jurisdiction over the west coast. Nor did the government have the finances to improve the infrastructure of the island, until a railway was started in 1882 with hopes of extending it across the island. The first census was in 1845 when 2,180 settlers were counted from Bonne Bay to Cape Ray. Twelve years later the next census treated the Bay of Islands separately. The district was called River Humber and contained only 143 residents. Some of these were from Jersey, who were often descended from French Huguenots, and others from England or France; most had originally lived in other Newfoundland settlements, and some were Mic Mac Indians. At this time they were described by an observer as tall and well built and different from the settlers in Bay St. George. Others describe them as ragged and ill clad. But they were tough. There is a legend that young lads would cross the Bay barefoot when it was frozen, which seems hard to believe. Clothing was probably a patchwork of skins and rags with sealskin moccasins—the likely footwear perhaps obtained by trading with the Indians or made by Indian mothers.

Wool would not become available until sheep were introduced into the Bay in the latter half of the 19th century. Houses were becoming more substantial, with frame construction using log pillars and rough hewn wall boards made from pine, but they were poorly insulated with moss and probably caribou skins. Farming was very important in contrast to most settlements on the rocky east coast of the island. The climate, sheltered as it is by hills, is similar to that of the Annapolis Valley in Nova Scotia, but without the depth of soil necessary for intensive cultivation (except in the Codroy Valley and Humber Valley). Early visitors commented on the stands of very large pine in the Bay. When the old houses in Water Street, Curling, were demolished to make way for Marine Drive a few years ago, several houses were found to have massive beams of over a foot in diameter.

One result of the Napoleonic War was that the west of England's seasonal fishing activity declined from 276 vessels in 1792 to 48 in 1817, making St. John's the centre of fishing activity on the Grand Banks and east coast. After Representative government was granted in 1832 the St. John's merchants soon began to complain about the French fishing rights. The French subsidy had been reinstated and thus they could undercut the price of Newfoundland fish in the European markets. But the French were also anxious to limit further settlement of the French shore and to restrict settlers' use of fishing gear to baited hooks and smaller boats. By this time the French were using seines and bultows— long lines with baited hooks a hundred yards long. These could only be operated with large crews. In 1836 Count Sebastian, the French Ambassador, requested exclusive fishing rights; this request was firmly rejected by Palmerston, the British foreign minister, denying any claim of the French exclusive fishing rights "either of codfish, or of fish generally."[21]

But the matter did not rest there, and from 1844 to 1857 negotiations continued between France and Britain. The French wanted fishing rights in Labrador (now becoming a lucrative fishery) and the right to fish for bait on the south and west coasts, as there was insufficient bait available at St. Pierre. Conversely, Britain wanted to confine exclusive French fishing to the coast between Cape Norman and Green Point, north of Bonne Bay, so that the rest of the west coast, including Bay of Islands, could be fished concurrently. In 1857 an agreement seemed to have been reached, although it appeared to be a reversal of Palmerston's policy, no longer Foreign Minister since 1851. The French agreed to limit their exclusive fishing rights to the coast from Cape Norman to Cape St. John as well as five harbours on the west coast including Little Port, just outside the Bay of Islands. In between there could be concurrent fishing. In addition French naval officers would be given authority to enforce their fishing rights when no British officer was available.

This 1857 agreement was strongly resisted in St. John's as one might have expected. But this seems to have come as a surprise to the British government. Eventually the British gave way and part of the famous "Labouchere Dispatch" of March 26th reads: "The proposals contained in the convention having now been unequivocally refused by the colony they will of course fall to the ground. And you are authorized to give such assurance as you may think proper that the consent of the community of Newfoundland is regarded by Her Majesty's government as the essential preliminary to any modifications of their territorial or maritime rights."[22] The letter was hailed in St. John's as the Colony's Magna Carta, and interpreted as giving the Colony a veto power over any subsequent negotiations.

As a result of this impasse, both French and British governments agreed to send a commission to the west coast in 1859 to assess the situation first hand. In 1858 the French had continued to demand inter-

[21] Palmerston to Sebastini. July 10, 1838. Journal of the Assembly 1857. Pp. 175-9.
[22] Prowse, D. W. (1896). A History of Newfoundland.

pretation of the Treaty to include the right to fish for salmon in the rivers on the French shore. Both governments sent their own commissioners. The British sent Captain Dunlop and John Kent, Premier of Newfoundland, and the French M. Montaignac de Chaurance and M. de Gabineau, both parties travelling in separate vessels. Although relations between the commissioners appear to have been fairly cordial, nothing concrete came out of their reports and proposals, which were biased in favour of their respective governments, as one might expect.

The Newfoundland government was anxious to grant title to the land occupied by the settlers on the west coast. A man named Kennedy from the Bay of Islands was the first to apply for title to his land in 1864, but Lord Cardwell, the Colonial Secretary in London, refused on the grounds that the French might be upset if this were permitted. Governor Musgrave, who appears to have been quite a diplomat, in siding with the Newfoundland government, wrote to Cardwell advising further review and subtly introduced to him the potential for mineral discoveries on the west coast. This was later confirmed by the geologist Alexander Murray who confirmed this potential after a geological survey of Newfoundland from 1864 to 1869. Meanwhile, Governor Musgrave decided to take a first-hand look at the situation on the west coast and after his visit in 1864 described the Bay of Islands as follows: "Marble, which seems to be of valuable description, has been discovered in large quantities on the Humber River; the timber on its banks and those on the lake called Deer Pond is of fine quality."[23] He was impressed with what he saw in the settlements on the west coast, especially when he compared the prosperity of the settlers there with those on the east coast.

A French perspective of these times is now possible to read in English by the translation of a book written by Joseph de Gobineau, one of the French Commissioners who had visited the island in 1859.[24] M. Gobineau was very conscious of his social status—we would call him a snob or a social climber—and his description of the Bay of Islands is flowery and romantic. He found the scenery of the Bay impressive in June and was particularly impressed by the entrance to the Humber River, reminding him of a pirate's lair. In fact the only pirate alleged ever to have operated in the area had been the blood-thirsty Eric and Maria Cobham, and Sandy Point in St. George's Bay was used as their hideout. Gobineau has little to say about the inhabitants, mentioning a few shacks and a few people who fished in summer and trapped in winter. He deplores the fact that they do not feel the necessity to be married or baptised. One of the interesting things mentioned in the report is the

[23]Governor Musgrave's report 1864. [24]A.de Gobineau(1861).Voyage a Terre Neuve. Paris . A translation of this book entitled "A Gentleman in the Outports" by Michael Wilkshire is worth reading. [25] Downer, D. Turbulent tides. See bibliography..

presence of "mounds of lobsters in several sites."[25] He did not realize that this crustacean would be a further cause of friction between the settlers and the French in years to come.

The canning of lobsters had been started in the United States but Nova Scotians took up the process and introduced it first to the Bay of Islands in 1856. Lobsters were found to be large and plentiful at that time. They were not exported live but were canned in factories established along the west coast. Some were owned by merchants and some by settlers themselves; most plants were family owned but one plant was said to have employed 80 persons. Later in that century, lobster was hailed as a gourmet dish and so the French joined in, building canneries in Middle Arm and on Tweed Island. They also claimed the lobster fishery for themselves, as part of their treaty rights. The Newfoundland government, on behalf of the settlers, responded by asserting, quite correctly, that the lobster was not a fish but a crustacean and therefore not covered by the treaty. But conflict continued to occur and canneries were destroyed by both sides. The cans used in this new industry were probably imported from the US. The settlers cooked, shucked, cleaned and packed the lobsters in one pound cans, 48 cans to a case. In the early days all the fishermen earned was 1 cent a lobster! Later in the 20th century a tradesman named George Graham from Nova Scotia imported metal and made cans and cases for a merchant named Auguin in Birchy Cove.

Besides the lobster industry, development of the Labrador fishery now encouraged further immigration to the Bay of Islands. Fishermen found it profitable to pursue the Labrador fishery in the summer for cod and then to winter in the Bay of Islands and continue there with the fall and spring herring fishery. Some of them eventually brought their families and settled mainly on Woods Island and in Lark Harbour. Most were from Conception Bay, Fortune Bay, and St. George's Bay originally. Although herring were so plentiful in the Bay that they could be caught through the ice, the main migration of the fish occurred southwards from the Straits of Belle Isle in the spring and northwards in the fall. It was a relatively safe fishery, carried out mostly in Humber Arm but also in the other arms. But in 1877 something unusual happened to the migration patterns of the herring, and the fishing did not recover until 1884. Perhaps the fish temporarily moved to Port au Port Bay or Bonne Bay or the water temperature changed, or that the herring had simply been overfished (Monsignor Sears states that 70,000 barrels were filled with herring in 1868). The absence of herring caused great distress in the Bay of Islands. In 1880 the diocese of St. George's raised money and goods in the communities south of Bay of Islands to provide relief for the destitute, suggested by that great west coast pioneer Monsignor Sears.

The third important development which increased settlement of the Bay of Islands was the construction of a sawmill in 1868 in what was to become Corner Brook. In 1870 the population of the Bay of Islands was about 1000 people, mainly Protestants, and in 1875 there were 1500 residents. These numbers include the growing communities on Woods Island and Summerside, where another sawmill was already operating in addition to two in Birchy Cove. Incredible as it may seem, an ocean-going schooner called the Ceres was built and launched from a wharf at Summerside in 1834. It sank in the Atlantic in 1838 but its construction indicates that some settlers built and owned their own vessels and did not rely on visiting ships to export their products. The first vessel known to have been built in Bay of Islands was built in 1818 by the pioneer settler Ralph Brake. Registered in St. John's, it was called Hope and displaced 43 tons. Between 1880 and 1949 no less than 26 vessels were built in the bay, mostly at Summerside.

The sawmill owned and operated by M.W. Silver from Nova Scotia was built in Corner Brook, using the Corner Brook stream for power and utilizing the extensive forests of white pine and spruce extending along the Humber River. These logs were then floated down the river and hauled by cart or sled to the mill. There were about 60 men employed in that mill, mostly from Nova Scotia with trade skills. Some brought their families and others lodged in the staff house managed by a man called Frank Gissue, later anglicised to Gushue, and believed to have jumped ship from a French vessel. It appears likely that he was one of the first residents of Corner Brook. Some of his descendants still live here. Other settlers came from the east coast of Newfoundland, fishing in Labrador in summer and logging for the sawmill company in the winter.

In 1871, the mill was bought by the Halifax firm of Byrnes and Murray and managed by a Mr. Tupper. It was probably expanded at that time as records indicate more artisans arrived from Nova Scotia, including a Christopher Fisher from Musquodoboit. When Tupper was lost at sea in the vessel Cassie Mae in 1880, Christopher Fisher bought and operated the mill successfully for the next 41 years. Some of his descendants still live in Corner Brook.

The man eventually chosen in 1864 by Bishop Feild for the mission

Rev. U. Z. Rule in his later years

in the Bay on Islands was the Rev. U. Z. Rule. Born in Gibraltar in 1840, he was the son of an English Methodist missionary and preacher. After meeting one of Bishop Feild's assistants in London, he decided to become an Anglican minister and to come to Newfoundland. He worked under the Rev. George Hutchinson as a lay reader and teacher in Battle Harbour, Labrador for a few years. He was ordained as deacon in 1864 and agreed to serve in the Bay of Islands ministry, arriving at Birchy Cove on July 12, 1865, as the first resident clergyman. It is recorded that he was rowed ashore from his arrival vessel by two small boys, James Parsons and William Bagg, as all the men were away fishing.

Soon after his arrival, Rule established began schools and built small

RIGHT REV. THOMAS SEARS, P.A., D.P.
First Prefect of St.George's, (1868-1885)

churches at Birchy Cove and at John's Beach. He must have been a strong and active man, as his diocese extended as far as Cow Head, including Bonne Bay. To cover this territory he would travel by boat in the summer whenever possible, travelling on foot or by dog team or horse and sled during winter. He gradually won the trust and friendship of some of the settlers and seems to have been less judgemental in his attitude towards the social habits of the settlers than Edward Wix. Perhaps these habits had changed over the intervening 30 years with a new generation and a modest increase in new settlers.

He was particularly friendly with Edward Brake, the son of John Brake and grandson of Ralph, and his family, with whom he stayed at Meadows Point when he visited the north side of the arm. Maurice Derrigan helped with teaching at the school in John's Beach and Charles Parsons at the school in Birchy Cove. Parsons was the father of one of the boys who had rowed Rev. Rule ashore and, accompanied by William Bagg, had arrived by boat in 1863. According to the <u>Records of West Newfoundland Anglican Synod</u>, both were originally from Nova Scotia.

Rev. Rule sent a letter to the Bishop at the time of his departure describing the character of his parishioners and church officers for the benefit of his successor, descriptions which appear fair and objective. He does not say much about the people in the Bay except to note a difference between the old and new settlers and the cleanliness of Mic Mac women as compared to some of the white women. He left the Bay of Islands in 1872 after serving for 7 arduous years, retiring to England and later writing an autobiography <u>Reminiscences of my Life</u>.

Two other great churchmen had a powerful and lasting influence in the development of the west coast and the Bay of Islands. The first of these churchmen was Monsignor Thomas Sears, born in Ireland and appointed as the resident priest in the St. George's Diocese in 1868. Succeeding Monsignor Belanger, Monsignor Sears arrived on the west coast in the Bay of Islands by boat from Port Mulgrave in Nova Scotia on the November 2, 1868, spending a few weeks there before going on to his future centre in Great Codroy. He first came, as it were, on loan from his diocese in Nova Scotia, as Monsignor Belanger had taken ill and had died shortly thereafter. However, Sears eventually stayed, and made the care of the people of the west coast his life's work. I append a letter written from the Bay of Islands to the Rev. J. T. Mullock, Bishop of St. John's, which indicates Sears' breadth of vision and enthusiasm. Perhaps he went too far when he stated that some thought the soil in the Bay of Islands is more fertile than in P.E.I.!

"To the Right Revd. J.T. Mullock, D.D.
Bishop of St. John's.

My Lord:

I left Port Mulgrave on the morning of All Saints, 1ˢᵗ inst., and arrived safe in the Bay of Islands on the following evening. I have now spent some three weeks here. There is no way of getting to Bay St. George till the vessels are ready to leave here. I was very fortunate in the circumstances of Captain Jackman of the Steamer Hawk from St.

John's coming to trade in this Bay this fall, otherwise I should have great difficulty in getting to Bay St. George. Captain Jackman kindly proffered to see me sent safely.

My Lord: this seems to me a very important portion of the grand Island of Newfoundland. This Bay, with its tributary rivers, as well as several other localities along this Coast, affords better inducement (at least in my estimation) than the United States, to the fishermen of St. John's and other places, who are emigrating. In this Bay alone there are now as many vessels at anchor as will require, it is estimated, seventy thousand barrels of herring to load them—still although the herring did not strike in till after the 22nd of this month such is the quantity taken, the last five or six days that they are all in hopes of getting fair cargoes. They tell me that the Codfish is quite plentiful in the Bay if they could attend to it. There is another advantage I perceive that this Bay enjoys, and that is the fertility of its soil and the magnificent forests that line the Bays and rivers especially. It seems that there is no land superior to this for the cultivation of green crops and hay. Potatoes grow as well as in any part of North America. Oats and barley of course will do as well. Cabbage can be produced in abundance. There have been two saw mills erected here lately; one will be in operation in a few days; it is constructed on the most approved method and will drive as many saws as will saw the largest pine logs in a pass. The pine is of enormous size, as large as any I have ever seen in Nova Scotia or New Brunswick and farmers who come here from Prince Edward Island say that the land is far superior in point of fertility to that of the Island. Add to this the fact of this Bay having (as it is calculated) always been the winter resort of the Labrador herring which swarm along the coast and which can be taken in the dead of winter as well as in summer when people are idle in all the other harbors of our fishing coast. I am very much mistaken then if this Bay does not hold out inducements to the poor fishermen who have to leave other parts of this Island, superior to the most glittering prospects held out by Gloucester or any other fishing district in the United States, with this difference that while in the latter places the fishermen are exposed to such and so many dangers that numbers of valuable lives are yearly lost, in this River the fisherman is safe while catching his fish as he is sitting in his house in the bosom of his family. The consequence of this is that several families from St. John's and Carbonear have already settled here for the last five years: but as there was no priest visiting the place, or but seldom, many

Rev. Joseph James Curling, who served the Protestant west coast mission from 1873 to 1886.

of them never felt contented. But now it appears to me they will soon be able to support a priest in this Bay itself; with this in view I am looking around to see where I could select a good site a Chapel and Glebe House.

It would be most desirable that the Government of St. John's do something towards establishing some sort of civil authority and some-

thing for the cause of Education on this Coast. Another great want is felt here—they have no roads, not even pathways. I hope the day is not far distant when some Government will take charge of the place and open roads from one locality to another and then look after the interests of the poor people who are now at the mercy of cupidity or caprice of heartless traders or merciless petty merchants. Hoping that these few lines may find your Lordship in good health.

I have the honor to remain
Your Lordship's most obedient servant
THOMAS SEARS "

He was to continue working in the diocese from 1868 to 1885, basing himself in the Codroy Valley and travelling great distances by boat or on foot without sparing himself. He continually petitioned members of the House of Assembly by letter or in person, pressing for better roads or a trans island extension of the railway and actually persuaded some west coast settlers to build a rough road with free labour to connect the Codroy Valley with Channel.

The second influential churchman was Joseph James Curling, who served the Protestant west coast mission from 1873 to 1886. Rev. Curling was an Englishman from a wealthy family and had been educated at Harrow, an English public school. He then graduated with the "sword of honour" from the Royal Military Academy at Woolwich in London. He served in the Royal Engineers as a subaltern and it was while in Bermuda as A.D.C. to Sir Frederick Chapman from 1869 to 1870 that he first met Bishop Kelly and later Bishop Feild, and got on extremely well with both these men who were to play such an important part in his later life. He accompanied Sir Frederick back to England and seems to have enjoyed London life to the full, entertaining liberally and spending as much time as he could sailing a 72-ton yawl he had bought—the Lavrock. Although clearly destined for a great career in the army, Curling gradually became more interested in missionary work. Indeed, when he learned that Bishop Feild's mission ship, the Star, had been wrecked in 1871, he immediately offered the Lavrock to replace her. He spent most of the next spring fitting her out as a church ship and then sailed her across the Atlantic with a crew, arriving in St. John's May 28, 1872. After handing over the ship he proceeded on a tour around eastern Canada and the United States, arriving back in Britain in July to resume his military duties. But his growing interest in the church had been established; after hearing sermons from the great missionary preacher Canon

Liddon, he decided to offer himself for the Church of England Foreign Mission.

He sent in his papers to the War Office, which were accepted with much regret by his chief Sir Frederick Chapman, and he was gazetted out of the British Army in August 1873. He sailed to Newfoundland, arriving on June 11, 1873. Although a comfortable room was provided by the Rectory he characteristically preferred to have his quarters on his old love the Lavrock. It was then decided that his charge should be the Bay of Islands mission, extending from the Bay of Islands to St. John's Island near Port aux Choix, including Bonne Bay. Bishop Feild was about to make his visitation tour in Lavrock at this time. Curling joined him and they reached the Bay of Islands on July 1. There he met as many of the settlers as possible and arranged for a parsonage to be built that winter, before he would arrive to take up his duties next year. After returning to St. John's he was ordained Deacon on November 1, 1873, and set off to Bay of Islands the next day in a chartered schooner. He arrived there with two schoolmasters, two servants, and an assistant, setting up Anglican schools in the Bay of Islands and Bonne Bay. School opened from 9 until 12 noon and from 2 until 4 each weekday afternoon. The first hour was for religious instruction. Schooling cost the family $1.50 for the first child, $1.00 for the second, and $0.50 for each of the others.

There seems to be no doubt that this unusually talented man made a great impression on the "unruly and turbulent" settlers in the Bay of Islands. His friends in both St. John's and in England were devoted and found him modest and unassuming. He was also determined, self reliant, and resourceful. He was certainly wealthy, and that did help him to add expensive imported items to the buildings and churches he built on the west coast.[26] His wealth also enabled him to help members of his own flock financially during the failure of the herring fishery in the years 1878 to 1885.

Though widely admired for his modesty and benevolence, Curling was chiefly admired by the settlers for his prowess as a seaman. In the first winter of his mission, the charter of his hired schooner the Velocity was due to expire when it was returned to St. John's. In January, having no further immediate use of the vessel, he ordered the Captain and crew to take her back. Some days after leaving, Curling heard that the vessel had not left the Bay of Islands. So he took a small fishing boat and went out after her, finding the vessel anchored near Lark Harbour. The Captain said he could not go any further because of ice which was forming

[26] St. Mary's church in John's Beach was a fine example but unfortunately burned down a few years later.

around the vessel. Curling realised that if the vessel remained there all winter it would cost the mission further leasing dues for the ship and full pay for the Captain and the crew. Curling disregarded the Captain's concerns, asserting he would sail the ship himself. Sail her out he did, reaching the port of Channel safely. When we remember some Newfoundland winters, when Bowater paper boats have been stuck in the Bay, and rafting ice has prevented ice breakers from entering port, this must be accounted a remarkable achievement. Furthermore, he returned to the Bay of Islands from Channel _on foot_ with snowshoes—over 200 miles!

There is no doubt in my mind that Monsignor Thomas Sears and the Rev. Joseph Curling were chiefly responsible for drawing attention to the natural resources of the west coast and the plight of its settlers. Sears repeatedly petitioned the House of Assembly and appealed to the Roman Catholic hierarchy in St. John's, while Curling used his influence with the Anglican community and colonial authorities; he married Emmie, youngest daughter of Sir Brian Robinson, a Judge of the Supreme Court of Newfoundland, in 1876 and brought her back with him to accompany him in his work in the Bay of Islands diocese.

But there was disagreement and opposition. In 1873 the Attorney General of Newfoundland stated that the French were justified in alleging that the settlers on the west coast had no concurrent fishing rights; this was repudiated by later statesmen. In 1884 the French government denied the Newfoundland government's proposal to build a trans-island railway through to Bay of Islands and Channel. And several MHA's deplored "wastage" of revenue on inhabitants of the west coast. Customs levies had been imposed but were difficult to collect and served to increase barter trade with Halifax merchants and the Americans, whose ships were now numerous in the bay in summer having had fishing rights on the west coast from Quirpon on the Northern Peninsula to Ramea on the south coast ratified by the Anglo-American Convention of 1818.

A school superintendent wrote to Sears in 1879 commenting on the unfairness of custom duties being levied because, first there was no political representation in the House of Assembly from the west coast and, second, there was no significant expenditure return to the area from the duties paid. At that time money for schools was given by special grant to the church school superintendents. This special grant was only $2000 in 1879 for the whole west coast. Most complaints from settlers on the west coast at this time seem to be directed at the lack of help and support from the Newfoundland government rather than complaints against

French behaviour.

Better times laid ahead. In 1865 J. S. Hayward was sent to Bay St. George to determine needed resources; he recommended a magistrate and customs officer as well as a lock-up at Sandy Point. Some of the settlers petitioned the House of Assembly against this, as they feared that other taxes would result. Hayward estimated the population of the Bay of Islands at 1500 inhabitants and noted that imports were mainly from Halifax, including a total of 2700 gallons of liquor, and that herring was the main export. He also alluded to a decline of salmon stocks because of weiring and spearing at the river mouths.

A major crime with important consequences for the Bay of Islands was the death of John Carter on December 18, 1875. Carter was a 35-year-old unmarried man from Nova Scotia who had lived in the Bay of Islands for 5 years and was master of a schooner. He died of gunshot wounds at the hands of Benjamin Brake, thought to be a full blooded Mic Mac Indian and no direct relation to the original settler, Ralph Brake. Some of Benjamin Brake's descendants allege that the crime took place in Trout River, not in Brake's Cove or Riverhead, Bay of Islands and that Benjamin Brake and his family settled in Brake's Cove, Middle Arm after his release from prison, but the census of 1871 lists a Benjamin Brake residing in the Bay of Islands.

The details of this incident are obscure; Benjamin Brake was the only witness and he was apparently drunk at the time. In a July 7, 1946 article in the Western Star, A. J.Barrett,who at one time edited the newspaper, states that Benjamin Brake and John Carter lived close to one another at Riverhead. Carter apparently visited Brake's house while he was away trapping. Brake became suspicious and one day returned early to find Carter in the house with his wife, and confronted him. This story is probably based on rumour, as Brake's own testimony indicated that Carter forcibly entered his house for payment of a small debt and had threatened him. When Carter seized the gun that Brake was brandishing to defend his property, Brake said that the gun discharged and Carter was accidentally shot in the leg. But Brake apparently made no effort to assist Carter, whose leg was practically severed; he bled to death.

In the absence of a magistrate an examination was held by Rev. T. Sears and J.S. Jacobs.[27] The result was that he was taken into custody by a person empowered to do so in the absence of a Royal Naval vessel, possibly that same J. S. Jacobs.[28] Don Morris tells this story in one of his weekly column in the Western Star, "Vignettes of the West Coast."

[27] Jacobs was unlikely to have been a doctor, as some aver.
[28] A Royal Naval vessel would be unlikely to visit in the Bay in December.

Benjamin Brake, died July 5th, 1911 age 76 years
earlier im prisoned for manslaughter

Communication at that time was significantly better with Halifax than St. John's—the account of this "murder" was first published in a Halifax newspaper in June, 1876, only later picked up by a St. John's newspaper. A police officer was sent to investigate and brought Brake to St. John's to stand trial before Judge Brian Robinson. He pleaded guilty to manslaughter and received a sympathetic judgement. The judge commented on several mitigating circumstances, noting that Brake had already had several months of imprisonment and had also suffered because his home and property had been violently destroyed by fire a day or two after Carter's death, by person or persons unknown. He also noted that two other crimes had been perpetrated on the west coast within a short period of time and that, because of the lack of a magistrate, nobody could be brought to justice. He admitted that unless people defended their lives and property by their own hand they had no other means of protection. In conclusion the judge stated that the west coast needed competent authority to preserve law and order.

Judge Robinson sentenced Brake to imprisonment for one more year, with hard labour, admitting that he had a right to defend his property but asserting that he should have used less violent means in doing so.

On May 2, 1877, Benjamin Brake petitioned the Governor, Sir John Glover, for early release to be able to prosecute the summer fishery so that he could support his wife and family. This petition was penned by a Mr. Bensting; illiterate, Brake made his mark. Many other prisoners would send petitions asking for remission of sentence at this time of the year for the same reason. But Brake's petition also reiterated the absence of any police or magistrate to protect himself and his property and the unavailability of medical attention to save John Carter's death. Although his petition was refused, local editorial comment provoked a popular outcry and an appeal to the British government.

One of these articles appeared in the <u>Newfoundlander</u> in 1877 and claimed that the Bay of Islands area had been for some time a refuge of outlaws, people who considered themselves beyond the reach of the law. The Minister of Justice had also received numerous letters from concerned citizens regarding drunk and disorderly conduct and assaults on citizens, including robbery even in daylight. A factor leading to this situation was the presence of the large fleets of American, Nova Scotian, and Newfoundland schooners in the Bay, loading with herring in the fall and releasing hundreds of sailors to look for drink and comforts ashore during their leisure hours, with no persons possessed with authority to enforce the laws.

Eventually these protests resulted in the appointment of police and a magistrate to the west coast in that same year. The magistrate was Captain Howorth, formerly of the Royal Navy, and who had previously served on a warship on the west coast. He was accompanied by one head constable Constable Edgar Kelland, from St. John's, and two other constables. One half of his salary of £500 a year was paid by the Imperial government for 4 years, the other half by the Colonial government.

His duties included maintenance of law and order and collection of customs in a huge area from Bay of Islands to the Northern Peninsula. He was instructed to abstain from any interpretation of treaty rights.

In 1879 Sergeant W.Bartlett from St John's was transferred by the Newfoundland Constabulary to Birchy Cove to command the Bay of Islands detachment. He was promoted in 1895 and transferred back to St John's but returned to Bay of Islands as District Inspector,retiring on Nov 1 1918 and succeeded by H.C. Peet. The following year he had the distinction of receiving the prestigious Imperial Service Medal from the Governor. He had a large family and Isaac,one of his sons, wrote some poems about the Bay of Islands, according to Olga Eastman, one of his descendants. Another descendant, Charles Bartlett, was a a prominent fish plant owner. A strange and curious event[29] which also influenced the authorities to provide a magistrate and police for the area is recorded by Otto Kelland, the son of Edgar Kelland, the head constable who had accompanied Captain Howorth to the Bay of Islands in 1877. Detailed by Otto, the event still divides local popular opinion to this day; it throws further light on the justice system as it applied to the Bay of Islands in those "lawless and turbulent times."

The strange event concerns the disappearance of Captain Rideout and his crew after the grounding and wreck of the brig <u>Flirt</u> near Wild Cove on the shore to the south of Little Port outside South Head and the Bay of Islands. This occurred in the fall of 1874. Rideout had a 20-man crew with him, with several coopers and a carpenter, and was known to be carrying a quantity of gold in a canvas bag to purchase herring and to pay off his crew. Rideout and his crew were never seen again. During the next 3 or 4 years their relatives petitioned the Colonial government for investigation of their disappearance, while dark rumours began to circulate around the Bay of Islands concerning possible murder and theft by persons who had been hired to guide them to safety.

The rumours circulated around three brothers, Gil, Exaviour, and François, who lived with Gil's daughter Agnes and her grandmother in Benoits Cove. There were whispers that these men made a habit of murder and robbery and were responsible for the disappearance of the crew of the schooner <u>Adonis</u> which had grounded in Wild Cove earlier in 1874. Eventually the government agreed to investigate the disappearance of the crew of the <u>Flirt</u>. However, there was not yet a magistrate. So the government appointed Captain Erskine of HMS <u>Eclipse</u> to head the enquiry. He was later aided by Judge Willy of the Newfoundland Supreme Court, Inspector Carty, and two constables. They ques-

---

[29] From Kelland, O. (1997). <u>Strange and Curious</u> (2nd. ed.). St. John's, NF: Creative Publishers.

tioned an old man called Jacko living in a tilt on the shore of Wild Cove. But he could not or would not give them any information, and despite his failure to find any bodies or record of a crime, Erskine committed the three brothers to stand trial in St. John's.

François, the youngest of the brothers, died in custody protesting his innocence. The volatile St. John's newspapers and their correspondents, who had previously published the wildest kind of slander about the Benoit brothers, at once gushed with sympathy for the two remaining brothers and blamed Captain Erskine for incompetence when they were later released for lack of evidence. As a result of this fiasco and the reports of the trial of Benjamin Brake in the same year, Captain Howorth was appointed magistrate and travelled to Bay of Islands on the steamer Hercules.

More petitions from the Flirt crew's relatives persuaded the Justice Department to reopen the case. Chief Constable Edgar Kelland was ordered to proceed to Wild Cove and reinvestigate the disappearance. He found evidence that masts and timbers had been removed from the wreck, probably as salvage. He discovered that the crew members had apparently reached shore, as he found that sails to provide rough tents were still there, as well as tools, bedding, and an old musket. A table had been set up in a sheltered location.

As he stepped out of the woods to return to the shore, he felt a tug on his tunic and was amazed to find a 14-year-old girl behind him. This was the girl Agnes, whom he had seen when he had visited the Benoit home. Her father had pointed her out to him and had stated that she was crazy.

She insisted that she was not crazy and told him, quite voluntarily, that she and her grandmother disapproved of the things that her father and uncle did. When asked to explain what she meant by this, she said that one day, 3 years ago, they came back to the house with their clothes and boots covered in blood. Her grandmother asked them the reason and they said that they had been out at Wild Cove shooting gulls. "No gulls you kill, you kill more poor men, now," she said, implying that she knew that they were in the business of murdering and robbing seamen. They told her to mind her own business and both withdrew to the bedroom. Agnes then said that she went around the house to a chink in the wall and saw them empty a canvas bag full of gold onto the bed. They divided the gold into two heaps and each pocketed their share.

When they returned to Wild Cove, Agnes said that she followed them at a distance and saw them dig up 20 bodies on the shore, dismem-

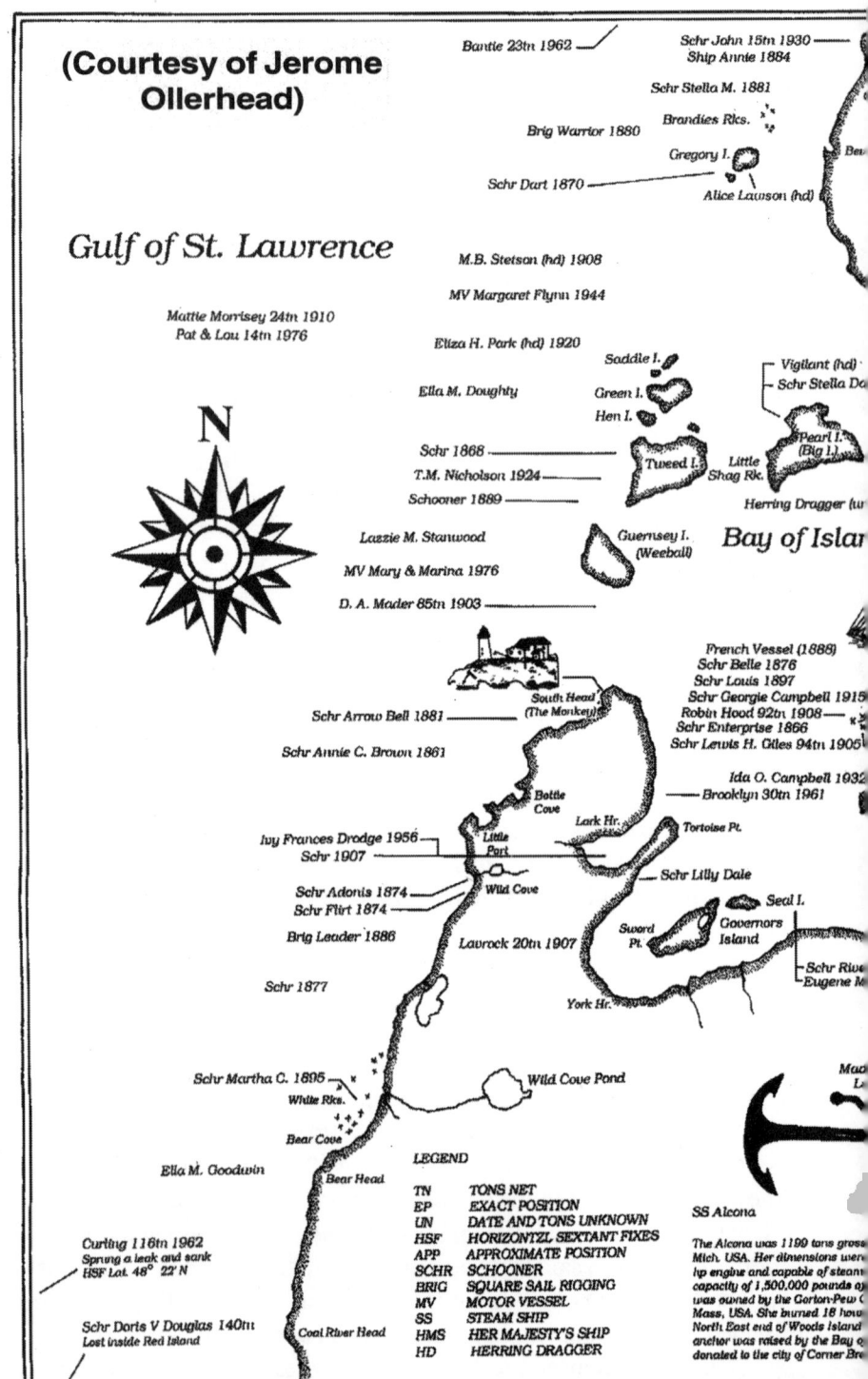

(Courtesy of Jerome Ollerhead)

Bantie 23tn 1962

Schr John 15tn 1930
Ship Annie 1884

Schr Stella M. 1881

Brig Warrior 1880

Brandies Rks.

Gregory I.

Schr Dart 1870

Alice Lawson (hd)

Gulf of St. Lawrence

M.B. Stetson (hd) 1908

MV Margaret Flynn 1944

Mattie Morrisey 24tn 1910
Pat & Lou 14tn 1976

Eliza H. Park (hd) 1920

Saddle I.

Vigilant (hd)
Schr Stella Da

Ella M. Doughty

Green I.

Hen I.

Pearl I.
(Big I.)

Schr 1868

T.M. Nicholson 1924

Tweed I.

Little
Shag Rk.

Schooner 1889

Herring Dragger (tr

Lazzie M. Stanwood

Guernsey I.
(Weeball)

Bay of Islan

MV Mary & Marina 1976

D. A. Mader 85tn 1903

French Vessel (1888)
Schr Belle 1876
Schr Louis 1897
Schr Georgie Campbell 1915
Robin Hood 92tn 1908
Schr Enterprise 1866
Schr Lewis H. Giles 94tn 1905

South Head
(The Monkey)

Schr Arrow Bell 1881

Schr Annie C. Brown 1861

Ida O. Campbell 1932
Brooklyn 30tn 1961

Bottle
Cove

Lark Hr.

Tortoise Pt.

Ivy Frances Drodge 1956
Schr 1907

Little
Port

Schr Adonis 1874
Schr Flirt 1874

Wild Cove

Schr Lilly Dale

Seal I.

Brig Leader 1886

Lavrock 20tn 1907

Sword
Pt.

Governors
Island

Schr Rive
Eugene M

Schr 1877

York Hr.

Schr Martha C. 1895

White Rks.

Wild Cove Pond

Mad
L

Bear Cove

LEGEND

Ella M. Goodwin

Bear Head

SS Alcona

Curling 116tn 1962
Sprung a leak and sank
HSF Lat. 48° 22' N

Schr Doris V Douglas 140tn
Lost inside Red Island

Coal River Head

TN	TONS NET
EP	EXACT POSITION
UN	DATE AND TONS UNKNOWN
HSF	HORIZONTZL SEXTANT FIXES
APP	APPROXIMATE POSITION
SCHR	SCHOONER
BRIG	SQUARE SAIL RIGGING
MV	MOTOR VESSEL
SS	STEAM SHIP
HMS	HER MAJESTY'S SHIP
HD	HERRING DRAGGER

The Alcona was 1199 tons gross
Mich. USA. Her dimensions were
lp engine and capable of steam
capacity of 1,500,000 pounds a
was owned by the Gorton-Pew (
Mass, USA. She burned 18 hou
North East end of Woods Island
anchor was raised by the Bay o
donated to the city of Corner Br

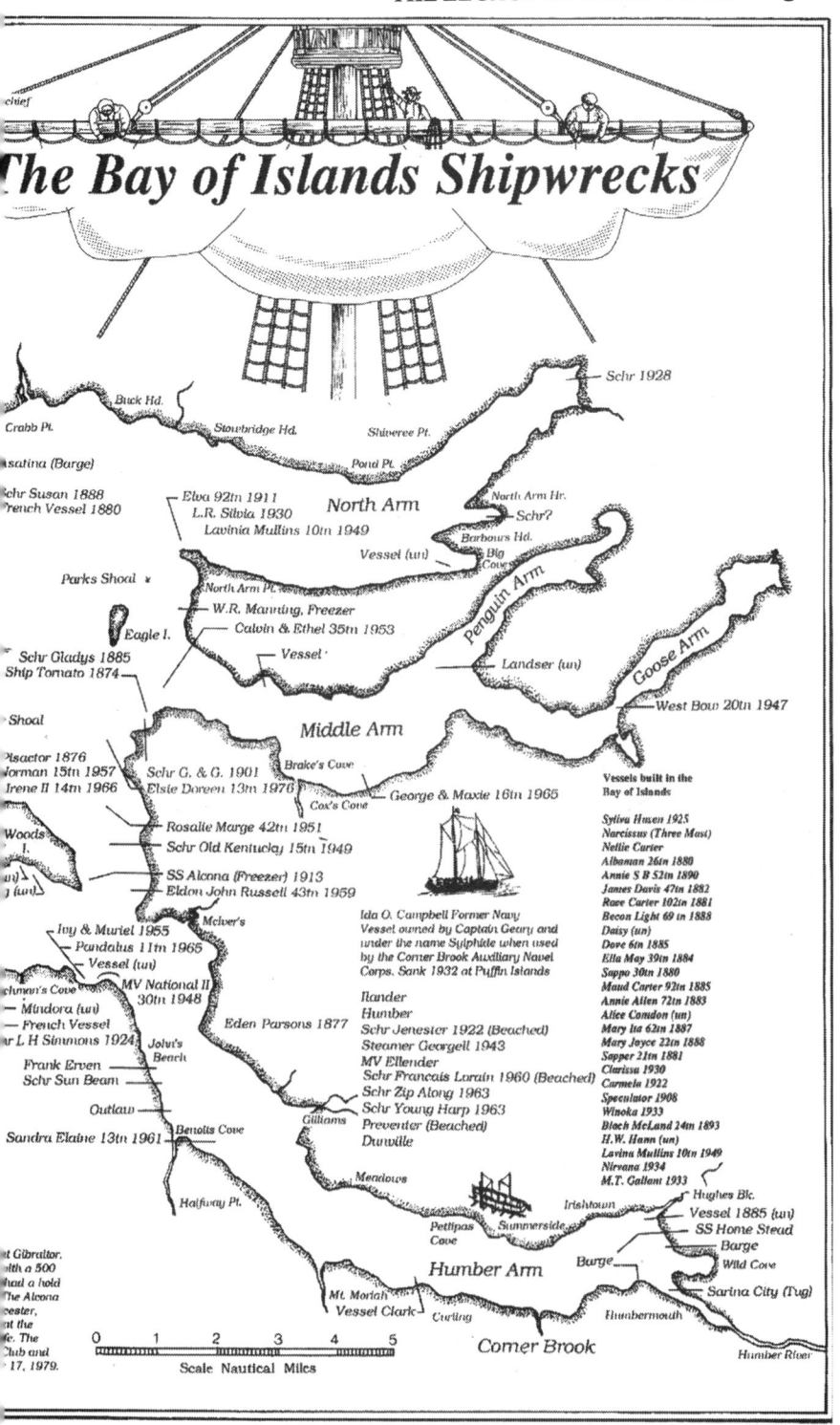

The Bay of Islands Shipwrecks

chief

Buck Hd.

Crabb Pt.

Stowbridge Hd.

Shiveree Pt.

Isatina (Barge)

Pond Pt.

Schr 1928

Schr Susan 1888
French Vessel 1880

Elva 92tn 1911
L.R. Silvia 1930
Lavinia Mullins 10tn 1949

North Arm

North Arm Hr.

Schr?

Barbours Hd.

Vessel (un)

Big Cove

Parks Shoal

North Arm Pt.

Penguin Arm

Eagle I.

W.R. Manning, Freezer
Calvin & Ethel 35tn 1953

Goose Arm

Schr Gladys 1885
Ship Tomato 1874

Vessel

Landser (un)

Shoal

Middle Arm

West Bow 20tn 1947

Pisactor 1876
Norman 15tn 1957
Irene II 14tn 1966

Schr G. & G. 1901
Elsie Doreen 13tn 1976

Brake's Cove

Cox's Cove

George & Maxie 16tn 1965

Vessels built in the
Bay of Islands

Woods I.

Rosalie Marge 42tn 1951
Schr Old Kentucky 15tn 1949

Sylvia Husen 1925
Narcissus (Three Mast)
Nellie Carter
Albanian 26tn 1880
Annie S B 52tn 1890
James Davis 47tn 1882
Rave Carter 102tn 1881
Becon Light 69 tn 1888
Daisy (un)
Dove 6tn 1885
Ella May 39tn 1884
Sappo 30tn 1880
Maud Carter 92tn 1885
Annie Allen 72tn 1883
Alice Comdon (un)
Mary Isa 62tn 1887
Mary Joyce 23tn 1888
Clarissa 1930
Carmela 1922
Speculator 1908
Winoka 1933
Black McLeod 24tn 1893
H.W. Hann (un)
Lavinia Mullins 10tn 1949
Nireana 1934
M.T. Gallant 1933

SS Alcona (Freezer) 1913
Eldon John Russell 43tn 1959

McIver's

Ida O. Campbell Former Navy
Vessel owned by Captain Geary and
under the name Sylphide when used
by the Corner Brook Auxiliary Navel
Corps. Sank 1932 at Puffin Islands

Ivy & Muriel 1955
Pandalus 11tn 1965
Vessel (un)

Rander
Humber
Schr Jenester 1922 (Beached)
Steamer Georgell 1943
MV Ellender
Schr Francais Lorain 1960 (Beached)
Schr Zip Along 1963
Schr Young Harp 1963
Preventer (Beached)
Dunville

tchman's Cove
MV National II
30tn 1948

Mindora (un)
French Vessel
ar L H Simmons 1924

Eden Parsons 1877

John's Beach

Frank Erven
Schr Sun Beam

Outlaw

Gilliams

Sandra Elaine 13tn 1961

Benoits Cove

Meadows

Hughes Blk.

Vessel 1885 (un)
SS Home Stead
Barge
Wild Cove

Irishtown

t Gibralter,
ith a 500
had a hold
The Alcona
cester,
t the
e. The
Club and
17, 1979.

Halfway Pt.

Pettipas
Cove

Summerside

Burge

Humber Arm

Sarina City (Tug)

Mt. Moriah
Vessel Clark

Curling

Humbermouth

Corner Brook

Humber River

0   1   2   3   4   5

Scale Nautical Miles

ber them and carry them into a small muddy pond in the woods. She was sure that she counted 20 bodies, not 21. After witnessing this grisly act, she took a short cut through the woods and was back in Benoits Cove before the brothers' arrival.

Constable Kelland found no bodies and none were ever discovered, although the pond was later dragged with hooks. He discovered no other clues but did note that the board that the crew had used for dining was grooved on both sides resembling marks that could have been made by musket balls. He spent the night in the tilt, Jacko having disappeared to parts unknown some weeks previously. On his return to Curling he obtained a search warrant hoping to find the canvas bag belonging to Captain Rideout, but a search of the Benoit home found nothing. The Benoit brothers denied having anything to do with Rideout and his crew or even to have seen them.

After receiving Kelland's report, which suggested that the crew might have been shot and then clubbed to death while sitting together at the table, Magistrate Howorth felt that he had enough evidence for a charge of murder and the two brothers were committed to trial in St. John's, arriving there in September 1877 on SS <u>Curlew</u>. The grandmother was not brought as a witness as her testimony was felt likely to be unreliable, but Agnes was brought in as the prosecution's key witness. She testified to the same story as she had given to Kelland and kept to it in spite of fierce cross examination. Kelland's theory of the murder was rejected as hypothetical and the Benoits were acquitted due to a lack of bodies and other evidence. Unfortunately, the transcripts of the trial have been lost, probably in the 1893 fire in St. John's.

The Benoits were sent home scotfree. Agnes' return was felt to be inadvisable. She obtained work as housekeeper to a priest in St. John's. It is not known how long she stayed there, as a resident reported that she returned to Benoits Cove and was reported to be looking after Gil, her elderly father, as recently as 1912, after her uncle had died. The relatives of the missing crew members continued to demand an explanation for their disappearance and eventually Chief Constable Sullivan was sent out to make a further investigation. He found nothing except for a single skeleton on the shore, perhaps that of Jacko?

So the disappearance of captain and crew of the <u>Flirt</u> remains an unsolved mystery. Edgar Kelland seems to have had no doubt about the guilt of Gil and Exaviour Benoit. François was never implicated by Agnes and may well have been quite innocent. Kelland theorised that the two brothers had ambushed the crew members while they were eating, perhaps drunk and seated on both sides of the table. The brothers crept up and fired at them in a simultaneous volley of buckshot (hence the grooves on the table) and afterwards had despatched them with the butts of their muskets, using them as clubs, as they would not have had time to reload.

George Cammie, who has done some research on the mystery, feels that the brothers were guilty and that Agnes' story was true. He thinks that the bodies may have been dumped in the surrounding bog rather than Wild Cove pond, as the pond is located quite a distance from the shore and above a small incline. When I pointed out to him that Benoits Cove is at least 25 miles distance from Wild Cove, with the Blomidon Mountains and Lewis Hills intervening, he felt that the return journey was quite possible for a 14-year-old girl in those days. Kelland had noted that when she had left him she broke into an Indian trot, which the MicMac Indians used to cover long distances quickly.[30] The practice of luring ships onto the shore where they could be robbed was not uncommon in parts of Newfoundland. Perhaps Jacko lured the Flirt ashore with a lantern to resemble the light on South Head and then aided the brothers in killing and robbing the crew?

Communications with the rest of the world were improving. A post office was built in 1872; prior to this letters had to go by an Indian courier on foot to Channel, at the cost of $1. In 1877 a telegraph station was built at Birchy Cove, first operated by G. Lemoine. At last the Bay of Islands was connected to the outside world, and it was a telegram to Rev. Curling in Bonne Bay in 1881 that alerted him to the fact that Captain Howorth was dying, worn out by his arduous assignment to this apparently lawless area. Curling immediately returned on foot in the middle of February, nearly losing his own life in the process. Also in 1878 the Supreme Court of Newfoundland held its first session in the Bay of Islands. The court house was situated at the present site of the Bay of Islands war memorial. Eventually, in 1881, Sir Frederick Carter, the Prime Minister of Newfoundland, authorised his government to make grants with title to land on the French shore and to allow west coast residents to elect two representatives to the House of Assembly. Michael H. Carty was the first to be elected. This entitlement ended the period of political isolation from the rest of the island.

I cannot leave this period without again referring to our first two great heroes, Monsignor Sears and Rev. Curling. They met on several occasions and established a good relationship. However, on July 20, 1876, Rev. Curling wrote to Rev. Sears admonishing him gently for

[30] George has already written a poem about this strange incident which he has put to music and I hope that this will be used in a sketch about this mystery that may be performed by the Grenfell College Drama Group.

rebaptising some of his Anglican converts while he was in Bonne Bay. Two years later Rev. Sears wrote to Rev. Curling protesting that the school at Sprucy Point, which was at that time the only one in the Bay, was not granting Catholic children exemption from the first school hour of religious instruction, according to their previous agreement. Rev. Curling had a boat of 33 tons called Sapper built in the Bay of Islands to replace his Lavrock, and lent it to Monsignor Sears to visit Bonne Bay on one occasion. Monsignor Sears was responsible for building four schools; books were in short supply but were circulated through the school system. Several churches were built including St. Joseph in 1870, Our Lady of Mercy in Benoits Cove in 1874, and the Church of the Holy Family in 1875. He estimated Roman Catholic population at that time at about 700, out of a total of about 1500, and they were from England, Nova Scotia, Bay Chaleur, and some Acadian French and Irish. The Monsignor's health started to deteriorate in 1883 and, although he was joined by his sister from Ireland, he was forced to resign and retired to Nova Scotia where he died soon after on November 7, 1885. Searston in the Codroy Valley is named in his memory.

Rev. Curling resigned soon after, in 1886. He too had been in poor health since his arduous return journey to Bonne Bay in 1881. He had been appointed Rural Dean for the whole area in 1880. The school he had built in Sprucy Point burned in 1877 but was rebuilt, and in 1882 he enlarged the church of St. Mary in Johns Beach quite elegantly but that also burned down. In 1886 he returned to England and took up residence in Oxford, intending to take a degree in Theology and to give his three children some further education. He returned to Newfoundland to accompany Bishop Llewellyn Jones on a tour of his Rural Deanery in 1887, again visiting Bay of Islands in 1889. At this point, it was decided that he would not return to the west coast again. So this remarkable man packed up his belongings and sailed back to England in 20 days in the Sapper. He later obtained his degree at the age of 46 and returned to St. John's in the fall of 1890 to work again, serving several nearby outports and settlements. That winter, exceptionally severe, was arduous work, but his wife usually accompanied him, having left the children in the good care of her sister in Hamble, Hampshire. Next April he was appointed Principal of Queen's College in St. John's but at the same time the vicarage at Hamble became vacant and he was urged by family and friends to apply for it. So he only served 1 year at the St. John's training college, and returned to England for good in 1892. He nevertheless continued to take a great interest in Newfoundland and in

Lavrock

Sapper

Above pictures courtesy of the West Newfoundland Anglican Synod

missionary work in general, dying in 1906. In 1904 Birchy Cove was renamed Curling in his memory. <u>Lavrock</u> continued as a mission ship until 1909 when, ironically, it grounded near York Harbour, a total loss.

Sears and Curling had departed, but the potential of the Bay of Islands was now being increasingly recognised by the rest of the island, and the next phase of the development was only impeded by the vexatious French shore question, involving an increasingly angry and impatient House of Assembly in St. John's with what they considered to be a pusillanimous British and an intransigent French government.

CHAPTER 6

The Arrival of the Railway

Communication with larger communities was initiated first of all with the mainland of Canada when a regular steamship service was started from Halifax in 1888, visiting communities on the southwest coast and Bay of Islands; regular communication with St John's had to wait for the Newfoundland railway to be extended. Indeed, commercial development in the late 19th century was primarily initiated by entrepreneurs from Nova Scotia, who built the sawmill in Corner Brook, and who offered their technology, along with that of the Americans, to help develop the lobster fishery. Once this steamship service was introduced, post offices were opened at Birchy Cove, where the postmaster was William Bagg, at Summerside where the postmaster was Thomas Carter, and at Benoits Cove, where James Evitt managed the service.

St. John's and its merchants were now at the centre of the east coast fishery, with the influence of the west of England merchants declining. The merchants of St. John's were anxious to develop commercial and mining activity on the west coast after a favourable survey of mining prospects in Newfoundland had been published by Alexander Murray in 1867. But the vexatious French shore question remained an immovable obstacle to exploitation of the west coast's natural resources. In 1884 the French government refused to allow Newfoundland to extend the railway to a terminus on the French shore. To avoid irritating the French, the British government refused to allow the Colonial government to grant mining licences on that shore in 1867.

In 1893, the Whiteway government decided to proceed with plans to build the railway from St. John's to Port aux Basques in spite of French objections. An agreement was reached with the Scottish industrialist R.G. Reid to construct the railway. A letter from Austin Chamberlain in the British Colonial Office to Governor Murray, dated March 23, 1898, referred to the Reid contract as an "extraordinary measure" and expressed regret that "the colony, after more than 40 years of self government, should have to resort to such a step." In fact, the Reid Company would own a large amount of land, a telegraph system—and the railway itself! This major construction project employed 3,000 men, proceeding steadily across the island. Once the track down the Humber Valley to Humbermouth had been completed, engineers were faced with a choice of three routes. The first option involved grading up along the future route of the Trans Canada Highway. The second option suggested following the course of Bell's Brook. The third option, ultimately decided upon, was to proceed along the shoreline from Curling to Petries and Mount Moriah, then following the grade up Cook's Brook.

When the first train to cross Newfoundland left St. John's on June 29th, 1898, it took 27.5 hours to reach Port aux Basques. In 1900, a railway station and roundhouse were built, and a machine shop was constructed in Humbermouth to enable repairs to be carried out to locomotives and rolling stock. In the same year, a railway office opened in Curling, occupying part of the old Western Star building. There was, however, no railway station in Corner Brook.

With a marked lack of foresight, the railway was built to a narrower gauge than on the mainland. Moreover, it was poorly maintained while owned by the Reid Company, with frequent delays due to snow during winter. George Tipple, a railway engineer, recalls a time when a train was snowed under for 2 months at Gaff Topsail. The passengers had no choice but to leave the train and walk about 30 kilometres to the nearest community—Deer Lake. On December 31, 1917, an avalanche on the track near Shellbird Island on the Humber River, killed Joshua Peddle. According to the records of the Curling Constabulary dated Jan 2, 1918, Peddle was employed as a section man and fellow workers testified that they saw him swept into the Humber River by an avalanche near the quarry. His body was recovered the following May on Woods Island.

In railway's inaugural year, a large fire devastated the communities of Mount Moriah, Petries, and part of Birchy Cove. Starting near Cook's Brook, its progress through Birchy Cove was arrested at St. Mary's Brook, although the railway trestle across the brook was destroyed. There is no consensus on the date of this first great fire; it is generally thought to have started on the afternoon of June 11, 1899, whereas the Evening Telegram suggests that it began June 12. Spreading quickly due to the dry summer and absence of men away at sea, the fire ultimately destroyed 54 buildings and left 48 families homeless with few possessions. None had fire insurance. A few days after the fire, Mr. Gibbs, MHA for the district of St. George's, appealed in the Evening Telegram for financial help for the 300 or so destitute men, women, and children. Although the full amount donated is unknown, the first three contributions came from railway owner R.G. Reid for $100, M.P. Gibbs for $25, and " an anonymous friend" for $5. Rev. Curling heard of the disaster in England and immediately arranged for a shipment of blankets and supplies to be sent to the homeless. Two years after the fire, most families had rebuilt. To commemorate the 40th anniversary of this great fire, the Western Star produced a column that identified sources of shelter for the dispossessed—in the homes of friends, in the Brittania and the St. Patrick's church halls, and aboard schooners offshore. Fires in this area were not uncommon, usually occurring annually and in increased numbers when the weather was dry. Burnt Brook and Burnt Pond, though, did not acquire their names until another big fire in 1938.

Many men were employed to extinguish brush fires in the early days of the wood burning locomotives. Others found employment in cutting birch for railway ties, and were paid 10¢ for each birch tie. Financial losses amassed, and on July 1, 1923, the Reid Company was bought out by the Colonial government. The ensuing Monroe administration modernized the railway, improving track and equipment, converting the locomotives to coal. Trains changed from only three carriages with a small locomotive in the early years to 17, even 20, carriages in later years, with corresponding increase in freight cars upon the advent of diesel engines in 1953. Unfortunately, no government was able to finance a wide track rail system to conform to the mainline gauge, even after Confederation, and the "Newfie Bullet," as it was nicknamed, still took 22 hours to travel between St. John's and Port aux Basques and was the only trans island land route until the Trans Canada Highway was completed and paved in 1965. The completion of the Trans Canada Highway across the country foretold the death of the railway. Assuming control of the railway after Confederation, Canadian National lost millions of dollars a year maintaining it. Beside increasing competition from road transport, it also faced competition from ACE shipping, which brought freight from Halifax and Montreal direct to St. John's and Corner Brook. The Newfoundland railway closed for good in 1988, after the ACE group successfully purchased Ellison Butt's shipping company, which had maintained a commercial shipping operation to West Newfoundland ever since the Clarke Steamship Company closed their Corner Brook service in 1982.

The successful construction of the railway encouraged the Newfoundland government to allow the opening of a copper mine in 1897 in spite of protests from the French government who objected to the construction of a proper wharf. Discovered by Simeon Wheeler, the mine was situated on a site east of York Harbour on the north shore. It closed in 1912, changing hands for $110,000 in 1905. After the settlement of the French shore dispute in 1904, a new wharf was built and at peak operation the mine employed 30 men working in two shifts of 12 hours each and earning 20¢ an hour. Ore was hoisted out of the mine by a system of pulleys, crushed using sledge hammers, and conveyed down to the shore by cars. The property is now owned by Noranda. Copper ore bodies are still in the area but further mining of the original adit has been impeded by faulting along the track of the ore body, according to a company spokesman.

Two slate quarries were started in the Bay of Islands, the first in Summerside in 1902 and the other near Birchy Cove in 1907. Several experienced miners were brought across from Wales to work these mines, but both operations ceased after a few years because of financial and marketing problems and most of the Welshmen and their families returned home. The first manager of both quarries was Owen J. Owen, a shadowy character who was a promoter rather than a quarry manager. Although the Reid Company had ordered 30,000 slates with which to roof the new railway station in St. John's, and a good number had been

Drawn from a photograph submitted by Norval Oxford

produced at Summerside, none were actually shipped, and still remain at the old site under debris. A few were used by school children as slateboards! The Birchy Cove quarry worked on and off for less than a year, beset by poor markets and by strikes by the Newfoundland workers for equal pay with the Welsh workers.

Several commercial attempts were made between 1869 and 1908 to quarry marble from the deposits on the hills alongside the Lower Humber River but all were unsuccessful. Probably the quarrysite until recently used by moose hunters for sighting in their rifles was the area leased by Captain Philip Cleary. His company managed to make only one shipment of marble to the United Kingdom before the manager quit and the business collapsed. This quarry, now known as the Limestone Junction Quarry, was mined by the paper companies from 1925 to 1943 to provide limestone used in the sulphite pulping process. It's use was then discontinued because of the close proximity to the road and to the railway. Bowaters then began mining the Dormston Quarry situated near the top of West Valley Road for the same purpose until 1956, producing that disfigureing scar on the side of the mountain overlooking Corner Brook. Rock from this quarry was also used in the construction of Western Memorial Hospital, and later in 1958 in the harbour development at Seal Head. In 1961 quarrying was terminated after an RCMP officer on duty was killed by a rock from a blasting operation. The paper company then bought limestone from the Leonard House quarry, on the right side of the highway close to the Riverside turnoff, until it's use was phased out when thermo mechanical pulping was introduced.

Most of the international fishing activity by the Americans and Nova Scotians was related to the Bay of Islands herring fishery and was centred at Curling, Summerside, and Woods Island. An American company based in Gloucester, Massachusetts, had owned a base on the east end of Woods Island since July 1911 comprising a supply store, storage shed, and a packing plant, all managed by the genial Chaine Hall. Another packing plant was located in North Arm and a firm of buyers owned by Forsey and Moulton also had a plant in Lark Harbour. The American schooners were mostly crewed by Newfoundlanders, some of whom lived in New England and had become US citizens. The Americans loaded their schooners with lightly salted herring, called bloaters, from the fall fishery and transported them to Gloucester. This trade petered out after the Second World War and after confederation with Canada.

The promotion of "Scotch Cure" was said to be responsible for this decline in the herring fishery trade, though the relaxation of strict religious observance of dietary customs in the world was also a factor. For example, after Vatican II there were no longer days when Catholics were obliged to eat fish. It is true that Scotch Cure was a more wasteful and expensive process. It involved bleeding and degutting herring, known as "popping," but provided more secondary processing for the fishermen. Experts could carry out the process in a few seconds and could earn $2 a tub instead of $1.25 for a barrel of bloaters (two tubs). The Americans were often unwilling to pay the extra money for Scotch Cure.

Even after the decline of this international fishery the herring fishery continued to be pursued by local merchants with some success. After Gorton Pew left Woods Island, the fishermen formed a co-op to export live lobsters to Boston and to supply a plant in Summerside with material for a fish reduction process, which continued to be operated until some time in the 1960s by the Crosbie organization.

Fishery-related enterprises were nothing new to the Crosbies. In 1941, Chesley Crosbie, a well known St. John's fish merchant and businessman and known to all as Ches, bought a piece of land in Summerside from Alfred Quigley.[31] He formed a company called Newfoundland Dehydrating Process Company Limited with 50% equity owned by US interests in Boston, Massachussetts. It cost half a million dollars to finance and was intended to produce fish meal and oil from Bay of Islands, and herring for sale in the North American market. The operation would need large quantities of herring to make it economically successful, and this meant that supplies from the local residents, who used gill nets and small boats, would have to be supplemented by the use of purse seines operated from larger boats and employed by a subsidiary company called "Herring Unlimited", it's very name evocative of nonconservation. But there had been a government ban on purse seining for herring; this method of fishing was able to corral far greater quantities of herring than the small gill nets. However, Crosbie's partner Olaf Olsen had already persuaded the Newfoundland Fisheries Board to rescind this ban after he had taken the President of the Board to Norway in 1936 to show him how fishermen used herring seining in their industry.

The plan had a capacity of processing 300 tons of herring a day into fish meal and oil, but the enterprising St. John's merchant also learned of a use for herring scales in the fashion industry. The scales were removed from the herring in a fairly simple process using wire mesh, and a lucrative contract with an American firm enabled these scales to be used to provide the sheen for artificial pearls, sequins, buttons, and iridescent paint.

[31] This account is taken, with permission, from Michael Harris's well written and well researched book, <u>Rare Ambition, the Crosbies of Newfoundland</u>, and from the <u>Western Star</u>.

The Crosbie company needed large vessels suitable for seining and intended to equip them with sonar to locate the schools of herring. He applied to the Commission of Government for money for a survey to research the habits of Bay of Islands herring and the most efficient method of catching them. Instead, the Commissioners agreed to give Crosbie a $100,000 loan at 3.5% to build herring seines. The Governor of Newfoundland explained the decision in a telegram to the Department of Dominion Affairs in London: he "attached great importance to this business which is [the] first real step in proper development of herring industry in Bay of Islands."

The new plant was in operation by 1942, supplied by a fleet of seiners and by a collector ship called <u>Western Star</u> that could pick up herring from the local fishermen. One would expect that the new plant would be appreciated by the fishermen as it would enable them to sell to the plant fish that were too small for Scotch Cure processing. But they were resentful of the use of large seines and suspicious of the use of sonar which they believed would frighten the fish away. More than likely, the Curling fish merchants encouraged their mistrust of the St. John's "townie." But the fire which completely destroyed Crosbie's wooden frame plant in 1944 appears to have been due to natural causes.

Ches Crosbie's response to this growing resentment was to persuade the government to provide financial support to build a more modern plant and wharf. Up to this time he had personally managed the herring operations, living in style in the Glynmill Inn away from his wife and family in St. John's and enjoying his favourite pursuits of "wine, women, and song." His marriage to his wife Jessie was disintegrating and he allegedly had a mistress in Corner Brook to console him. But when the new plant was completed his other businesses were requiring more of his attention, as his partner Olaf Olsen had recently died. He therefore brought in Bill Crosbie, his youngest brother, to carry out the executive responsibilities. Bill had just returned from service with a Canadian tank regiment in World War II, where he distinguished himself and was awarded the Distinguished Service Order (DSO) for service in Italy and western Europe, finishing his army career as Major. Young Bill Crosbie was going to need all the skills he had learned from confronting Germans to enable him to deal with the angry fishermen from the Bay of Islands.

Shortly after the start of the 1946 spring herring fishery he was asleep on board the <u>Western Star</u> at Woods Island, having spent the previous day and most of the night loading fish on the collector boat. He was woken early in the morning by his chief assistant Robert McCarthy who told him that some men had seized a bar seine and were setting the herring free. He wondered what he should do, but before long some men landed on the wharf intending to seize the other seines. Seizing other men's nets is considered a very hostile act and is not part of the fisherman's culture in Bay of Islands or anywhere else, and Bill and Robert were able to defy the intruders on this occasion. But later on, shortly after they had returned to work, a large flotilla of boats with several dozen men appeared, took the seines, and tried to seize the ship. Bill reacted bravely and resourcefully by raising the ship's flag and instructing his mate to man a powerful water hose to be used against anyone who attempted to board. He went up to the front of the ship and got McCarthy's son to call out the names of the men in the circling boats, noting them down and telling the men that he would prosecute the men for attempting to seize the ship. They dispersed.

That evening Bill went to the Glynmill Inn to discuss the matter with Ches. They decided that Bill would go to Magistrate Timothy Wade and swear out summonses against the men on his list. He did so, and later that Sunday morning Magistrate Wade and Pierce Fudge, the president of the Labourers Union, accompanied by two police officers, set out in the fishery inspector's boat to serve the summonses. They were met with a volley of stones from the shore at McIver's, their first stop, but Pierce Fudge persuaded them to show respect for the law and to allow the magistrate to land and listen to their grievances. After the men told the magistrate that they had not stolen the seines but had only removed them until the fishing season was over, when they intended to return them, Wade said nothing about the summonses. He also said nothing about summonses at other communities.

Next morning Robert McCarthy told Crosbie what had happened, and said that the magistrate had even tried to persude him to join in the protest against the Crosbies when he landed at Woods Island. Ches was furious, and Bill called on the magistrate to find out what was going on. Magistrate Wade maintained that his discretion had avoided a riot but Bill insisted on appealing to Albert Walsh, the Commissioner for Justice. He asked the Commiussioner to send an adequate police detachment to reclaim the stolen property; the Bay of Islands only had a 7-man force at the time.

Bill ventured to the Glynmill Inn, but when he went to his brother's room later on he found that Ches, probably half in the bag, had been unable to restrain himself and was grabbing Wade by the throat. He was probably shouting something like "You son of a bitch, you little Jeezler, you don't think I don't know what you were up to yesterday!" when Bill tried to get Ches away from the magistrate, but he eventually got to calm him down and listen to reason.

The suggestion was made that instead of sending more police, the herring fishery would be closed down, enabling the seines to be returned. But Raymond Gushue, the Chairman of the Newfoundland Fisheries Board, refused to close the season 5 weeks early. He said that there were international quotas remaining to be filled, and that the Newfoundland government needed the foreign exchange. Instead it was decided to convene a public meeting, attended by representatives of the owners and the fishermen and a member of the Fisheries Board, to discuss differences.

The meeting was held in the Majestic Theatre in Townsite on Sunday, May 26, and as a precautionary measure all taverns were closed. Over 800 fishermen attended. According to the May 31st edition of the Western Star, they were first addressed by Pierce Fudge and Magistrate Wade. Raymond Gushue then informed the audience that no other country, including Canada, now fished for herring without using seines. He then went on to make the unfortunate remark that in his opinion the use of seines could not possibly destroy the stock. After guaranteeing to take all the herring that were offered to the plant by the fishermen, Ches Crosbie left his lawyer, Gorden Higgins, to appeal for order to prevent more police being brought in from St. John's. After discussion from the floor, which was likely noisy and heated, the meeting resolved to give the seines back at once to the Crosbies. In return, another meeting would be held after the season was over to determine the location of the fishing zones where the use of seines would be authorized.

But next morning when Bill returned to Woods Island he was told by Robert McCarthy that the fishermen had changed their minds and would not give up the seines. He suspected that the seines were stored in a 2-story loft near the wharf at McIvers but when he landed on the wharf he was confronted by the men in the settlement. When he asked them whether they were going to live up to the terms of the agreement he was met with a stony silence. He held his ground, lead pipe in hand, at the end of the wharf and firmly ordered Robert McCarthy to enter the loft and to throw the seines down and load them into the ship's dinghy. McCarthy must have been a brave man too, as he carried out his orders, while the men murmured and discussed whether to throw both Robert and Bill into the harbour. Eventually they decided to let them go, impressed by their bravery. Bill Crosbie later said that this episode was as frightening as anything he had experienced in wartime.

There was no happy ending for the Crosbies and the Newfoundland Dehydrating Process Company. When the meeting was convened at the end of the herring season it was resolved that seines would only be allowed outside the headlands of the Bay of Islands, which considerably handicapped the Crosbie operations. Herring became scarce in the Bay in the 1950s and the plant became increasingly unprofitable, losing $2,000,000 before it was finally closed. Ches Crosbie later headed the party promoting Responsible government for Newfoundland in the 1949 referendum campaign. It seems possible that the animosity towards his herring operation in the Bay of Islands was at least partly responsible for the large vote cast for the Confederation Party in this riding.

Inshore fishermen in the Bay of Islands were still using dories and still do, but after World War II the use of outboard engines began to replace oars and sail. Fishing activities using lobster traps, gill nets, and bait lines were continued, as in other parts of the island, and transportation by dory was essential until roads around the south and north shore were constructed. Boys would usually leave their denominational schools in their early teens to work in the fishery with their fathers or relatives. No one really considered other occupations.

The barter system was still used by the merchants and the local fishermen, but cash rather than credit was beginning to be used more and more as the 20th century progressed. Money was provided by trade in fish with Nova Scotian and American vessels, and the Americans usually paid in gold up until the outbreak of the First World War. Now there was also seasonal work in logging for the sawmills and wages were also paid to gangs of workers to keep the railroad clear and free of fires. The herring and lobster fisheries continued to be the main fishing activities, with some cod fishing. A whaling station was built in Lark Harbour in 1911 but it soon closed due to lack of markets. Local legend says that they did catch one whale before the plant closed. A barrel of herring, salted, now fetched $5 and a barrel of Scotch Cure herring with gills and guts removed would sell for $20. Codfish would be caught in the outer Bay of Islands; the men lived in shacks close to the fishery from May to August, using codtraps or baited hook and line. Lobsters were caught in two types of traps, most using the familiar type of wooden trap in general use today. Lobster pots and nets needed repairing in the slack season and some fishermen, like William Noseworthy of Cox's Cove, were even capable of making their own barrels. He recalls that he first fished for herring from a 60-foot row boat when he was a young boy, using a net.

The introduction of cash as a means of exchange brought with it the banking system. The Colonial banks in St. John's had collapsed in 1894 under mountains of debts and mismanagement. This had brought the Canadian banks into the island by invitation, and the Bank of Montreal opened a few branches in west Newfoundland, opening a branch in Birchy Cove in 1902 in the Western Star building. A new building was constructed shortly afterwards on Main Street, Curling, rebuilt twice after being ravaged by fires in the next few years.

The railway made a big difference socially to resettlement of the small communities on the Bay of Islands as people tended to migrate to the railway side of the Bay, especially Curling, which then became the main trading centre. Before the coming of the railway, Meadows, Summerside and even Corner Brook all had a significantly higher population than Curling. In 1857 the population of the whole Humber River area was only 157 people, increasing to about 2000 in 1891. Then only half the population could read or write, although there were small schools in Benoits Cove, John's Beach, and Birchy Cove and Summerside. In 1901 there were 2,820 in the census, which included Deer Lake, settled first by George Nichols in 1870, and approximately 60% of these were Protestant. In 1911 numbers had risen to 4,473, about a quarter of whom now lived in Curling. A surprising number of persons still lived in small communities in the outer Bay of Islands, including Goose Arm, Middle Arm and Penguin Arm as well as Lark and York Harbour. In 1921 there were still only 4,700 people living in the Bay of Islands. In that year, the census recorded six families in the settlement of South Brook, a small station on the railway between Deer Lake and Corner Brook which amalgamated with Pasadena in the 1980s.

Corner Brook, the site of the largest sawmill in the Bay of Islands but as yet with no railway station, was described in 1881 by a visiting Presbyterian minister as "The quiet Nova Scotia settlement of Corner Brook." Many of the sawmill workers were from Nova Scotia and of the Presbyterian faith. As long ago as 1866 a Presbyterian minister the Rev. R. Archibald had visited the community but the main immigration came in 1872. The Rev. David Creelman arrived as the first resident minister in 1876 and built the first Presbyterian church in Birchy Cove and Sunday schools in both Petries and in Corner Brook in 1877. A building in Corner Brook was also used for worship until a church was built and opened in August 1898 on the side now occupied by the Coop Store on Fishers Hill.

Rev. H. Petley

This large church, seating 120 people, was designed by the Rev. W. C. Morrison. Building material was supplied by sawmill owner Christopher Fisher, and granite was supplied by Gaff Topsail Quarry. The church was built with free labour and contributions from the congregation. When no longer in use as a centre of worship, this building was carefully dismantled in 1940. Some of its contents were then incorporated in the Curling Memorial Church, and Don Thistle, who grew up in Corner Brook, says that he remembers the building itself being dragged across by a horse and a system of pulleys (which fascinated him)to form part of the future United Church on West Street.

A Methodist church was built in Birchy Cove in 1890, later destroyed by fire in 1943. Rev. Peter Bryce, later the Moderator of the United Church of Canada, was the first resident minister of the church in 1903. The congregation joined the United Church of Canada in 1925. The Rev. Petley was the Anglican Minister in Birchy Cove from 1904 to 1935. Beside being a well liked minister, he was also a well rounded sportsman—an accomplished fly fisherman who was usually accompanied on his visits around the bay by his fly rod. Summerside already had a Roman Catholic church, built in 1870.

Communication with the outside world had improved with the onset of the regular mail service in 1888 and the opening of telegraph service in 1878. A group of investors, including Christopher Fisher and Walter March, started a weekly newspaper, first published on April 4, 1900, and at first its type was entirely hand set under the management of Walter S. March. Its ownership changed hands several times and was eventually assumed by Arthur L. Barrett in 1924. Mr. Barrett and his family had been associated with the paper since its first issue and managed and edited it up until the Bowaters purchase in 1941. After Bowaters bought the paper, production was moved to Corner Brook. Following the installation of modern equipment, it was published daily. In 1952 the Herder family purchased the Star from Bowaters. It was later sold to the Thompson group and in 1996 purchased by Conrad Black and the Southam group. For a few years in the 1920s the Star faced some competition from the Humber Herald, but that paper failed to survive. The Humber Log, a weekly paper, was started in 1981 and confines itself to local news and events.[32]

Indeed, the Western Star has served the community well. There have been many editors over the past Century but its editorial columns usually reflect the west coast's positive and progressive outlook and it has avoided the scurrilous reporting and partisanship common in earlier days of the St. John's papers. The "Roamer" column is good at pointing out defects in the function of City Hall and civic services and there is no censorship of the "Letters to the Editor;" people are able to express their sometimes bizarre views and vent their anger. The paper has also tried hard to publish news from the west coast from Bay of Islands to Port

[32] Copies of old issues of the Western Star have been preserved on microfilm in the Western Star building and in the Corner Brook Library but unfortunately its early printings had deteriorated before they were microfilmed. However, future writers interested in the history of the Bay of Islands might like to know that Bruce Stevenson on O'Connell Drive has copies of all the old editions of the Western Star donated to him by Arthur Barrett.

*The Petries Hotel, Birchy Cove, Bay of Islands, Newfound-
land, Destroyed by fire in 1929
—Courtesy of Mrs Olga Eastman*

aux Basques.

In 1901, a few years after the trans island railway was completed,
the population of Bay St. George was still more numerous than the Bay
of Islands and surpassed it in production of salmon and agriculture. Cod
and lobster production was about the same in the two bays, but the herring fishery, though variable from year to year, was much greater in the
Bay of Islands. And this bay was still the only place on the west coast
that built vessels of more than 100 tons. Several familiar family names
now appear for the first time in trading records. The Pynn family from
St. John's operated a small sawmill and the Barry and Dunphy families
of Irish origin became involved in the herring trade. Traders from the
east coast included the Murphys, Bolands and Petries, who originally
came from Sligo in Ireland and who operated an elegant tourist hotel at
Petries Point, used by American sports fishermen who fished the Humber River. The hotel was completely destroyed by fire on May 14th,
1929.

By 1906 a bakery was in operation at Meadows. Charles Farnell
came from Nova Scotia in 1859 and at first lived in Summerside, working in the sawmill at Pynn's Brook. In 1870 he moved across the bay
and operated a blacksmith forge and cooperage as well as a small general store and dispensary on land to the west of the Corner Brook
sawmill. This versatile man had apparently learned some medical remedies and techniques from Dr Preble in Bonne Bay, an unqualified apoth-

ecary. Olga Eastman is related to the Farnell family and says that her grandmother told her that Charles even performed a successful appendectomy on a Miss Jones on the kitchen table!

In this early part of the 20th century and through the First World War the west coast remained "on the fringe of the hinterlands of St. John's and Halifax, an entrepreneurial backwater in a rapidly specialising and centralising commercial world."[33] In the Bay of Islands agriculture failed to flourish on a commercial basis, fur and salmon stocks became depleted, and readily available stocks of white pine were soon used up and logging confined to a few sawmills. The lack of roads and the difficulty of communications between the settlements limited further commercial expansion, despite the railway. Between the census of 1911 and 1921 the Bay population only increased by 162 persons. Many of the young people were moving away to find employment as the population of the Bay virtually reached the limit for dependence on a subsistence economy. In 1921 the population of Corner Brook was still only 411 people out of a total population in the Bay of 4,700.

There were, however, about 22 resident merchants in the Bay in 1921 who still carried on the traditional barter system, providing the fishermen with supplies in spring in return for their produce in the fall. This produce was then conveyed to St. John's or Halifax and resold, and further supplies purchased. Most of these merchants were located in the Curling area, with others in Lark Harbour, Benoits Cove, and on Woods Island. Other merchants were transient and traded for a few years before moving back to St. John's or the mainland. There was of course some retail trading stores and there were also peddlers called "nunnybacks" who walked or rode from settlement to settlement selling goods. One of the first of these was Lebanese-born Tanius Basha who was later successful in the herring fishing industry. Before his death in April, 1936, at the age of 95, he became known as Tom Basha. After the Second World War, a character called Mosey Murrin carried on the nunnyback tradition and was a familiar sight on streets and roads in west Newfoundland with a wheelbarrow or a sack on his back. He never engaged in traditional work in his life; nevertheless, he had a sharp wit. One of his renowned stories took place after some tourists off a cruise boat asked him where all the Indians were. He replied, "They haven't come off the boat yet!"

The denominational churches had opened schools and provided a centre for some social interaction, but health care was sadly lacking. Early doctors such as Dr. Miller charged $6 for treating an entire family

---

[33] Mannion, J. (1990). The Peopling of Newfoundland. Toronto: U of Toronto P.

for a year. In addition, the family paid $2.50 to the minister and $2 per child for schooling. Every family in Birchy Cove was expected to cut a load of wood for their minister and one for their church and school. According to Captain Joe Hackett's records, Dr. William Whalen practised on Woods Island from 1908 until 1914. Dr. Frank Fisher, son of Christopher Fisher, returned to practice in Curling before 1910 and Dr. Webber, who was an apothecary or druggist, also provided some service there. Dr. Ames and Dr. Carnahan are alleged to have also practised briefly in Curling before Dr. Fisher's arrival, although I have been unable to confirm this from any reliable source. However, no hospital operated in the area until after the paper mill was built in Corner Brook in 1924.

The concept of a paper mill in the Bay of Islands was already being considered, given the successful operation of a paper mill in Grand Falls earlier in the century. The timber rights had been bought from the Reid Company by Newfoundland Products Corporation Ltd., free of taxes and stumpage. Around 1910 a report from an engineering company signed by a Mr. Wallace stated that a hydroelectric power site was feasible at Deer Lake and that wood supply was adequate for the operation of a large pulp and paper mill. Deer Lake town was to be the site of the mill, and unbelievably, the deep water port was planned to be close by at lakeside! The engineering plan called for a series of locks on the Humber river to enable ocean going paper carriers to travel to and fro. The threat of World War I fortunately prevented these ecologically disastrous plans from being pursued. When the proposal was again considered after the war the Prime Minister was Sir Richard Squires, an ardent salmon fisherman of the Lower Humber, who helped promote an alternate, final plan which ensured that this potential disaster was avoided.

CHAPTER 7

World War I and Beyond

The outbreak of World War I in August 1914 put all plans for economic development on the west coast into abeyance. The Newfoundland government immediately telegraphed the British government offering to raise a land force, remustering the Newfoundland Regiment and mobilising the Royal Naval Reserve. Most of the reservists were busily employed fishing. Nevertheless, St. John's went ahead with the recommissioning of the Regiment and 500 men, mostly from the Avalon peninsula, volunteered for service "for the duration of the war, not exceeding one year." The power to organize, equip, and direct this force was delegated to the Newfoundland Patriotic Committee, headed by Governor Davidson and composed of 50 appointees, mostly St. John's businessmen. On October 4th, 1914 the first contingent of volunteers, called "The Blue Puttees" on account of the atypical colour of their puttees, sailed from St. John's. A few residents from Bay of Islands were aboard, including Peter Daniels from Curling and Ralph Tulk. Little did they know, the war would last 4 years. They and the others that followed would have a magnificent record of service in Gallipoli and on the Western Front. Of the Regiment's total enlistment of 6242 men, no less than 1305 were killed, a percentage twice as high as that of the Canadian Expeditionary Force.

The total number of men from the Bay of Islands who enlisted during the First World War is not known. Two score or more served in the Newfoundland Regiment, but many others served in the Royal Navy and the Forestry Unit. After the war, several ex-servicemen migrated to Corner Brook when the paper mill started up, including one renowned officer of the Regiment Major Bert Butler, who had been awarded the Distinguished Service Order, the Military Cross and Bar. Men who were decorated from the Bay of Islands include Sgt. Charles Curnew of Curling who won the Military Medal in 1918 at the Battle of Bailleul, Private Pierce Power who won the Military Medal at the Battle of Cambrai— it was after this engagement that the regiment was permitted the designation "Royal"—and Private Thomas Corbin of Corner Brook who won the Distinguished Conduct Medal at Ledeghem in 1918. The Bay of Islands War Memorial in Curling records the names of 21 men who lost their lives in the war. Several others became prisoners of war.

Recruits had to support themselves in St. John's prior to enlistment. Consequently, recruiting for the Regiment was slow in the outports and the Bay of Islands was no exception. Sir Walter Davidson, the Governor and head of the Patriotic Commission, visited Bay of Islands in December 1915 and only recruited two persons, one for the Navy and one for the Regiment. Later in the war the Curling magistrate mentioned that 18 had volunteered from Curling. Many inhabitants were unsure of what the war was all about and in some areas the Governor would be met by the comment "What, fight with the French? Why, we've always fought against the French!"

Stories from WW1 include one related to me by Rev. Petley's daughter, the late Mrs. O. W. Frost who told me that the boat which was carrying her father to a visit to Chimney Cove encountered a U-boat in the outer Bay of Islands. It surfaced, and was preparing to sink or seize Petley's vessel when the captain noticed the church flag flying instead of the British Ensign. He thereupon saluted smartly and ordered the U-boat to submerge and depart. Another interesting fact is that the constabulary office in Curling looked after 7 German prisoners during World War I. One of the prisoners sent a letter of thanks back to his warder in 1920 after he was repatriated. This letter is on display in the Corner Brook Museum. Its beautifully written English is strikingly interspersed with some of the colloquial Newfoundland terminology he must have picked up during his stay in the Bay of Islands. The prisoners were apparently well treated, and spent some of their time in captivity building a wall in Doman's Lane, parts of which are still visible.

The Bay of Islands shared in the whole island's prosperity during that war and in the early postwar years, with good prices for fish and lumber. But prices fell sharply in the early 1920s. A government headed by Sir Richard Squires, elected in 1919, revived the idea of a paper mill in the Humber Valley. The first people to become interested were a Norwegian engineer Mr. Blackstad and a Canadian publisher Mr. Greenwood. Their project fell through when the government wisely refused to guarantee the principal and interest on the loan; a second proposal from different sponsors was declined for the same reason.

The third proposal was different. According to Mr. Smallwood, the full credit for nurturing this proposal and bringing it to fruition was Sir Richard Squires, and he recognised this when he later became Premier by naming the provincial building constructed in Corner Brook the Sir Richard Squires Building. There seems little doubt that Sir Richard's energy and enthusiasm were responsible for the procurement of financing for the final proposal to build a mill in Corner Brook. For this reason, if for no other, he should be saluted and remembered by the residents of the Bay of Islands despite his subsequent gross financial irresponsibility.

After the war, Curling was the centre of commercial activity in the

Bay and had surpassed Summerside and Corner Brook in population. In 1921, Curling had 569 people, Humbermouth 369, and Corner Brook 411. But now with declining employment in the sawmill the Presbyterian population in Corner Brook of 87 was outnumbered by Roman Catholics of 298, with other denominations totalling 26. There were trails between communities but no roads anywhere. A narrow muddy track ran from Curling to Humbermouth capable of use by horse and sleigh in winter or horse and cart in summer, but it was often blocked with snow in winter. Most people walked between the communities along the railway track. The George L ferry, a sailboat, or rowboat were the only ways to cross the bay in early days. In later times, the outboard motor dory served that purposed until 1956 when the Ballam bridge was completed. When the ice was thick enough, the bay could be crossed on foot or by horse and sleigh. The main herring fisheries in the spring and fall ceased when ice formed in the bay, although hardy individuals might fish through the ice for herring in winter instead of going trapping. They would make holes and channels through the ice with the rope and attachments for a net threaded from one hole to the other. A fisherman once complained to the magistrate that a neighbour had stolen his holes and had spread his own net there. But by the time the case came to trial in the spring, the ice in the Bay had disappeared and with it the evidence!

Winter ice in the Bay has always played a big part in the lifestyle of the communities and seems to have been a good deal thicker in the first part of this century. It has always rafted outside the Bay when driven onshore by westerly winds. Even now, large ships are sometimes unable to enter the Bay except when preceded by an ice breaker.

The presence of thick ice made travel across the Bay quicker, but more hazardous, as squalls of wind and snow are notorious in the Outer Bay. William Noseworthy came from Labrador to settle in Cox's Cove at the age of 9 when only 4 families lived there, 3 Cox families and the O'Grady family. At that time, the settlement was known as Middle Arm. Noseworthy describes how it would take him 3 hours to travel to Curling by boat in summer to sell his produce and obtain his supplies, but in winter only 2 hours over the ice by horse and sleigh. Annie Wheeler had arrived in 1921 from Fogo as a teacher in one of the three denominational school in Summerside. She recalls that her marriage was delayed for 3 days because the George L became stuck in the ice while conveying Rev. Petley from Curling to marry her.

Now that land could be bought and sold, most families owned fields in which they could produce hay, and grow a few crops like potatoes, turnip, cabbage, and cauliflower. These would be stored in a root cellar for winter use. Most families would also own a few chicken or ducks and a horse or ox for transportation. Some owned sheep and milk cows, but strangely there is no folklore of cream or cheese making. Hay making was carried out in summer and enjoyed as a social occasion. Cutting the hay was men's work, using a scythe, but making the hay was women and children's work. This involved turning the hay over until dry and then piling it into heaps before carrying it into the barn or shed.

Hunting wild game was a seasonal activity. Turrs, more correctly called murres, were shot in the Outer Bay and ducks and geese locally. Older children would take off in groups into the woods in the fall to snare snow shoe hares, known as rabbits in Newfoundland. Like the moose population, their origin was from Nova Scotia. They were introduced into communities under care of the local magistrate from 1864 to 1876 and thrived, with bags of several dozen snared 30-40 years later. Ruffed grouse were only introduced here after World War 2. Caribou also seemed to be more plentiful and the allowed bag limit was 3 per person. Many men went trapping in wintertime. A bounty of $3 per pelt was paid for lynx, beaver hunting had a closed season, and musk rat, weasel, and foxes were also hunted. The skin of a silver or black fox could fetch $150.00. Parsons and Baggs tried fox farming, but it was unsuccessful. Hunters sold their pelts to the local merchants Parsons and Basha. Pine marten were probably hunted in those days, though now an endangered species. Beaver were said to be good to eat and black bear would also be shot for meat and skin.

A shed or root cellar for storing vegetables might still be a tilt, but houses were now mostly of wood frame construction faced with matched lumber with birch rind placed on the outside and shingled, though only partially insulated with hay, moss or kelp. The roof would be sharply sloping and shingled. Woodstoves were still in general use, requiring enormous quantities of wood and requiring many more hands in cutting the wood than nowadays, using axe and hand saws. Coal, imported from Nova Scotia, was beginning to be used, but unless the woodstoves were attended through the night, they would go out, so beds would have to be well covered, often with hand-made quilts made of old clothes. Many children recall getting up to go to school in a freezing cold bedroom, and leaving their nice warm bed. Other bed coverings might be made of sail cloth, filled with hay or feathers. The craft of quilt making is still carried on and some are very ornamental—Mrs. Brake of

Summerside turned out some exquisite quilts in the late 1950s.

An outhouse was an important part of the domestic establishment and visitors are said to have judged the social quality of a family in those days by the cleanliness of its outhouse. The outhouse would enclose an earth privy; septic tanks did not come into use until much later in the century. Some built a shed on a stage and used holes in the floor leading to the seawater. Unfortunately effluents were also constructed leading directly to the sea. Some of these are still in use in outports such as Lark Harbour—even the Corner Brook sewers all still run directly into the Humber Arm. Wells were often the source of water, especially in Curling and Woods Island. In winter, water would be stored in a 40-gallon pork barrel in the kitchen. Washing and bathing would take place in a large tub filled with warmed water. Soap was made from lye, or wood ash strained through water and mixed with boiled fat, cooled and cut into cakes. Large families were common and the small dwellings provided little domestic privacy. Infant mortality was high and respiratory and deficiency diseases were common in childhood. Dental hygiene was appalling and practically nonexistent.

The population of Birchy Cove (Curling) increased from 142 in 1857 to 316 in 1874, primarily because of immigration from overpopulated settlements in Conception Bay. The Bay of Islands attracted immigrants with its excellent access to the Labrador fishery and winter employment in logging, trapping and in the herring fishery. New settlers built their homes close to the waterfront, their properties often extending nearly a mile inland, though the railway construction in 1896 often separated the land lots.

Farming, too, was an essential part of the early life of settlers in the Inner Bay of Islands and made them more self sufficient than those on the east coast and indeed than those in the Outer Bay. These settlers cleared the land with an axe, pulling out the stumps with block and tackle hauled by an ox and then burning the tree limbs and stumps. The land was then dug and usually planted with potatoes as a first crop, manured with kelp, caplin, or fish guts. The Irish method of growing potatoes was usual with 4-foot-wide beds. This arable land was fenced off and turnips, carrots, parsnips, beet, and cabbage were grown later, as well as oats and hay for feeding the livestock. Crop rotation was practised but, although up to 25 barrels of potatoes might be grown in a good year, most was stored in root cellars for family use and little was sold outside the community. Fruit trees were also common in Birchy Cove—plum, damsons, apples, and greengages, as well as currant and gooseberry bushes. The fruit was preserved in jars.

Most people used oxen for hauling, but the more affluent such as businessmen, used horses. Families would often have one or two cows, milked daily by the children. After sheep were introduced from Nova Scotia, up to a dozen would be kept, sheared in May, and then turned loose. The wool was washed, carded, and then spun, usually at home. Goats were infrequent, as they were a nuisance, destroying fences and fruit trees. A family would also usually own one pig, importing it in springtime from Nova Scotia for about $5. This saved the cost of feeding a pig through the winter months. It would also be barred up and fed waste, including the whey from butter making. The pig would be slaughtered for Christmas.

Cattle were important, not only for their milk and butter but also for their meat and for their skins, which were fashioned into rough boots. They were also usually slaughtered in the fall, as were the chickens. Chickens would be bought in spring as pullets and laid eggs through the summer, preserved over winter in a jug containing flour. Ducks and geese were unpopular, as ducks are dirty and geese are noisy. Turkeys were also uncommon. Reliance on farming as well as the herring fishery enabled settlers in Curling, Summerside, and Corner Brook to weather the Great Depression in the 1930s better than those solely dependant on the fishery in the Outer Bay of Islands.

The settlers had the convenience of two sawmills in Birchy Cove employing 15 men. The Parson's mill was located near the mouth of St. Mary's Brook. These sawmills enabled settlers to purchase shingles and matched lumber, and the wood that they brought to the sawmill could be processed for $5 per thousand board feet for use in their houses, boats, or wharf.

As always, women had important work to do. Responsibilities included looking after the children, picking berries in the fall, growing vegetables, packing fish, and sawing wood. Besides all this, a woman had to be skilful with wool, shearing her sheep, washing the wool, spinning and knitting it. Women wore woolen stockings, mitts and cap, rarely using makeup. "Sunlight Soap" was often used for washing, although some families made their own soap. Little time remained for leisure, and neither swimming nor dancing were considered proper for young ladies. Young boys and men, on the other hand, swam in the buff in summer and went sliding, skating, and even skiing using barrel staves in winter.

Regardless of a child's denomination, the quality of his or her education varied according to the quality and availability of a teacher. One room schools attached to or part of the church structure were usual. In some instances, the school room became the church meeting place on Sunday, universally observed in the province as a day of rest. The first school in Corner Brook was a one-room school at the bottom of Fishers Hill, while in 1921 Summerside had no less than three schools of different denominations.

According to former students of the area such as Anne Dormody of Petries, a surprisingly wide range of subjects were taught including Grammar, History, Geography, Bible history, Writing, French and Algebra, as well as shorthand, knitting, and sewing. High school education was only available at this time in St. John's and there was no degree conferring university in the province until Memorial University was founded there in 1924. Few availed of this level of education; boys were expected to leave school to go to work fishing with their families, often as young as 9 years old.

The first organised sport is recorded in 1901 when two football teams were formed in Petries and Birchy Cove. Later an annual match was played against Grand Falls. Hockey began to be played on natural ice in the bay, though no one seems to know when it first started. Horse and sleigh races were also popular when the Humber Arm ice became sufficiently solid. The game of cricket was still very popular in St. John's at the close of the century and the Western Star records a cricket team from Birchy Cove playing against Grand Falls and one of HM ships in 1928. Originally designed as a cricket pitch, cricket was played on Jubilee Field in Corner Brook until 1955. Youth organisations included the Church Lads Brigade and the Catholic Cadet Corps and the Boy Scouts and the Girl Guides. Lord Baden Powell, the founder of the Scouting Movement, visited Bay of Islands with his wife in 1935. After World War 2 Army, Navy, and Air Force cadet units were formed and the Newfoundland Regiment was reformed as a Militia unit, as well as an Engineer company and a unit of the 1st Medical Company, all parading in a new building named Gallipoli Armoury on O'Connell Drive.

Several accounts from those days assert that, although marriage was often delayed for several years until the husband could support his family, children born to unmarried mothers were uncommon. In the absence of effective contraceptive methods this would imply a degree of chastity rare in modern Western society, and the Curling Constabulary records do indeed record several charges of "bastardy" from 1917 to 1922. Petty crime, especially larceny, appears to have been fairly common, and often carried out by juveniles, but major crime was rare.

The biggest concern of the customs offices was bootlegging and rum running and stories abound of these pursuits, not perceived by the inhabitants of the Bay of Islands as a serious crime, then or now. Liquor was purchased from "rum boats" in earlier days, who would sail round the outports in summertime. It was cheap and readily available up to the time of Prohibition in 1915. In that year, the House of Assembly, in a surge of puritanical zeal promoted by the head of the Unionist party in the government William Coaker, passed an Act of Prohibition that was to extend to 1924. This Act served to increase the old lucrative business of rum running from St. Pierre through Port aux Basques, and by other routes from Quebec and Nova Scotia. Liquor, chiefly rum and usually black Demerara, was conveyed in kegs containing several gallons of 200% overproof rum, later diluted by the purchaser according to his taste. George Basha stated that a 12-ounce bottle cost 75¢. Cox's Cove and Lark Harbour were the primary ports used by the rum runners, with stocks subsequently delivered by smaller boats to other destinations in the Bay of Islands. After a cargo had been successfully landed, distribution was by word of mouth. During prohibition some stores, known as "blind pigs," stored homebrew, selling it by the glass.

Being a customs official during that period had certain benefits as well as risks. M. S. Leggo, a well known resident of Curling, said that his father was a customs official and often returned from visiting a vessel with bribes, or shall we say gifts, of produce. Frank Colbourne related that one customs official despatched from St. John's to stop the rum running, was met with force when he boarded a vessel for inspection. He was disarmed and beaten up and cast adrift in his boat and was unfortunately so injured that he had to spend the rest of his life in a St. John's hospital. Most people took a more relaxed approach to the situation. Legend describes a hotel owner who maintained a pipe leading to a barrel in his basement from the shore to import the smuggled rum more discreetly; other local merchants were allegedly actively involved in rum running. With only one customs inspector to cover the entire island, illicit cargo could slip into the Bay with relative ease. An anecdote related by Ethel Rowsell records such an episode. She herself was bringing a keg or two from Port aux Basques by train when this customs inspector boarded the train; she knew the man personally and her cargo remained unchallenged. Rum running from St. Pierre and bootlegging continued actively in the Bay of Islands through the 1920s and 1930s. It still continues on the south coast, though now the runners have to contend with the RCMP radar and a fast police cutter.

After prohibition ended in 1924, liquor could be legally ordered from St. John's and delivered by train.Before that, so I am told, liquor could only be obtained on a doctor's prescription. Later, when a government liquor store was opened on West Street in Corner Brook, 3 bottles of spirits could be purchased per week per family. After prohibition, Curling brewery began selling a reputedly potent brew called "Old Bills Special;" most families, however, continued to brew their own. If homebrew was above a certain alcohol strength, it was illegal. Walter Mugford, one of the detachment of 4 constables and 1 sergeant for the Bay of Islands, recounts that in the 1930s when he suspected a brew was too strong he was authorised to seal a bottle in the owner's presence before sending it to St. John's for analysis. Pat Callaghan recalled that when he delivered coal in Corner Brook he would usually be offered a glass of homebrew before he left the customer's house. Moonshine distilled from homebrew was also made by some more daring individuals though this involved a heavier penalty if convicted.

After the American Base in Stephenville was constructed in the Second World War and was designated as an overseas posting with duty free status, duty-free liquor found its way into use in Corner Brook. US airmen, who came to the area for R & R (Rest and Recreation) were allowed to bring liquor into the city, officially for their own use, and residents who visited the base would often bring a few bottles, or more, back with them. RCMP officers would periodically organise a road block on the Stephenville highway outside Corner Brook to deter this smuggling. Other sources of contraband and liquor in the Bowater era were from the UK shipping fleet that carried paper from the mill to US ports, but this source seems to have dried up with the Kruger operation.

According to the constabulary, overt drunkenness was not particularly common, at least in the larger centres of the Bay. Nevertheless, I recall that alcohol consumption was generally fairly high in the Corner Brook area as late as the 1960s. There would be the usual drunks in the Hospital Casualty Department at night, and after Christmas the familiar "drying out" problems with withdrawal symptoms. Alcohol related accidents were also much more common 30 years ago than they are now. The breathalyser and strict alcohol limits for driving are chiefly responsible for this decline, although they have led to a marked drop in social activities in clubs and taverns and fewer private parties, again most noticeable in the larger centres.

The first recorded church socials occurred in 1878 and were probably organized by Rev. Curling's wife, as she appears to have been a soloist. They were called "Penny Readings" and consisted of popular songs and rounds and story readings and magic lantern shows. When the first bank was opened on August 26, 1878, in St. Mary's Parsonage under the sponsorship of the Bay of Islands Mission, it was known as the "Penny Savings Bank" and was intended to promote the virtue of thrift in the community.

Once established, social occasions took place often in church halls and usually involved dances and card parties. The game of 45's was

Programme of Penny Reading
given by the Bay of Islands Church Institute on 17th April 1879.
Commander Howorth R.N. in the Chair.
1. March. "The British Grenadiers."
2. Solo. "Twenty years Ago". Mr Adams Tupper.
3. Trio. The Canadian Boat Song". Mr Curling Mrs Stone, Mr E. Weir
4. Solo and chorus. "Hard Times" Solo by Mr R. Weir
5. Reading. "Nothing to wear." Mr Pope.
6. Solo. "Kathleen Mavourneen". Mrs Curling.
7. Solo and chorus. "In Woods". Solo by Mr James Parsons.
8. Solo. Mary Blane". Mr Meredith.
9. Reading————Mr Barron.
10. Solo & Chorus. "Come where my Love lies dreaming". Solo by Miss Stone.
11. Reading. How to steal a feather bed". Com. Howorth. R.N.
Second Part
1. Solo. "Home Sweet Home". Mrs Curling.
2. Solo & Chorus. "The Three Knights". Solo by Mr R. Weir.
3. Reading. "A tale for the Marines". Com. Howorth R.N
4. Solo. "The fine old Irish Gentleman". Mr Adams Tupper.
5. Duet. Flute & Harmonium. Mr Doman & Mrs Curling.
6. Solo. Come Lasses and Lads". Miss Stone.
7. Solo and chorus. Ellen Bayne. Solo by Mr E. Weir.
Magic Lantern
GOD Save The QUEEN
T. Doman
Treasurer.
R. R. Pike

popular, a form of whist, known as "growl" in Newfoundland. The church denominations varied in their tolerance of these activities. An occasional play was acted, usually a simple folksy comedy such as Mother O'Leary's Cow or a sacred drama such as Pilate's Daughter performed on May 23, 1934, in the Curling Church Hall. Organised drama groups sprang up only after the Second World War.

The first movie theatres appeared in Curling and in Corner Brook after the mill was constructed. The Palace and Regent cinemas were on Broadway, the Majestic cinema in Townsite and another cinema was on Humber Road. Before that time itinerant movie operators might bring in his equipment and hire a hall for the occasion, charging 5¢ per person. Most entertainments, still known as "times," occurred among friends and families in the home during the long winter evenings with music provided by a fiddler or accordion player, occasionally accompanied by a person playing "the spoons" to keep the beat, or by the player stamping his foot to produce a similar effect. Refreshments would be served and the party would continue until all became tired or the liquor ran out, whichever came earlier. Pat Griffin senior said that he was much sought after as a fiddle player, and would often walk from Curling to play in Corner Brook for $15, quite a large sum in those days. Jigs were the most popular music and dancing mostly foxtrots and waltzes, though sometimes a person would show off with a step dance, a type of tap dance. Jiving and jitter bugging did not come in till the Second World War, when the Americans came in for parties at the so-called "White House" from the Air Force Base in Stephenville. Minnie White, the well known accordion player from the Codroy Valley, lived in Corner Brook before the Second World War and although she did not play here herself she recalled the use of accordions, fiddles, banjos, ukuleles, and mandolins at dances. Such musical environments fostered the development of two well known musicians on this coast, the fiddle players Emile Benoit of the Port au Port Peninsula and Rufus Guinchard from Port au Choix.

The railway company forbade people to use the track, but of course they did. Although train service was often quite erratic during the winter months, the service provided was better than no service at all and people gradually became to feel less isolated and more a part of the island community. It continued to be the only land link between the east and west coasts until the completion of the trans island highway in 1965. There was genuine sorrow when the railway was finally closed in 1988 and the railtrack was removed.

CHAPTER 8

The Arrival of the Paper Mill

After World War I ended in 1918, a marked drop in fish prices soon threatened the Newfoundland fisheries—the Bay of Islands operations were no exception. The quest for a stable industrial base, which had started in the late 19th century and was to continue all through the 20th, increasingly concerned the colonial government. Central and western Newfoundland had the potential resources to form that base. In 1915, the paper mill in Grand Falls started production; there was also a proposal for a fertiliser plant in the Bay of Islands. This proposal was put forward by the Reid brothers and by a Mr. Wilson but fell through when Sir William Reid and Mr. Wilson both died. When Sir Richard Squires became Prime Minister in 1919, though, the idea of a paper mill in the Bay of Islands was revived. Squires used his personal charm and enthusiasm to woo financiers and industrialists in Britain and the United States.

Eventually he struck a deal with the Bank of England and the Armstrong Whitworth Company of Great Britain, who were anxious to diversify out of the arms industry following World War I. This final proposal was to form a production company called Newfoundland Power and Paper Company Limited to run the mill, with Armstrong Whitworth owning a majority of the common stock shares, and the Reid Newfoundland Company owning the remainder. Approximately $20,000,000 worth of bonds were to be issued, with the British and Newfoundland governments each agreeing to guarantee half of the interest due on the bonds for the next 20 years. A sinking fund for repayment of the principal on these bonds was to be created. Armstrong Whitworth were also to be the contractors to construct the mill, with the Townsite and the power installations in Deer Lake to be taken over by their subsidiary company, Newfoundland Power and Paper Company, on completion.

To the surprise of many, the agreements were signed, and what was termed "The Humber Enterprise" started on July 8, 1923. Construction started on the development of the mill site and power plant simultaneously. The power plant project included a power house and turbines at Deer Lake as well as a penstock and forebay. Main Dam was built to dam Junction Brook, raising the level of Grand Lake. A head of water was then conveyed to the generators in the power house by a man-made canal called the Humber Canal. The plant was capable of generating 98,000 HP of electricity, transmitted to the mill 32 miles away by overhead cables supported by pylons.

The paper mill was built near the mouth of the Corner Brook stream, used as a water supply by constructing a dam on the stream near the

Glynmill Inn. The foundations were built on mainly reclaimed land, using steel and concrete. About 40 acres were available for the construction of mill buildings, offices, shipping piers, and paper storage sheds. Finally the machinery for four paper machines was installed, each capable of producing 100 tons of newsprint a day.

Besides the construction of the mill and the hydroelectric project in Deer Lake, the Armstrong Whitworth Company built roads, sewers, water mains, and about 100 houses in the 1st year in a permanent site for mill workers to be known as Townsite. The streets were named after some of the principal shareholders of the company; the staff house was called the Glynmill Inn after Sir Glyn West, the chairman of the company. Houses of frames construction were built on Marcelle Avenue and Cobb Lane, some large and imposing. Others were built on West and Park Streets and the lower parts of West and East Valley Roads, Central and Reid Streets, and Armstrong Avenue. Construction workers started living in tents along the shoreline but later a shanty town of wood and tar paper huts were built—popularly known as "Shacktown"—that provided little protection against the winter cold.

This construction phase proceeded at breathtaking speed and was completed on time in 2 years. But the capital cost came in at $51,771,066, double the estimate. Contemporary observers point to evidence of gross waste and mismanagement to explain this overrun. Incompetence was

How many remember those days? . . . Corner Brook in 1922, June 23rd to be exact . . . before the development . . . "nothing but a fishing village, with a cluster of little houses and a saw mill."

Courtesy of Humber Log

also apparent later when the project was turned over to the Newfound-land Power & Paper Company, who simply did not have the expertise to run a paper mill.

Construction workers came by railway or boat from all parts of the island. They were initially paid about 10¢ an hour. Men worked 12 hours a day, 7 days a week. Although some of these Newfoundlanders became foremen and were paid higher wages, most of the senior construction staff came from Great Britain. Dock workers were only getting about 12¢ an hour at first, but a strike for an increase of 5¢ an hour was quickly settled by Armstrong Whitworth with a smaller wage increase. There was no union for the workers at this time. Meals, though, were provided by the construction company in cookhouses and there were few complaints about the food, although most of the cooks were from England, a country not known for its culinary expertise.

Most people who worked in the construction phase recall scenes of frantic activity, long hours of work without opportunities for leisure, and a sea of mud. Mud or dust was everywhere—people had to walk around in rubber boots. Horse drawn carts were often up to their axles in mud and often were only able to haul half loads. Rumour has it that a tractor disappeared completely in the mud; some say that this occurred in a bog in front of what is now the Majestic Cinema. And, of course, the flies! In winter things seemed better, as horse driven sleighs could be used. Another type of sled, known as a "go devil" was used

The Fisher sawmill around 1910

even in the mud of spring and summer. Corduroy duckwalks were used to get around the construction site.

The inhabitants of the communities in the Bay of Islands must have been amazed at this drastic change in their quiet and secluded life. Most had never seen concrete poured and had never encountered construction equipment, tractors or pile drivers, nor the noise which accompanied them. Some came to work, sleeping in their boats rather than in the tar paper huts in Shacktown. According to Annie Wheeler, some fishermen from Summerside sold their nets and worked for wages in the construction site, only to regret it later when they found that the work was temporary and seasonal. Others came to gawp and returned to their fishing pursuits.

The problem for most married fishermen was that, unless they lived near by the construction site, they had to leave their wife and family behind when they started working. Most of the construction workers and later the mill workers came from other areas of Newfoundland, especially the east coast and central Newfoundland. This seems to be

Wood boom at the Fisher sawmill. Doubless many of the logs were pine like the big tree in the foreground. These pines once grew in abundance on the banks of the Humber. White pine was said to run from 12 to 36 inches in diameter at the butt and up to 40 feet before a limb is reached. The trees grew from 40 to 70 feet tall.

confirmed by the fact that the census of 1935 indicated a population of 3701 in the Bay of Islands, including Curling but excluding Corner Brook, little more than that recorded in 1921. Townsite, Corner Brook West and East Sides and Humbermouth numbered 8603 residents in 1935.

Residents of Curling in particular say that they were glad to be living in a civilised town in those days, away from the filth and noise of "Milltown." There was still a lot of seasonal work available there in the herring fishery and George Basha recalls that he paid his fish plant workers 25¢ an hour in 1932, only a little less than the wages then being paid to mill workers. Photographs of the Curling waterfront at that time showed many fish plants. James Furlong owned four plants at one time, and others were owned by Alex Dunphy, Jim Barry, George Allen, H. T. Porter, Charles Bartlett, and Ayre & Sons.

The herring fishery remained active and profitable until the early 1950s, when the fish disappeared from the Humber Arm and had to be located elsewhere in the other Arms, Bonne Bay, or Port au Port Bay. This was probably the result of overfishing, though increasing pollution, not only from the paper mill but also from untreated sewage from Corner Brook could also have been responsible. Effluents from the mill have recently been much improved, but regrettably, not the city's sewage.

Tourists and Humber River sports fishermen still stayed in the hotel in Petries or in the two then located in Curling. Although communication with Corner Brook was now possible by a narrow road, Pat Griffin said that he always walked to work in Corner Brook along the railway track. The railway company had objected to people using the track as a road because of the danger of accidents, especially in winter when snow was piled up on either side by the snow ploughs, making escape from an oncoming train difficult. The Curling magistrate even threatened to prosecute pedestrians for trespass, but people still preferred to use the track rather than wallow in mud along the narrow road. From 1925 to 1935 a steam coach ran from Petries to Humbermouth and back, costing 10¢. This was more than most people could afford and Ett Webber, a former resident, told me that when social activities and dances started to become popular in the 1940s the young people still walked back and forth to Corner Brook.

Incredibly, the construction work finished on time and the four paper machines started up in June 1925, with the first delivery of paper overseas to Boston in September by the newly constructed SS <u>Humber Arm</u>. This vessel and its sister ship the SS <u>Corner Brook</u> were the first

Photographs courtesy of Dave Gillard

vessels to be built exclusively as paper carriers. On August 24, the Western Star became the first newspaper to use Corner Brook newsprint in publication. When the company arranged a banquet and ball to mark the opening of the mill, several hundred guests were entertained in one of the large paper sheds, as there was nowhere else in town suitable for the occasion. They stayed overnight, probably in either the sleeping cars on the trains from St. John's or at private homes and hotels in Petries, Curling, and Townsite. On the following day they visited Main Dam and the Deer Lake powerhouse. No doubt they were impressed by what they saw, the fine modern machinery, the vast shipping sheds and woodpiles, the powerhouse, and the neat Townsite housing development. They would also learn about the manufacture of newsprint.

Papermaking has changed considerably in the years since those first rolls of newsprint came off the machines in the Corner Brook mill. In those days it was much more labour intensive but as much an art as a science, with skill and experience needed to produce good pulp and paper. Nowadays, the computer has replaced the experienced skill of the papermaker, who used to tap the new roll to detect air pockets or moisture problems. The production of chemical pulp, with its unpleasant smell from the gases emitted when the digester was "blown" has been replaced by a thermomechanical process. Waste bark is now used as fuel instead of being dumped into the Humber Arm, and other toxic effluents have been eliminated.

In those early days a very basic description of newsprint manufacture would start in the company's timber concessions in the forests on the west coast. Woodsmen there used crosscut saws, requiring two men, as well as axes to cut and trim timber. Cords were then measured by a scaler (a cord of wood is a cubic measure of 128 cubic feet), loaded on a cart or sledge and transported to the nearest railway or floated down a river. All down the Humber River logs were corralled and stored in booms, released when the water level was suitable, gathered in a large boom at the mouth, and conveyed to the mill by tugs. Logs could also be floated in booms from other logging sites along the west coast to the mill in the same way.

The logs were piled into large pyramidal stacks by jack ladders and irrigated to prevent combustion. They were then conveyed to the debarking machines when needed. Some would be chipped to be used in the production of sulphite pulp, others were sent to large stone grinders to make groundwood pulp. When I went on a tour of the mill some years ago, I was told about a worker who was dragged into one of these

The building of the first General Hospital, unknow medical doctor in foreground

East Valley Road, Central Street and Reid Street

Humbermouth Road—1924

grinders—a gruesome anecdote. Sulphite pulp was made by boiling a chemical mixture of wood chips and an acid bisulphite solution for a few hours in a digester. This dissolved the lignum binding the wood fibres together, and a proportion of this pulp was mixed with groundwood pulp to form the raw material for paper making.

The paper making process essentially consists of starting with a "wet end" and rolling and drying the material on a wire mesh (now a fabric). This sheet is calendared to form a smooth surface to take the printer's ink, cut into customer sizes of newsprint, then wound onto rolls of paper, packaged, and labelled. The rolls of paper are then conveyed to the wood sheds to await loading on a paper carrier for export, with the majority still going to the American market.

This process appears to be straightforward but requires experienced people to operate the machinery successfully. Furthermore, an industrial project based on exports requires experienced salesmen. Although some mill workers were experienced, and had worked in the Grand Falls mill or elsewhere, and some of the management had experience, the new workers were keen but untrained and some had little basic education. All had to work in conditions which were appalling, with suffocating heat in summer, no ventilation, and frightful noise from grinders and paper machines. It comes as no surprise that most of these early paper makers experience significant hearing loss. Most of them worked in the lightest possible clothing with bare feet to avoid slipping on the wet floors. Safety shoes were not commercially available until 1938.

The construction company built the first hospital in Corner Brook on the site of the present Eddy's Bus Station on Humber Road, just above the old railway station, according to Bill Herdman. It was a tar paper shack with 5 beds. Dr. Joe MacDonald was the first doctor, followed by Dr. Frank Fisher, the son of Christopher Fisher who had owned and operated the saw mill in Corner Brook and had sold his land holdings to the construction company. A new hospital of frame construction was opened in August, 1925, located below the present O'Connell Centre on Hospital Hill and now demolished. These first company doctors must have been fully employed, as accidents were frequent, including several fatalities in the mill and woods operations. It was not until the early 1930s that safety guards were put around the machines and a safety education programme was started which began to reduce the number of accidents.

Inexperienced workers were not the only problem the mill faced. Management was largely inexperienced in operating a pulp and paper mill and the four spanking new machines rarely worked to their potential capacity of 400 tons daily output. But the albatross around the new companies neck was the service of the debt. Shortly after the start of operations the Bank of England worried about the huge construction overrun, and, in order to try to protect its financial interests, sent Frater Taylor as its representative on the Board. Although he was an able man, he was unable to save the company from near bankruptcy. The mill manager, Frank Stadler, and the woods manager resigned soon after the startup, and although experienced business men were brought in as replacements the mill still failed to make a profit. The parent company in Britain, Armstrong Whitworth, was unable to help as it was also in financial trouble, so a decision was made to sell the mill to the International Power and Paper Corporation of New York in June of 1926. A financial deal acceptable to the Bank of England and the Newfoundland government, who had both guaranteed the payment of interest on the original bonds, was necessary for completion of the purchase.

The International Power and Paper Company (I.P.&P.) was a large and experienced North American Company and ran the mill for 12 years. The potential daily capacity of 400 tons was achieved and then increased by additions to the working capacity of the four paper machines and by the introduction of two more machines. This increased production required increase in the generating output of Deer Lake Power Company, which was also achieved. It did not last. Production was to be reduced because of soft markets as the global economy headed into the Great Depression, and downtime at the mill would become more and more frequent.

Not many residents are alive today to tell us what it was like to live in Corner Brook and the Bay of Islands in the time when IP and P owned the mill. When Florence LeDrew arrived in the 1930s she found it very much an American town. Townsite was well laid out and orderly and bore signs of its British influence, later enhanced by Monty Lewin, the popular Bowaters manager who was responsible for beautifying Corner Brook House and the Glynmill Inn pond as well as for planting the chestnut, maple, and linden trees down West Street. But the area around Broadway was more like a Wild Western town without the Stetsons and cowboy boots. On both sides of Townsite dwellings and shops had grown up all over the place, as land could not be purchased in Townsite.

Although paper companies had reserved houses in Townsite for their workers, and charged quite reasonable rentals, not everyone was considered suitable to work in the mill or consequently to live in Townsite. Protestants took precedence over Catholics, and Jews and Lebanese and Chinese were simply unacceptable. These outcasts built their homes and businesses on what was to be known as the West Side, including Broadway, and on the East Side along Humber Road and Humber Heights. To be fair, the IP and P Company had offered to include these areas in their serviced town, but Frank Colbourne asserts that this offer was turned down by the Newfoundland government under pressure from St. John's merchants.

There was no water and sewerage to the buildings on the East and West Sides. Pit privies were in use but even these could not be constructed in some areas because of the rocky terrain. And the steep sides of the hills meant that sewage would inevitably flow downwards and contaminate drinking water from the brooks and wells. So it is not surprising that gastrointestinal infections were common, the most noteworthy being a typhoid epidemic in the autumn of 1925. This was dealt with in a manner that would not now be tolerated although compulsory isolation had been enforced during the "Spanish Flu" epidemic of 1918. The new hospital had been opened, but the typhoid cases were "treated" in isolation in the tar paper shack on Humber Road, formerly the first hospital. The dwellings from which these cases had originated were placed under quarantine for the incubation period, with only the delivery of life's necessities. Fortunately these Draconian measures proved successful and in 1928, as the result of a government grant, water and sewerage were finally established in Broadway and Caribou Road.

Houses were heated by wood stoves. Coal, delivered by horse and sleigh, was also used if one could afford it. Distribution rights for electrical power were purchased by Charlie Ballam, who formed a company to hook up dwellings and businesses with power purchased from the mill. The family life of a mill worker has been somewhat satirised in Percy James' book House of Hate, but a man walking to work and working for 12 hours without a break might be expected to be interested in little more than eating and sleeping when at home, with an occasional evening for drinking or "for a piece of tail," as we say in Newfoundland.

Broadway merchants, especially the clothing store owners, were often buying from Montreal and New York, purchasing last year's fashions cheaply and selling them at fancy prices, so people grumbled, as they usually do, about the high prices. The store owners, Jewish, Lebanese and Chinese apparently all got on well together. For example, Johnny Noah, born in Havana and of Lebanese origin, came to Corner Brook in 1923, acquiring agencies and eventually opening a store on Broadway. Norah Alteen, daughter of S. E. Tuma, owner of the first jewellery store on Broadway, recalls other stores on Broadway in business in the 1920s, including Rumbolts and Abbott's Barber Shops, Peter Coleman and Pete Burns blacksmith's forge, as well as stores owned by Ernie Levitz, Tom Coombs, J.A. Basha, Joseph Noah, Joe Solo, and Peter White.

The first radio station was located in the Glynmill Inn. It opened in 1943 under the managership of Cliff Herlihy and its call sign was VOWN—the Voice of West Newfoundland. Before this station was opened, radio programmes could be obtained from St. John's or even from the mainland if conditions were right. The Gerald S. Doyle programme was listened to as an important way for families to communicate with their menfolk at sea or in the woods.

These families tended to be large and six, eight, ten, or even more children were quite common in a family, whether Catholic or Protestant. Schools had started with the churches, and denominational control of the school boards was later enshrined in the terms of union with Canada. Education was not compulsory until 1944. Funded by government, the first teacher on the west coast on the government's payroll was Miss Anne Collins of Placentia who arrived in Corner Brook in 1882 to teach at the Roman Catholic school. Miss Rose O'Reilly and Mr. McKenzie were also employed at about the same time to teach at schools in Summerside and Benoits Cove, respectively.

One of the first schools in Corner Brook was a one-room school at the bottom of Fisher's Hill. Interestingly, this was the first interdenominational or amalgamated school in Newfoundland and was initially refused approval by the provincial government. Fortunately the paper company agreed to support it financially and it continued to be the only school until 1926 when the Park Street School opened on the present-day site of the Holiday Inn, and it was the first amalgamated high school in the province. In 1927 St. Henry's school was opened, situated behind the present site of the Columbus Club. The early Roman Catholic congregation worshipped in the basement of this school. Father Desmond McGrath, later a pioneer founder of the Fisherman's Union, was one of the first teachers at St. Henry's. In the same year of 1927, six Sisters of Mercy came and founded Mount Bernard Academy.

One of the pioneer founders of Corner Brook was William "Bill" Herdman who served on the Public School Board from 1924 until 1942. He came to work in the construction company from Newcastle on Tyne, England and was later employed by the paper companies. Herdman Collegiate, built in 1956 to replace Park Street School, was named in his honour.

During the Depression years, the mill unions cooperated in keeping schools going in Corner Brook by a contribution from mill employees. The schools were built for Townsite residents but, if there was room for them, students living outside Townsite could attend on payment of a fee. There was no school bussing in those early days. Children had to walk to school and, although there were some paved roads in Townsite, Marian Oxford said that she had to sew laces on the backs of her children's boots to prevent the mud sucking them off when they walked to school. Some paths and roads, including West Street, were covered by a form of rubberised fabric, and duck boards were also used. People would sometimes see rats scuttling beneath them!

Life in Townsite was appreciably different from life on the East and West Sides. Some families still kept some livestock, as they had done in their outport days. In 1942, the Bowater Company tried to stop this practice on company land. Dormston farm, built on land which is now part of the golf course, was able to supply Townsite with eggs and milk and vegetables in season. There was a company store for millworkers only, situated on the present site of the Post Office on Fisher's Hill and a voucher system was used for payment. The first bank in Corner Brook was the Bank of Montreal, opening in 1925 at a site at the top of West Street. Goodyear and House received a franchise to build a department store in a tar paper shack on West Street in 1925 and competed successfully with the company store.

There is a controversy regarding the owner of the first car in Corner Brook, but it seems clear that Thomas Blanchard of Searston was the first to own a car on the West Coast. Jack Fisher claimed that he owned one in 1924. Johnny Noah said that Ed Barry was the first and Amy Wiseman stated that Dr. Cochrane and T. Wall owned the first cars that she saw. In his book, Harold Horwood states that Mr. Stadler, the first mill manager, was the first to use a car. But Stadler resigned in 1925 and it is likely that he sold the car before he left for the mainland, as Newfoundland still drove on the left side of the road in those days, changing to the right hand side on Jan 2 1947; Walter Ruth apparently owned the first taxi. Cars were certainly popular in the area—Corner Brook received continental publicity in the late 1930s on a "Believe it or Not" programme on radio as a town which had 800 cars and only 8 miles of roads! But nobody could drive a car in wintertime until the roads started to be ploughed in the 1940's.

Strangely, almost all the people who were interviewed in the Oral History project commissioned by Bowaters in 1980 declared that class distinction was not a problem amongst adults in Corner Brook. However my personal impression is that there was class distinction when I arrived in Corner Brook in 1956, though it is hardly discernable nowadays. Religious rivalry existed amongst the children, especially in the interschool sporting activities between the Amalgamated Protestant schools and the Catholic schools, but it never became as marked or as violent as it used to be in St. John's and Conception Bay. Every sect or denomination had their own church and cemetery. There was even a synagogue on Concord Avenue for the small Jewish community; when they died their remains were shipped to Montreal for burial.

The people who worked and suffered the most in those days were the loggers, who lived in the woods camps in tar paper shacks with no insulation and poor food and sanitation. They were often men from outports or from communities in the Bay of Islands who tried to supplement their seasonal fishing with work in the woods camps. Walter Reid, a retired garage owner, told me that he worked in the woods when a young man and remembers sleeping communally on spruce boughs on the floor and later in wooden bunks. He still remembers the fleas and the lice.

At first loggers worked in pairs with a crosscut saw; later they worked individually with the bucksaw. The chain saw was introduced around 1940. Ralph Tulk was a scaler in the woods operations. A scaler measured the amount of wood cut by a logger to enable him to get paid. A cord of wood measured 128 cubic feet, or approximately 1.25 metres high and 2.5 metres wide. Tulk said that when the bucksaw was first introduced some loggers could not even cut one cord of wood a day and so were not paid, as they were paid at first by the cord. But an average logger working with a bucksaw might be able to cut two cords a day for which he would be paid about $2, less deduction for food and board. An exceptional logger might manager four cords a day.

Later on the Woods Department at the mill developed a system whereby individual contractors, often former woods department foremen, were allowed to run some of the camps under contract. Payment was changed to an hourly rate, with this rate set annually by the Woods Labour Board with a government-appointed chairman. There was no representation of the loggers on this board and conditions changed very little until 1957 when the International Woodworkers of America tried to organize the loggers, calling a strike that resulted in the death of Constable William Moss, a Newfoundland Constabulary officer and described more fully in another chapter.

A strike by millworkers occurred in 1931, shutting down the mill for 10 days. The cause of it was a proposal by the company to do away with the sixth hand on the paper machines, which was resisted by the Paperworkers Union. Feelings ran high, but were not inflamed by the newspapers of that period which now included the Humber Herald, employing the former Union organiser Joe Smallwood as a reporter. In an interview with Jean Smith in 1980, Father Costello even goes so far as to state that he believes that Smallwood was paid $100 a month by the IP and P Company to keep quiet and not support the unions. The strike was eventually settled and the company agreed to reinstate the sixth hand on the paper machines.

But both company and unions and everyone else in the Bay of Islands were now about to enter a dark period of the world's economic and social history known as the Great Depression, which still sends shudders through survivors when this period of history is recalled. In fact, although markets went sour and the mill had to go on a greatly shortened work week as a consequence, mill workers and management were still better off than the loggers and fishermen, who simply starved.

CHAPTER 9

The Depression Years

The Stock Market crash in 1929 was the start of the Great Depression, a period of financial uncertainty with the loss of capital investment, bankruptcies, and unemployment which affected all the industrial world. Governments reacted by trying to protect their national markets, but mass unemployment forced them to adopt a system of relief popularly known as "the dole." Although the depression did not begin to bite really hard here until 1933, Newfoundland proved no exception. The export market for fish on which the provincial economy depended collapsed to such an extent that 112 pounds of fish fetched only $5 in those years in the Bay of Islands, according to G. Tipple. Pat Griffin, senior, remembers that at one time 124 pounds of codfish would only fetch $3. Fish plant workers were similarly affected and George Basha recalls that they were still only earning 25¢ per hour in 1932.

Instead of the old barter system and the provision of credit by merchants, most fishermen now expected to be paid in cash to enable them to buy provisions and clothing in the growing number of retail stores. Nobody had much in the way of savings—perhaps some had a few gold coins stuffed under the mattress. Families began to suffer immediately, although fish were still plentiful in the bay. But fishermen could not sell the fish on the open market. Some tried hawking fish and vegetables door to door; a codfish might fetch 5 to 10¢ and a large cabbage 5¢. Several Townsite residents recall people at their doors begging for something to eat or clothing for their children. Many of them went about in rags, and many babies died from malnutrition.

Mill workers did not suffer nearly so much. But the export markets for pulp and paper were very soft and the mill was forced to shut down frequently to reduce inventory. At the worst time of this crisis mill, workers were only working 3 days a week. Mona Collins, who was working as a clerk in the mill at this time, recalls three pay cuts in 1 year, each of 10¢ an hour. Nevertheless, she says that she experienced no real hardship. Teachers, earning about $50 a month, were comparatively well off, especially as prices for fresh fish and vegetables were so low.

Perhaps the loggers, who were often part-time fishermen, suffered the worst. They were used to being paid in cash, but when the annual cut of wood for the mill dropped from 300,000 cords to just 40,000 cords a year, some earned only 90¢ a cord for a few weeks work. During the period of this reduced cut, the paper mill used up its inventory of stored wood in the mill yard. The woods operations in Lomond and Howley were closed down completely and the men went on the dole. It was not until 1935 that the woods department was able to increase its

The Curling Waterfront, early part of this century —
from a painting by Robert Pilot

annual cut to 150,000 cords a year. Some time during this period Kit Scott recalls seeing a crowd of men, mostly loggers, sitting on the railway track in Corner Brook waiting for work, any kind of work.

It is difficult for us these days to appreciate how the unemployed and their families suffered during the Great Depression. And it may have been similarly difficult for those in government then to fully appreciate it. Travel was slow and difficult, there was no television, and no local residents represented the riding in the House of Assembly. F. Gordon Bradley was the MHA for the district of Humber in 1932; this district had been separated from St. George's in 1928. In fact, all the MHA's for St. George's and Humber had lived outside their riding up until 1946, most of them in St. John's, except William R. Howley, fish plant owner on Woods Island. In any case Representative and Colonial government came to an end in 1932, collapsing under a huge mountain of debt due to financial irresponsibility and political corruption. The consequence was a marked loss of international credibility and a subsequent inability to borrow money abroad.

As a result of this chain of events, the United Kingdom Colonial Office appointed a Commission of Government. It was made up of three members from both Newfoundland and the UK, presided over by

Bartlett's Point and Mount Moriah (date unknown)
from a painting by Robert Pilot
— These reproductions by permission of Grenfell College

View of Meadows Point from Curling— From the original
by Robert Pilot

the Governor. There was no public referendum and none of the three Newfoundland members were elected by ballot, although William R. Howley, later a barrister in St. John's, had represented St. George's in the House of Assembly from 1900 to 1904.

The mandate given to this commission by the British government was to restore the Newfoundland economy to a sound footing. This they achieved in the years from 1933 to 1949, but little improvement was noticed in the years leading up to the Second World War. Admittedly, they were helped in achieving their goal by a buoyant economy in Newfoundland during and immediately after the war, but the UK commissioners seemed to have well represented the interests of the country as a whole, though of course they had no opposition. They have received somewhat grudging acknowledgement from some Newfoundland historians.

In the course of the next 17 years the Commission introduced the Education Act in 1944, which made schooling compulsory, constructed cottage hospitals, the West Coast Sanatorium, and financed part of the cost of building the Western Memorial Hospital, greatly improving social conditions on the west coast. For instance, the cottage hospital in Norris Point was built using free local labour and materials. There were also hospitals built at Port Aux Basques and Stephenville Crossing, providing basic low cost medical care.

Although quality medical care was now more readily available, dole conditions made life harsh. The dole allotted 6¢ per person per day as well as 1 pound of tea, 1 gallon of molasses, and 1 sack of flour each month. Those unemployed would be issued vouchers for these commodities for use in the stores. Frank Milley, who managed the Ayre & Sons store in Curling, relates that store owners also suffered during the Depression, as the vouchers were often not redeemed by the government until months later.

Dole was refused able-bodied fishermen, who were expected to go on fishing. Moreover, to avail of the dole was a last resort, generally considered a social disgrace. Widows and orphans were entitled to assistance. These unfortunate circumstances drove people to extremes of action; George Allen, a resident of Curling, relates a pathetic story of a man called Childs from Lark Harbour, an able-bodied man with a wife and large family who went by boat to Curling or Corner Brook to ask for the dole. When this was refused, he felt that he had no option but to shoot himself, which he did, in order that his orphaned family would be looked after by the government. Other fishermen from the Bay fought for the dole, regarding it was their right, with some success. In the following account, Ulric Sheppard from Lark Harbour recounts his experiences[34] with the Relieving Officer, a government-appointed official for issuing the dole. It is a long and entertaining account illuminating a grim period in our island history.

"I travelled to Corner Brook one time to the poor house to get me relief. When I walked into Halden's office, he was the relieving officer then, he asked me what I come fer and I told him I come fer me dole, he said 'There's no dole fer ya.'

Well we rowed but we never fight, no, but we done all the rest clear of fighten. I abused him, I called him down to the dirt but all I could get out of him was 'no dole.' Well, I said 'I'm goin to have me dole or I'm going to have your Jesus throat, one thing or the other. I never travelled 31 miles to come in here and get turned down by the likes of you; the Government got plenty of it and I'm going to have it. And I'm not going to Lark Harbour to make away with meself for you, that's one thing I'm not going to do. Before I does that I'll tear the Jesus throat out aya.' And that keeped on and on all day 'till five in the evening.

When I walked out of Halden's office, I got to the porch and there was two policemen there, it wasn't mounties they had at that time, it was policemen... two policemen now and I figured I was goin to end up in jail. So the policemen came along and asked me what was the trouble, they heard the two of us into the argument in Halden's office. So I told them that I come from Lark Harbour this morning and I had to get back with me wife and children before dark and here it is now five o'clock and no relief. So the policemen patted me on the back and said, 'Mister, you're here fightin fer your rights.' 'Yes,' I said 'that's what I'm going to do. I'm not going back to Lark Harbour with nothing to eat for me wife and children. I got nothing at all home so what's the good for me to go home.' So Halden came to the door and said 'I'll be at the Star Office tomorrow morning in Curling.' That was on a Wednesday.

So I stayed with me sister that night. They gave me food and a bed to sleep in and the next morning at nine o'clock I went down to the Star Office there in Curling, down by the Bank of Montreal. When I went in, Halden went through the back door so's I wouldn't see him, but I seen him just the same. I knowed it was him so I went up to the door and I knocked and there was no answer so I knocked the second time and the feller who was printin the Star came to the door, his name was John Barrett. He asked me what I wanted and I told him I wanted to see the Relieving Officer, so he told me to come in.

---

[34] Recounted by Sheppard in his own words, researched by Karl Childs, and rewritten by Mable Sheppard.

Halden was at his desk up in the corner, and the other feller was at his desk printing papers. I went up and I asked Halden fer me dole and he said, 'You're not getting any.' Barrett made signs for me to hit him, but I never, I'd put up a good battle before I'd do that. He told me a dozen times that I wasn't getting any dole and to go home. I said 'I'm not going home before I gets me revenge on you this morning.' I rose me fist and I come down on the table and paper was flying everywhere. 'Now, you can make this as big as you can because I'm getting out of patience.' He looked at me and said, 'Mr. Sheppard, I'll give you half a order.' I said, 'No you don't give me no half order. If you can give half a order, you can give me a full order and I'm not going with no less either, I won't settle on half a order.'

So he sat down to his desk and he wrote me out a order and a half. He passed me the order and I thanked him. He took out his cigarettes and he gave me a smoke, and he asked me if I had any smokes and I told him I didn't, so the cigarettes that was left in the pack he gave them to me. I looked at him and I said, 'Now, Mr. Halden, I came to your office yesterday morning nine o'clock lookin fer me dole, and you turned me down flat. I abused you which I believed I shouldn't have been doing. If you had done it last evening instead of this morning, I'd a been home with me wife and children now. It could have happened but instead of that, I got the same hope of dealing with the fog again this morning." 'Now' he said, 'take that order and don't mention it', cause there was about twenty men down Eugene Baggs. They was all up here before and couldn't get their dole.

The first man I ran into when I come down on the track was Walt Pennell from Frenchman's Cove. We all knowed one another then, and I was the oldest of them all. He looked at me and he said, 'How did ya get on this morning?' 'Well,' 'I said 'boy, I got me order. I come here yesterday and I was up there all day to the office in Corner Brook and I couldn't get it, but I got it this morning though. If I didn't get it this morning, I woulda killed the bastard. You go up to that door and knock and if he don't come out, put your fist through the door, bust the door open. Don't give him no slack, grab him by the throat, you're Pennell enough to do it.'

I went down to Eugene Baggs and there was about twenty men there. They had all been up to Corner Brook trying to get their dole and had to give up. When I come in with some fellars from McIvers, they asked me did I get me relief and I said, 'Yes.' So they said, 'You never got your relief,' and I said, 'I certainly did... I got a order and a half.' They wouldn't believe me so I picked up me paper and showed them. 'Now,' I said, 'boys, go up and get them and don't take nothing less than a order and a half.'

I passed me order into Eugene Baggs and he said, 'I passed Walt Pennell going down and when he came into the shop he was laughing. He musta done alright, I guess he got he's order and a half.'

All I had was a little sleigh and two dogs to come down the bay. Walt said, 'Wait fer me,' and I get me parker and the two of us go out together on me sleigh and let the dogs run along behind. We went down to Frenchman's Cove, and we got there early and I had me dinner at Walt's. He done up he's pony and brought me out to Blow-Me-Down Point. The ice was so rough, he couldn't come no farther. So I took me two dogs and they brought me the rest of the ways home."

Ulrich's story may be embellished a bit but it illustrates the extremities that fishermen had to do to survive in the "dirty thirties." Fortunately, some help was also available from the church organizations that were active in the Bay in those years. The Salvation Army is particularly remembered. Other denominations also did what they could.

People in the Bay of Islands, the north shore in particular, also remember the efforts of a kind, courteous and hard working doctor who practiced in the Bay of Islands at that time. He worked out of a surgery attached to his house in Curling but was ready to answer a call for assistance anywhere in the Bay, later using a motor dory to make his house calls.

This man was Dr. John O'Connell.[35] He was born in Sydney, Nova Scotia, in August, 1875. His grandparents were of Irish descent, from County Tipperary, probably some of the many thousands who emigrated from that country in the time of the potato famine. Working as a boy on his father's farm and in the coal mines of Cape Breton, he later taught school for a few years. Afterwards, he went to St. Francis Xavier University in Antigonish, graduating with a Bachelor of Arts in 1898 with the honour of the Governor General's Medal. The next year he went to Dalhousie to study medicine and graduated in 1905. He then went into general practice in St. John's, Newfoundland. In 1915 he volunteered for service overseas with the Canadian Army Medical Corps, serving in France for 3 years with distinction during which time he was mentioned in dispatches for bravery in keeping his post with the wounded under heavy fire. His first wife died in childbirth on his return to Newfoundland, where he practiced in Harbour Breton, Change Islands, and then

---

[35] I am grateful to his son, Dr. Charles O'Connell, for a biography. Regrettably, Dr. John O'Connell's career is not even mentioned in the Encyclopedia of Newfoundland, although many old party hacks and nonentities mostly from the St. John's area are included.

Placentia where he met and married Bridget Collins.

It was not until 1926, at the age of 51, that he and his family took up residence in Curling, serving all the communities in the Bay of Islands except Corner Brook. The work was rough and demanding—he had to venture by motor boat or dory to visit the sick in their homes when they could not come to his clinic—but he did initiate some medical advances in the communities, starting a program of inoculation against infectious diseases and lecturing at schools on public health. Home deliveries were carried out, often with the help of the local midwife or "handy woman," at all hours of the day and night and in all kinds of weather. His wife Bridget also helped him in his surgery or office when she could, and the Western Star also records that she would "pull a tooth" or dress a wound when the doctor was away on a long trip.

So for the second time in the history of the Bay of Islands, a strong, experienced, and caring individual was there to help the sick and needy during a time of great suffering. Rev. Curling had been this man in the 1870s and Dr. John O'Connell was the man in the 1930s. Like Curling, he often helped out families with his own money and often took no fee for his services. He was greatly loved and appreciated by his patients and went on working well into his 80s, dying in Curling on September 23, 1963. A touching epitaph was written to the Western Star by Annie Wheeler, the Post Mistress in Summerside:

"Sir: On the North side of the Bay of Islands in particular, the passing of Dr. J. I. O'Connell is felt as a personal loss. Our flags flew at half-mast in respect for him, billowing out, fluttering, and drooping sadly, just as our thoughts do—as we look back over the past years during which he was our doctor. Ours more so than anywhere else in the area. People of Curling and the South Shore could if need arose, get another doctor, for they were not isolated as we were.

No bridge or road connected us then with Corner Brook; only by boat, or in winter, on ice, could we get a doctor and for thirty years that doctor was Dr. O'Connell.

I remember well the first time I had occasion to call for his services. Our small son had terrified us by a sudden onslaught of spasmodic croup. It was late in November, the fall had set in, seas were piling high, and winds were wild so no motor boat could cross the bay. The mail steamer of that time, the gallant George L, was dispatched for help and while we waited anxiously Johnnie seemed to recover.

There were now no signs of the terrifying spasms of the night before

Dr. John I. O'Connell and his wife Bridget (CIRCA 1930)
—Courtesy of Dr. Charles O'Connell

and I feared that the doctor would think we had got him out on such a bad night for nothing. But as soon as he saw the child he said, "You were badly worried last night about Johnnie; you will be worried again tonight and perhaps again tomorrow night, but he will be alright. You do exactly what I say and he will be alright."

How understanding he was and encouraging, and Johnnie got better.

I remember a neighbour taking his small son across the ice on a sled, over to see the doctor about an injury which was painful, but considered not at all serious. The doctor examined the boy and ordered him to Corner Brook hospital at once. Seeing the father hesitate, he sensed the trouble. Times were hard then for many, so putting his hand in his pocket he took out some money, and said, "Take this now, it will get you to the hospital and back again. Your child must have X-rays."

Once in the early spring when the ice was weakening after the long winter, a prospective mother was having difficulty and the attending nurse was beginning to despair. "Can we get the doctor on this ice this dark night?" Men went for him, explained the situation and he came. The ice was broken up around the shores and he had to make his way ashore on the loose pans, but he came and brought relief with him, and comfort.

I remember the long, hard journey one winter to the outmost parts of the Bay of Islands, away up in the bottom of Goose Arm, through snow drifts, on ice, by boat, and some part on foot to save a mother and her baby. He saved them too, and stayed with them until they were safely out of danger, before he left to begin the long hard journey back to Curling.

I remember the beads of perspiration on his brow more than once while he worked to bring relief. I remember his unashamed tears of frustration and his sympathy when all his efforts were of no avail.

I remember his warm, sympathetic handshake as he stood silently in the bereaved household.

I could go on and on until of my own knowledge I could fill a book; and I am only one of the many hundreds on this North Shore. From Irishtown through Cox's Cove and beyond, there must be hundreds who can tell of their own experiences of the gentle doctor's help under all sorts of conditions; and for them, also I speak, for I am sure they would like to be included in this small tribute. He came to us in pelting rain and icy sleet and biting cold; in boat, on horse sled, and often by dog sled.

We loved him, indeed and indeed we loved him, but did he know it? Why is it we wait until it brings no answering smile to say what we feel, to those who do so much for us?

Ah well! He has passed on, and if every tear shed for him today could be turned into a shining jewel; or, if each of his many acts of kindness and words of encouragement over and above his obligations could be turned as I say, into a bright and shining jewel; what a dazzling sight his crown would be!

And when our turn comes to render an accounting, if we could show on the credit side of our life's ledger just a small part of what he can, we would know that we too had earned the "well done."

Clearly I can hear the welcoming words to him: "Well done, good and faithful servant." For that is what he was—servant of God, servant of his fellowmen, and master of himself, and may God bless him and his.

ONE WHO REMEMBERS
Summerside,
September 27, 1963."

CHAPTER 10

Bowaters and World War II

The world slowly pulled out of the Great Depression and economies were fuelled, especially in Europe later in the decade, by the need to rearm to counter the increasing menace of Nazi Germany. But IP and P, close to bankruptcy, were anxious to sell the Corner Brook Mill, and in May, 1938, the whole operation was bought by British firm Bowaters Lloyd for $5,000,000 with financing through the Bank of Montreal. The man who accomplished this deal was Eric Vansittart Bowater, a personality of amazing force, daring, and creativeness who had succeeded his father in the chairmanship of the Bowater companies in England at the age of 29. He *was* Bowaters and ran the organisation as a personal fief with increasingly undisputed authority until his death in August 1962. Strangely, he never owned many shares in the Corporation and did not seem to wish to amass a great personal fortune. Nevertheless, he enjoyed living the good life, a life supported by his loyal shareholders. Bowaters annual meetings were legendary; buses would be hired to transport the hundreds of shareholders in England to one of Bowaters English paper mills to be regaled with wine and picnic lunches, a tour of the paper mill and a rousing speech from the Chairman, a man later knighted and known as Sir Eric to all and sundry.

Although running the company from England, Eric Bowater was no stranger to Corner Brook, having visited several times in the 1920s when Bowaters was appointed the sales representatives for North America for the Newfoundland Pulp and Paper Company. In fact, he was present at the grand opening of the mill in 1925. His influence on the development of the Bay of Islands and Corner Brook in particular was very great, and both he and the townsfolk looked forward to his periodic visits. After World War II, he built an imposing mansion on land overlooking Corner Brook Stream which he and his wife Margaret used from 1947 to 1955 when they visited Corner Brook. This residence has always been known as the Vipers Nest, probably derived from the anacronym V.I.P. When the Ball Diversion, now O'Connell Drive, was built, Sir Eric donated the land by the Corner Brook Stream to the city, to be called Margaret Bowater Park and his house to the Roman Catholic Diocese; Archbishop Raymond Lahey is the present resident. Bowater then built a large one-story mansion called Strawberry Hill on a particularly beautiful portion of the Humber River where he entertained publishers from North America and other dignitaries. Most notable was the 1959 visit of Queen Elizabeth and Prince Philip during their tour of west Newfoundland. This remarkable residence was donated to Grenfell College after Bowaters left Corner Brook. It is now a tourist home, with most of the original fixtures and fittings intact, including the Queen's bedroom—well worth a visit.

Sir Eric was also very popular with the Legionnaires. He authorised the purchase of the War Memorial in Remembrance Square and always visited the Royal Canadian Legion Club on West Street during his visits and where he would "shout the house" (Buying all present a free drink!).

The influence of Sir Eric and the Bowater company on the history and development of Corner Brook and the Bay of Islands cannot be overestimated. From a stumbling and sometimes bumbling organisation he raised quality and capacity of the Corner Brook mill within 2 decades for it to become the largest integrated pulp and paper mill in the world. This man was one of the most successful entrepreneurs in the 20th century and in dash and daring in his financial and business affairs he resembled some of the great military and naval commanders of history like Alexander, Napoleon, and Nelson. Like them, he had a gift for selecting and retaining the loyalty of able subordinates upon whom he could rely to carry out his orders and like them he had the charisma to retain the support of his followers (in his case, shareholders and creditors) through good times and bad. He was fortunate in having a commanding presence, tall and straight backed, with penetrating eyes and supreme self confidence. But he was not arrogant and could mix equally well with lords and paper barons or with shareholders or workers or legionnaires. In Corner Brook he was always treated with great deference but I am not sure that he really appreciated it or wanted it.

He was fond of Corner Brook, and I remember that when I attended him in 1961 after he had suffered from a stroke at his residence at Strawberry Hill he was quite enthusiastic about the future of Corner Brook and the west coast and encouraged me to stay and continue to practise here. I expected him to be a difficult patient but this was not the case, although I could not persuade him or his secretaries to allow him much rest, as it was obvious to me that he was a one-man show, and even when I was with him flunkies were popping in and out of the bedroom giving him the latest financial news from London, New York, and Zurich. Those were the days before currency hedging and derivatives, and Bowater's finances were potentially much more exposed to fluctuations between the US dollar, Canadian dollar, and the pound sterling.

The acquisition of the Corner Brook mill by Bowaters in 1938 is a fine example of Eric Bowater's enterprise and skill. Groundwood and pulp prices in 1937 and 1938 had risen sharply, but Bowaters had just taken over Lloyds Paper Mills in an audacious reverse takeover (Lloyds was a larger organisation) and were being financially squeezed by a Scandinavian pulp cartel. This resulted in low or nonexistent profits for the Bowater paper mills in Britain and Eric Bowater was determined to obtain his own secure supply of groundwood for these mills. The Commission of Government, then governing Newfoundland, were approached with a view to obtaining supplies from the Gander area. The Commission agreed, on condition that a pulp mill was built there, and offered to build the railway to it. The timberland was owned by the Reid Company, who were anxious to sell. But Bowater was not anxious to build the pulp mill, and the Commission were not prepared to continue export of pulpwood without "adding value to it" in Newfoundland.

While negotiations for the Gander project were proceeding, Eric Bowater became aware of the IP&P Company's desire to sell the Corner Brook mill through Frater Taylor, the Bank of England's representative on the IP&P Board in New York. He immediately began to work on the possibility of building a pulp mill at the site of the paper mill in Corner Brook rather than building a pulp mill on the Gander timberlands. In Corner Brook he would have the advantage of being able to purchase a paper mill, power company, and forestry operation with the benefit of

Sir Eric Bowater
— Courtesy of Humber Log

an existing work force and infrastructure. The problems lay in the financing, as the Bank of England still held debentures on the Corner Brook property and Bowaters were heavily indebted as the result of the takeover of Lloyds and some small mills in Scandinavia. Moreover, the Newfoundland government was reluctant to lose the chance of employment in the construction and production of a prospective mill in Gander.

After some difficult negotiations an Act was passed by the Newfoundland government, the Bank of England was mollified, and the successful sale of an issue of debentures cleared the way to Bowaters acquisition of the Corner Brook Mill as well as the Deer Lake Power Company. But many doubted the wisdom of this purchase, as the mill's balance sheet was a mixture of both sterling and dollar debt, guaranteed by another mixture of creditors including two governments, the Bank of England, and the three UK companies. And the paper mill had not made a profit for the previous 5 years.

What a gamble! Especially as the European political scene meant that another great war was likely. But taking a gamble, accepting the risk and making it pay off is something that distinguishes a competent businessman from a financial genius and that is what Eric Bowater was, right up until the final 4 or 5 years of his life. By then he had lost, by their deaths, several important friends and advisers, and in those later years it was almost impossible for one man to control the activities of many different and diversified companies all over the world. Indeed, it may have been a mistake on his part to try to maintain newsprint production in the United Kingdom after the war, but loyalty to his country and his roots probably prevented him from making Bowaters a totally North American company in his day, as it is now.

Corner Brook residents and mill workers immediately noticed a difference after the Bowater Pulp & Paper Company took over. The management set out to downsize and streamline administration and tried to increase production and net revenue. But those measures were still unable to cover interest payable on the debt incurred in the purchase of the mill. It is important to remember that profits from the UK mills were used by Bowaters to pay the interest on those debts in these early years. Ironically, when the same strategy was employed by Sir Eric later on to finance the two new mills in the USA with profits from the Corner Brook mill there was local criticism.

The first general manager after Bowaters bought the mill was H. M. S. "Monty" Lewin. Eric Bowater had been impressed by Lewin's han-

H.M.S. Lewin
—By Permission of theWestern Star

dling of a rather violent loggers dispute on the east coast in 1937, and appointed him general manager of the Corner Brook mill in 1938, a post that he was to hold for 19 years. Just as Eric Bowater dominated the Bowaters organisation, so too did Lewin dominate the Corner Brook organisation. Noel Murphy has referred to Lewin as a little dictator and indeed he was short in stature, but one would have to call him a benevolent dictator, as his overall influence on Corner Brook was very positive. For instance, he restored confidence in the mill workers by immediately initiating an 8-hour shift and a 6-day work week. He regarded Townsite as his fief, and set out to beautify it, and he is chiefly responsible for the attractiveness of the Townsite part of the city, often commented upon by visitors. He made the grounds of his residence at Corner Brook House into an English Garden complete with lawn tennis court, and built a boat house and an island on Corner Brook Pond, importing some swans from England, another unusual attraction in this part of the world. He was also instrumental in planting those linden, maple, and horse chestnut trees along the roads in Townsite and made sure that generous donations were given to sports and cultural organisations which were now beginning to emerge. Margaret Bowater Park was donated in 1957.

Monty Lewin was used to getting his own way but was quite reasonable to people who stood up to him. He was born in London, England, in 1900 of Welsh parents and, before he trained as an accountant, he had spent some years at sea in the Merchant Navy and also served as a Midshipman in World War I. He was popular with both management and men in the mill, but perpetuated some of the exclusiveness, some might call it snobbery, of the former management in retaining housing in Townsite for millworkers and a select few other families such as doctors, lawyers, teachers, and store owners. When war broke out in 1939 he organised a Home Guard to protect Main Dam and even commanded a company vessel called <u>Gertrude</u> which was supposed to guard the Humber Arm against the threat of a U-boat attack. In this latter war effort he was assisted by Captain Victor Campbell R.N., formerly a member of Scott's Polar Expedition, then retired and living in Black Duck, who organised a Canadian naval unit for the west coast of Newfoundland. Captain Campbell died in 1956 and was buried in Stephenville with full military honours. A collection of photographs from his Polar expeditions can be seen in Dhoon Lodge, Black Duck and worth a visit.

Before the outbreak of the Second World War in September, 1939, employment in the mill and woods camps was back to normal as far as the economy was concerned. Although conditions were still very bad in the woods camps, an unpaved highway had been constructed from Corner Brook to Deer Lake in 1938 and new woods camps had been established in George's Lake and Adies Lake, increasing the number of loggers. Fish prices had also improved. It is difficult to assess the population of the Bay of Islands at that time because the last census was in 1935, but probably 15,000 lived in the Bay, with about 10,000 of these residing in Curling, Humber East and West, and Townsite. A youth club was formed and a social club for community work. The Blomidon Club was centred in the Glynmill Inn. The Bowater Company were reluctant to part with any property in Townsite before the city was incorporated in 1956, and even then one had to get permission from Bowaters to sell property. It is unfortunate for the present generation of golfers that our present 18 hole course is still under lease from the paper company until 2001.

New schools had been built. Six Presentation sisters known as the Sisters of Mercy came to Corner Brook to teach in 1926. Father Desmond McGrath came with the Christian Brothers to teach in St. Henry's, then Mount Bernard Academy was built and owes its name to Father Bernard Coffey, a Redemptive priest who served here from 1937 to 1948. The first Mount Bernard was destroyed by fire; construction of Presentation High School and Presentation Elementary followed the fire.

The Anglican cathedral of St. John the Evangelist on Main Street in Corner Brook was opened on June 9, 1935, which happened to be the centenary of the Church of England Mission in Newfoundland. Bishop W. C. White, the first native Newfoundlander to be Bishop, and the Archbishop of Canterbury consecrated the building. The Right Rev. Robert Payne also officiated. Prior to this, Anglicans had worshipped in the basement of a church located on Humber Park, Townsite, but never completed. The first parish priest was Rev. Fred Vivian. The new church was built as a replica of Canon T. E. Loder's home church at Fogo. All Saints Church in Clarence Street and St. Michaels Church on Park Drive were both completed later and Corner Brook did not become the centre of the new diocese of west Newfoundland until 1976.

The First Anglican Church in Corner Brook, said to have been built in Humber Park

   Although St. John the Evangelist Church was built in 1935, the United Church was not built until 1941. Willis Eastman recalls a Catholic church on Fudge's Hill and a Salvation Army church in Humbermouth. The Citadel on O'Connell Drive came later, in 1967. In 1947, the Episcopal See of the Roman Catholic Diocese of St. George's was transferred to Corner Brook. Rev. Michael O'Reilly was the Bishop of St. George's at the time. He had previously served with distinction for several years as a priest at Lourdes in the Port au Port Peninsula. Soon after his arrival in Corner Brook he formed a committee to organize the raising of funds and the design of the new cathedral because a new place of worship was needed on account of the population growth and the inadequacy of the existing churches. The Rev. W. Brennan was the first parish priest and celebrated mass in a small chapel at the bottom of Fudges Road; this chapel was so small that he often had to celebrate mass in the open air to an overflow congregation. The first resident priest in the Bay of Islands was Father Andrew Sears, nephew of Monsignor Thomas Sears, who arrived in 1890. Rev. Father Michael Brosnan was the first Parish priest at the Sacred Heart Church in Curling. Sufficient funding was eventually collected and a group of architects from Boston designed

Corner Brook's First Presbyterian Church on Fisher's Hill

the cathedral which resulted in a modern and yet pleasing design with a layout based on the shape of a cross and containing many features based on the Catholic religion and history. The Cathedral Of The Most Holy Redeemer was opened on September 9, 1956.

In 1937 a group of citizens got together to form a Cooperative Society. The Paper Company neither helped or objected to the opening of the store at the top of Fisher's Hill which initially was a great success, both as a department store and as a grocery store. Shares were $5 each and the company cooperated with arrangements for payroll deductions on instalment. In fact both workers and some management helped to run the store, giving their time at first without pay. Other stores opened on West Street. Humber Pharmacy was the first pharmacy with "Pop" Fitzgerald as manager. Eatons followed on West Street and Woolworths later. On Caribou Road A. J. Coleman opened the first of what was to become a chain of family-managed grocery stores in west Newfoundland, moving with his family to Corner Brook in 1934 from Glace Bay.

In contrast to World War I, when most of the Newfoundland volunteers for service came from St. John's and the east coast, men from the Bay of Islands eagerly volunteered for service after Newfoundland entered the war against Germany in September, 1939. Several drafts were

Cathedral of the Most Holy redeemer

levied over the next 6 years of war, totalling about 600 men and women—all volunteers. The Newfoundland government had decided not to activate the Royal Newfoundland Regiment because of its heavy losses in World War I and the difficulties which had been experienced in keeping the Regiment up to strength. Instead the 57th Artillery Regiment, later to become the 166th, was formed and the first draft of 131 men sailed to Britain during the Blitz. In 1940 men began enlisting in the 59th Heavy Regiment, joining a convoy to Britain from Halifax. The Regiment spent the time from its arrival until D-day in May, 1944, preparing for the landings in Normandy in which it played an important part in the battle for Caen and in the advance into France and the Rhine crossings. Before the D-day invasion the Regiment was stationed in Brighton. An amusing story told by the veterans is that one night a party from a German U-Boat landed there and took 5 officers prisoner from a pub. They are proud to state that none of these officers were from the 59th; however, knowing some of these veterans it seems an unlikely story that none of them were carousing in the pub that night.

The 166th Regiment joined the Imperial forces in the North African campaign, and after securing defeat of Rommel's Afrika Korps joined in the invasion of Sicily and Italy where they stayed until the final German defeat. More volunteers joined the Royal or Canadian Navies where they often served in the smaller vessels, such as corvettes, although six Newfoundlanders went down with HMS Hood when it was sunk by the Bismarck. Others, several hundred from the west coast, served in the Merchant Navy and sailed in the dangerous convoys to Russia and across the Atlantic and in the Mediterranean. Not so many joined the Royal or Royal Canadian air forces but a few became pilots or crew members. Not to be forgotten are the Forestry Corps, a group of older men and experienced loggers who worked in Scotland during the war, nor the considerable number of women who joined up in one or another of the women's branches of the services.[36]

Men who worked in the mill were encouraged by Bowaters to volunteer with promises of their jobs upon their return. This promise was kept by Monty Lewin. Replacements were hired; the mill never employed women in pulp and paper manufacture during this war as the Grand Falls Mill did in World War I. In fact the mill worked close to full capacity and was quite profitable, exporting to the US and to Britain, although the paper carrier Humber Arm was sunk in one convoy to Britain.

The returning veterans, were and still are, greatly honoured by the

---

[36] A list of the men from the Bay of Islands who gave their lives in World War II and those that won decorations are given in the appendix.

Bay of Islands communities. While some would never return, casualties in the British and Imperial forces were lower than in World War I and were much lower than the Germans, Russian, and Japanese, especially where civilian casualties are included. Bay of Islands casualty figures were higher than World War I but enlistment from the west coast was far greater in the Second World War when compared with the First. Unfortunately, some veterans came back with illnesses and disabilities caused by the war; others happily returned with new brides from Britain. Two particularly happy couples were Bill and Vic Hann, two brothers from Corner Brook who married two sisters, Mary and Marian, from Scotland. And all returned with experience of the world beyond the still limited confines of the Bay of Islands and were thus able to make significant contributions to the post-war expansion of economic and social activity which was to take place.

Another beneficial effect of the war on the development of the west coast was the result of the agreement between Churchill and Roosevelt in 1941. Part of this agreement gave the British 50 desperately needed old US destroyers in return for 99-year leases on several bases in Newfoundland and the Caribbean, including one to be built at Stephenville for the US Air Force. Construction of this base began almost immediately and resulted in a large number of jobs in construction of the new air field and port, hangers and fuel dumps, and living accommodations. A railway spur line was built to connect to the main Newfoundland Railway system at Stephenville Crossing. The whole complex was known as the Ernest Harmon Air Force Base, after a pioneer US aviator, and the same security system was used as elsewhere on overseas bases, permitting only entry to nonmilitary personnel who worked on the base and to visitors who were authorised with a pass. This base housed a fighter wing and a transportation and refuelling unit when in full operation, but in the 1960s activity was gradually phased out as planes like the giant Hercules were being introduced whose ranges did not require refuelling to cross the Atlantic. The based closed in 1966, with the lease cancelled and all property on the base, including its hospital, returned to the provincial and federal governments.

This large new development in the Port au Port area also had several important effects on the Bay of Islands. First, the west coast at last possessed a world class airfield. After the war, Trans Canada Airlines initiated a service from Montreal through Stephenville to St. John's. People from Corner Brook could use this service by driving to Stephenville along rough woods roads, depending on weather conditions. These roads were upgraded in 1958 but not paved until the early 1960s. Second, there was civilian employment in support services on the base. Local businessmen also benefited from supplying services and one particular businessman in Corner Brook, W. J. Lundrigan, founded his business on the contracts to supply construction lumber to the base. Third, American servicemen enjoyed a visit to Corner Brook for what they called R & R (rest & recreation). They used to come in by a special train at weekends and many would be hosted by Corner Brook residents or would stay with girl friends. In fact, many married Corner Brook girls—I know of three ladies from one family here that married US servicemen. Chaperoned dances were held in a building known as the "White House". The Americans also competed in sports activities such as golf and baseball and considerably raised the overall standard of play in these sports. But not always. After the Blomidon golf course was opened in 1951, a group of golfers from Corner Brook were invited each year to play against the Americans on the golf course at the base. The American team usually included some really good scratch players but a combination of golf handicaps and lavish American hospitality often reduced the golf to a common level, while a good time was had by all!

CHAPTER 11

Confederation
and Civic Government

In the years immediately following World War II the economy of the Bay of Islands continued to boom. The cod and herring fishery benefited from a deal with UNRRA, the United Nations relief agency, to buy salted and cured fish to feed people in countries devastated by the war. Papermaking was also very profitable and pulp prices were good for a time. But Bowaters, still under Monty Lewin as manager, began to try to divest themselves of some of their commercial properties and to shed their responsibility for the upkeep of Townsite by proposing amalgamation of the four town councils into one civic authority. These town councils had been set up during or after the war.

Corner Brook West was the first, set up in 1942 after a petition to the Commission of Government, with H. J. Reader as chairman. Curling was incorporated in 1947 with W. P. Young as its first chairman, and Corner Brook East in 1948 with Allison Bugden as chairman; a later Act included the settlements of Brakes Cove, Humber Road, and Humbermouth in the Corner Brook East town area. Townsite, of course, continued under Bowaters supervision, who appointed the Town Manager. The formation of town councils in both Humber East and West was opposed by a majority of the populations of both areas. A petition containing 600 names was sent to the Commission from Humber East residents who wished to avoid paying the predictable property taxes. But government funds were not forthcoming for much needed water and sewerage projects unless a council was incorporated. This was enacted after a meeting of 40 invited residents in Humber East, chaired by H. J. Reader, had forwarded their own petition. A majority of voters does not always produce the right result, it would seem. Perhaps someone in the Parti Quebecois might mention this gambit to M.Bouchard!

Sir Eric Bowater visited the mill in 1946 and apparently gave an inspirational speech in which he promised expansion both of the mill and of the town. Authorization was given for the building of another paper machine, No. 7, which was to increase newsprint production to 800 tons a day and eventually to over 1000 tons, making the mill for a time the largest integrated pulp and paper mill in the world. But Monty Lewin made a great mistake, which he later admitted, by allowing the machine to be built "in service" instead of contracted out. This temporarily increased local employment of course, but resulted in the work being done inefficiently and over budget, and No. 7 paper machine took many years of continued adjustment to approach its full potential.

The paper mill yard was expanded to allow more wood to be stored. The land was owned by D.M. O'Callahan and his relatives assert, rather bitterly, that it was expropriated by Bowaters. To help pay for these investments Monty Lewin set up a holding company called the West Newfoundland Investment Company whose mandate was to dispose of certain commercial properties still owned by Bowaters to interested investors. Properties sold in this way included:

-The Glynmill Inn, bought by the Islands Hotel Company in 1947.

-The Western Star, purchased by the St. John's Herder family and published as a daily paper in 1952. The Humber Herald was bought out in 1941.

- Crown Laundry and Dry Cleaners and Corner Brook Stores on West Street (both bought by Mr. H.O. House); Corner Brook Stores' name changed to Goodyear and House.

- Western Terminals(formed by Clarke Steamship Company &Bowaters in 1946)

- Newfoundland Engineering &Construction Company (formed in 1944)

Discussions regarding amalgamation of the town councils were at first overshadowed by the referenda on the future of Newfoundland as a whole. The Commission of Government had benefited from its cost cutting policies and from the economic windfalls accruing to the Newfoundland government from the American bases and the wartime boom. Debt had been almost fully retired and there was in fact a growing surplus of revenue, so there seemed no reason for any delay in returning to Responsible government, because before 1932 Newfoundland had claimed to be a self-governing British Dominion. Britain proposed a National Convention which was followed by a referendum. Although the majority of the Convention wanted a return to Responsible government or continuation of the Commission of Government, a minority suggested union with Canada. At Britain's insistence this third option was put on the first referendum. The campaign that preceded the referendum was intense, with a small majority for Responsible government, and confederation with Canada a close second. In this first referendum, 5,189 from the Bay of Islands voted for confederation, 2,837 for Responsible Government, and 2,225 for Commission of Government. The third option was dropped from the second referendum and the Confederation party won it by a narrow margin. But in Bay of Islands, 7,133 voted for confederation and only 3,245 for Responsible Government.

There is no doubt that the heavy pro-Confederation vote in Bay of

Islands, as well as in Labrador and the south west coast of the island made all the difference to ensuring a win for the Confederate Party. Monty Lewin was against confederation, but made no effort to influence the voters. Bowaters were afraid of losing their tax-free status under confederation and in fact they did lose it, although they retained their exemption from municipal taxation, which was to remain a thorn in the flesh of future city councils. But before the Commission was dissolved it had made an important contribution to the future welfare of citizens in Corner Brook and the Bay of Islands—authorization of construction of the Western Memorial Hospital and the West Coast Sanatorium, both of which opened in 1951.

The leader of the pro-Confederate party was Joseph R. Smallwood, the former Pulp Sulphite union organiser and Humber Herald reporter in Corner Brook. When he was elected Premier of the Canadian province of Newfoundland in 1949 he remembered his friends in Corner Brook who had helped him to obtain a majority in the Confederation campaign. He soon established authority over his party and cabinet and always enjoyed massive popular support outside the city of St. John's. He resolved to attempt to industrialise the Newfoundland economy to diversify it away from over-dependence on the fishery. Later, of course, he used more direct measures with the controversial resettlement programme. When his government took over from the Commission there was a sizable surplus of more than $40,000,000, and he spent a large part of this money in establishing factories on the east coast, all of which eventually failed. The exceptions were the two industries set up in Corner Brook, which succeeded because of the presence of raw materials nearby and the city's location as a seaport.

One of the successful Corner Brook developments was North Star Cement, built by the West Germany company Miag, and completed in November 1951. The Germany company operated this plant for the first 7 years but ran it at a loss. Interestingly enough, the original site proposed for the mill was at Mount Moriah, which has a nearby limestone deposit, but the site was changed to Humber Heights, closer to harbour facilities and to a huge nearby limestone deposit. In fact, large commercial limestone deposits are only found on the west coast of Newfoundland. Arthur Reibling, born in West Germany, was the first manager and continued to manage the company after it was purchased by a local group in 1958. It became successful and debt was paid off in 12 years; production was reduced and became intermittent in later years but has recently improved. Initially the plant employed several senior employees who were European expatriates, and these families brought with them European styles and customs and appreciation for the Arts which had a significant effect on Corner Brook society. While the plant boosted employment in the area, the neighbouring residents were not so pleased with the pollution in the form of light dust which affected some parts of Humber East, causing annoyance as well as respiratory problems and forcing management eventually to install modern equipment with pollution control.

The other less successful industry introduced by the Smallwood government was a plant which manufactured gypsum wall board, using gypsum from a large deposit in St. George's Bay. Originally owned and operated by the government of Newfoundland, it was completed in 1952 by the Benno-Schilde Company of West Germany. It produced a high quality product but it suffered from poor markets and never reached its full capacity. Ownership passed through several companies, first a UK company, then a partnership with Flintkote who operated the gypsum mine, then Domtar who expanded the mining operations. Twenty years ago, the Lundrigan organization bought the mill and after the collapse of that company a private consortium bought and operated it with intermittent downtime ever since. At one time the plant employed 180 people. The first manager was Ernest Leja who came to Newfoundland from Latvia.

Immediately following Confederation there was a marked increase in family income because of the addition of the Old Age Pension, unemployment insurance, improved veteran's pensions and allowances, and of course the "baby bonus" which families were now entitled to receive from Ottawa. In spite of infant mortality, which was still unacceptably high in the Bay, families were large, often in double figures, and nobody had yet discovered The Pill. Other changes from confederation included a sudden overnight switch to right hand drive on the roads, such as they were, to conform to the rest of North America, and the institution of a regular ferry service from Channel to North Sydney, as one of the terms of union. Some other changes were not so advantageous. Store owners had bought goods from the mainland and had paid duty on them; there had been no duty on UK goods. Frank Milley, who managed Ayre & Sons store in Curling, says that after confederation the sale of duty-free goods from the mainland undercut him and he was forced to sell many articles at a loss. H. O. House, who then owned Goodyear & House store on West Street in Corner Brook, claims that he lost $200,000 for the same reason. But when the Western Star drew attention in an editorial to the fact that stores were not lowering prices following the elimination of customs duties the uproar caused the resignation of the editor. According to the late Mary Powell, a long time resident of Corner Brook, his name was Bernard Gill.

Another result of Confederation which was to prove controversial in later years was the inclusion of Article 17 in the Terms of Union, continuing the control of school boards by the Christian denominational churches. Discontinuation of the Denominational System had been planned by the Commission of Government but was never implemented. The Newfoundland railway system was taken over by Canadian National, but the intention to construct a broad gauge railway system conforming to the mainland system was also never implemented. As a result the railway system was never profitable and passenger service was discontinued in 1969 following the opening of a paved Trans Canada Highway from Port aux Basques to St. John's in 1965, allowing trans island transportation by tractor trailers. The railway was finally closed completely in 1988 on the understanding that the federal government would upgrade the Trans Canada Highway in Newfoundland, permitting the construction of a four-lane highway in certain places, the road from Corner Brook to Deer Lake being one of the sections chosen.

The closing of the passenger service on the Newfoundland railway was deeply regretted by some people. Confederation had resulted in Trans Canadian Airways operating regular aircraft flights through Stephenville and Gander to St. John's, but many people still preferred the leisurely, if bumpy, journey by train to St. John's. One always met or made friends on the journey and could enjoy a game of cards, and you or someone else could usually provide a nip or two of Screech or Scotch in the smoking room, and the food in the dining room was surprisingly good. Sleep was a different matter, because of the stops and starts at the stations, and clanging bells and whistles at the level crossings and there was always the chance of encountering a moose or snowbank, particularly at Kitty's Brook (near Sheffield Lake) in the wintertime. The opening of the paved trans island highway in 1965 resulted in the death of the passenger train, as many now preferred to drive across the island in less than half the time.

Later results of confederation were also very important to working people in the Bay of Islands over the course of the next few decades. Unemployment insurance changed the subsistence economies of some fishermen and fish plant workers into an occupation where one could survive and feed one's family all the year round without recourse to the dole or welfare. Women started to enter the work force in greater numbers, especially after the introduction of reasonably safe and effective contraceptive measures to enable them to control the size of their families. In spite of the introduction of new industries to Corner Brook the fish plants in the Bay still employed many people, mostly women, although the work was seasonal. For example, Dunphy's fish plant in Curling employed 250 people at the height of the season, almost as many as were employed at the Cement Plant and Gypsum plant combined.

In the late 1960s the Pearson government in Ottawa enacted a series of measures which again profoundly altered the economy of the province, the undeveloped west coast in particular. The Canada Pension Plan was intended to ensure that those elderly and retired would not be so dependant on their families and welfare, although it was not fully funded. But a more revolutionary development was the completion of the Medicare program in 1969, allowing all Canadian citizens access to "free" hospitalisation and "free" medical care, where available. Some of us would like to have seen the system based on some type of user pay system, as the word free is a misnomer, because it is still paid for by taxation or borrowing, which means that there are upper limits to the amounts that can be borrowed or raised by taxation. This upper limit has, in fact, bedeviled the scheme in recent years, and means that services have had to be restricted. This will continue unless more money is made available from other sources.

The Smallwood government had anticipated this federal act by implementing some of its own. In 1957 an act was passed in the House of Assembly entitling all children under 16 to free hospital care, medical services included. This courageous and enlightened act, coupled with the opening of a children's hospital in St. John's (the Janeway, named after a famous US paediatrician) and the addition of Vitamin C to Carnation Milk (then a popular and cheap infant's food) resulted in a significant improvement in children's health and the virtual eradication of deficiency diseases. Dental care had been free since 1950 and the introduction of fluorine into the water system in Corner Brook by Mayor Murphy in his first term of office afforded local dentists more opportunity to employ conservation measures rather than emergency extractions.

As a result of the National Health Acts, plans were soon made to expand facilities and medical care in the province. Well could Dr. Leonard Miller, the Deputy Minister of Health, claim that these Acts were a "Bonanza for the Province," as until then the provincial government had been responsible for the Cottage Hospital system, the Waterford Hospital, the two Sanatoria, the General Hospital in St. John's, and the children's free health service, only partially assisted by federal funding since the onset of confederation.

Just before confederation, discussions on the future amalgamation of the four town councils were initiated in 1947, spearheaded by Monty Lewin. In 1950, as a result of a meeting at Bowaters of the Humber Municipal Association, a feasibility study by Carl Goldenburg of Montreal was authorised and completed and some initial planning was also carried out by the Association to resolve joint concerns. A public referendum in 1955 resulted in 75% of the votes cast by the population of the four towns in favour of amalgamation, and an act passed the House of Assembly in April 1955. In August 1955 a mayor and eight councillors were elected, representing eight separate wards of the city. This ward representation was an attempt to ensure equal representation from all areas, but in practice it was a failure as it caused councillors to promote schemes for improving their own wards without consideration of the good of the city as a whole. Internal bickering soon followed. The City Council took office in January 1956 and City Hall was completed in the same year. Sir Eric Bowater donated a civic mace, and a mayor's chain of office and a coat of arms was authorised by the British College of Heralds. The anchor in the front parking lot was from SS <u>Alcona</u> and was donated in 1979. This 1199-ton vessel was owned by Gorthon Pew of Gloucester, Mass. It burned and then sank off the south east coast of Wood's Island in 1913. The anchor was raised and donated by the Corner Brook Scuba Diving Club.

Also in 1956 there was an attempted implementation of a school tax by the newly appointed School Tax Authority. This was levied on taxable property, retired persons, and people who worked in the city for the purposes of financing education in the school system. There was bitter opposition to this tax, as schools had previously been largely financed by churches and government grants. A vigilante group headed by Ethel Rowsell collected 4300 names for a petition against this tax, but the petition was ignored by the Smallwood government. Rosie Tuma refused to pay the tax and invited prosecution, but lost the case both in the local court and later on appeal in the Newfoundland Supreme Court. Even after this there was widespread opposition and tax evasion, but some years later persons over 65 were exempted.

Physical linkage of Curling to the three other municipalities was achieved by the construction of the Ball Diversion by the provincial government (now called O'Connell Drive in memory of the Curling physician). The petty squabbles and feuds of the Corner Brook City Council over the next 7 years did not reflect on the growth and development of the area but demonstrated the failure of the ward system. They indicate the growing pains of a city still separated by local jealousies and rivalries, and of former town councillors still reluctant to work with a city manager and allow him to carry out policies reached by a vote in a meeting of city councillors. The stories of the so called Elliott affair led to the resignation of the town manager and Horwood describes the McNamara affair in his book, when the Smallwood government overruled a decision of the city council to allow the McNamara construction firm to set up business in Wild Cove, within the boundaries of Corner Brook. It is an example of Smallwood's increasingly dictatorial regime and resulted in his peremptory dismissal of City Council in April 1963.

After the Council had been dismissed, a Commission of Administration was set up. Allison Bugden, the former mayor, was asked to continue to serve on it and Bill Cossitt and Ben Pryde were appointed as councillors. Elot Penny, a long time resident, said that some people grumbled at Bugdens appointment, as the former council had incurred a loss of twenty thousand dollars for which the auditors could find no trace. It was a situation strongly reminiscent of the appointment of the Commission of Government by the UK. government in 1933, and both commissions inherited large debts and poor tax collection. Following the recommendations of a report by Peat, Marwick and Mitchell, this Commission improved the bureaucratic management of the city and collected taxes more efficiently but failed to make much impression on the debt, which had grown to over $9,000,000. Nor were any major public works carried out during these 4 years. Ben Pryde resigned when he became Bowaters Assistant Manager and Fraser Robbins, an accountant, took his place. Allison Bugden, now chief commissioner, was disliked by some as too arrogant, but had political skills, notably by keeping on good terms with Smallwood. He continued as chairman of the School Tax Authority while acting as mayor, and some interpreted this as a conflict of interest.

Many people felt that the Commission did little for the city during their term of office from 1964 to 1967, and it is true that there was little spending on roads and water and sewerage during that time. Fortunately other large projects were completed with federal or provincial money including the Sir Richard Squires building, opened in 1967, and the harbour development scheme at Seal Head. Also the Corner Brook

Housing Authority was set up in 1965, chaired by Sir Brian Dunfield. It began construction of a housing development in West Side, nicknamed "Jelly Bean Square" as the outside of these row houses were painted in different colours. The Holiday Inn was opened in 1966 on land formerly occupied by Park Street school; the Amalgamated Board were now using Herdman Collegiate built in 1956 and named in honour of William Herdman, as well as G.A. Mercer School for grades 7 through 11, S. D. Cook for grades 5 to 8, and Fern Street School for the early grades.

In 1967 elections were finally held for a new City Council. Apparently Allison Bugden was out of the province at the time the election was called, which seems hard to understand given his close relationship with the Smallwood government. Maybe he was just tired of municipal politics as he did not organize much of a campaign. Although he lost his office, he did not suffer long; he was appointed by Smallwood to the Workmen's Compensation Board soon afterwards.

The Council that was elected with Dr. Noel Murphy as the new mayor was one of the best that has ever served the city. Dr. Murphy himself had represented Humber East from 1962 to 1966 in the House of Assembly, sitting as one of the three Progressive Conservative opposition members. He was defeated by the young Clyde Wells in the election in 1966. Despite being Leader of the Opposition to the Smallwood government, Murphy had always remained on reasonable terms with Joey Smallwood, both sharing an interest in Newfoundland history and both being proficient in self promotion. In 1971, Dr. Murphy very briefly served in Smallwood's cabinet as a Liberal, something that made him many enemies in the Progressive Conservative Party and may have handicapped him during his second term as mayor. It must surely have contributed to his defeat by Pat Griffin in 1973.

But as a mayor Noel Murphy was first rate. He was at times authoritarian and at times whimsical but he had clear ideas as to the future of the city and was fair minded and hard working. He immediately recognised the need for increased public services and used his influence with Smallwood to obtain agreement for a 5-year plan to increase and improve these services in the city, with the provincial government granting $1,000,000 a year. Roads were paved, some rather lightly and some with matching contributions from residents, a scheme that had been introduced by the Commission. Water and sewerage was extended and sidewalks constructed. Snow clearing was improved and new housing lots were serviced and sold. The population of the city was now just

Mayor Noel Murphy

below 30,000 people and the city was planning for increases to 40 or
even 50,000. But Corner Brook was still essentially a one-industry town
and, in spite of an excellent year in 1966 when the mill ran 7 days a
week and made a profit, the Bowaters organization was suffering from

the loss of Sir Eric Bowater and A. B. Meyers, their North American sales manager who died in 1964. Inventory piled up, and the mill and its woods operations had to go on to short time. In addition to this, the national economy had slowed, unemployment was in double figures, and some fish plants had to close.

Noel Murphy's first two councils were comprised of businessmen who realised that the economy of the area could not depend on one industry. They attempted to do two things. One was to try to diversify the economy by attracting provincial and federal government initiatives. Harbour development was expanded and plans made for an arterial route into the city, opened in 1973 and named the Lewin Parkway after the popular former general manager of the paper mill. Planning started in 1969 for a new hospital and lobbying began for a regional university. An Arts and Culture Centre was completed in 1968, including an indoor swimming pool. And now that the Deer Lake highway was paved, an airport was opened in that town, used by Eastern Provincial Airways, providing easier access to North America as well as overseas.

But the second objective ended in failure. This was an attempt to force Bowaters to pay City taxes to their assessed value, which would have resulted in an annual amount of over $1,000,000 in taxes to the city instead of the $450,000 donation, increased annually and somewhat grudgingly. Bowaters management responded by calling attention to their extensive and varied donations made to the city over the years, such as parks, buildings, a gift of $200,000 towards the Arts and Culture Centre, and $1,000,000 to Grenfell College. The Murphy city councils did not push the matter in the late 1960's because of the poor state of the economy and of Bowaters in particular , but the 1973 council headed by Pat Griffin actually brought the matter to the courts and surprisingly won the case in the lower court, only to lose on appeal to the Supreme Court of Newfoundland. Later, when Kruger took over the mill from Bowaters in 1982, an opportunity to change the taxation system was lost when the city council failed to press its inclusion in the terms of sale; a donation in lieu of taxes is still in effect to this day.

Dr Noel Murphy, who is still alive and active in the city, deserves a great deal of credit as one of the pioneer doctors of the west coast and an effective mayor of the city of Corner Brook and former MHA. Noel Francis Murphy grew up in St. John's but was educated in England at Ampleforth School and London University where he qualified as a physician in 1942. He has an impeccably English accent but comes from a distinguished family in St. John's where his grandfather was a businessman and his father a physician who served briefly in the Morris government. Noel joined the RAF after qualification and served in England until 1945 when he was recalled by the Commission of Government to fill a vacancy in the Cottage Hospital at Bonne Bay on the west coast of Newfoundland. It is rumoured that while in medical school he paid his way by playing in dance bands and no doubt his musical talents entertained his fellow officers in the mess during those wartime years. He worked in Bonne Bay for 9 years, travelling on call up the west coast as far as Port Saunders. He used a boat in the summer and a horse and sleigh in the winter, much as those other medical pioneers Grenfell and O'Connell had done, as there were still no roads past Bonne Bay.

He married an English woman, Edna, and they had one daughter Edwina and an adopted daughter Gereen. The family moved to Corner Brook in 1954 where Murphy set up a family practice working out of his own home in Cobb Lane. He was never very interested in medical politics but built up a large general practice which he limited during his campaign against Jack Forsey for the Humber East seat in the House of Assembly. He was successful in that endeavour, winning the seat as a Progressive Conservative in 1962 to join a tiny PC opposition in the House of Assembly.

In that same year, Dr. Murphy, in company with Arthur Lundrigan and a group of investors, started a local broadcasting station called CFCB which eventually expanded by transmitting programmes to the west coast and Northern Peninsula and to Labrador. Being an excellent speaker, with a ready wit, he used to host talk shows and other programmes, and I wasn't the only person to be woken by a phone call very early on Christmas morning from Dr. Murphy at CFCB to tell me that I was on open line and to wish me a Happy Christmas and did I want to say something to the listeners! Given his ability to use the media, it was surprising that Pat Griffin defeated him in the mayoralty election of 1973. Indeed, in a community which valued loyalty highly, there was an element of distrust for a man who had switched his provincial party allegiance. Pat Griffin, also a former RAF veteran, later claimed that he owed his success to the hard working people from Curling in his organization who had felt neglected and ignored in civic construction programmes implemented by the previous council. Murphy returned to his general practice but kept active in voluntary organisations and business affairs and in 1978 was again elected mayor, retiring in 1981. In retrospect the early Murphy years were a time of optimism and expansion in Corner Brook. People began to feel good about themselves and their part in the affairs of the province and more importantly began to feel themselves part of Canada. Better communications with the outside world certainly helped, in the shape of a new airport at Deer Lake and the completion of the Trans Canada Highway, and perhaps the most important of all the arrival of television in 1959 and better facilities on Humber Heights for the Canadian Broadcasting Corporation. The construction of an Arts and Culture Centre which enabled important national groups such as the Winnipeg Ballet and Halifax Symphony orchestra and other groups and individuals to entertain and spread the national culture was another important milestone. No longer was Corner Brook "an entrepreneurial backwater." It was becoming part of the main stream.

Murphy certainly left his mark as mayor on the city of Corner Brook during his three terms. Apart from attracting able businessmen to serve with him, such as H. G. Harnett, Bill Hann, and W. McD. Brown to name just three, he was always full of ideas, some of which were impractical. But others, such as fluoridation of the water supply, were implemented with skilful persuasion and with much less opposition than that encountered in other cities. He was also active in many other voluntary organisations such as St. John Ambulance, VON, and the Red Cross. Later on he was promoted to Honorary Colonel of the Newfoundland Regiment and Aide de Camp to the Lieutenant Governor. He is still active in the Rotary Club of Corner Brook, twice President, and once District Governor, and with 38 years perfect attendance until 1998. In fact many people felt that he would and should have been given a term as Lieutenant Governor. No doubt his mistake in joining the ill-fated final Smallwood cabinet in 1971 as a Liberal served to discredit him as a potential candidate, as Progressive Conservative governments were in power from 1972 until 1989.

Municipal government in the city has been steady, if somewhat uninspiring in the past few years. George Hutchings succeeded Noel Murphy in 1981 and continued as mayor until 1985 when he was succeeded by Ray Pollett, a local realtor. These later city council meetings seem to have been tarnished by a lack of openness with the public, as exemplified by the use of private meetings and the delayed publication of the Cuff Report, which described many shortcomings in the city administration. After three terms of office Pollett was defeated in 1997 by Dave Luther, a former CBC broadcaster. Re-elected councillors in that election included Priscilla Boutcher, Jeanette Christopher, and Bernd Staeben and the new councillors were Kevin St. George, Charles Pender and Alton Whelan. The mandate given to this council by the electorate seems to have been directed at attempting to increase the economic base of the economy by encouraging new businesses, making municipal government more open and accountable, and ensuring that the new Canada Games Centre pays for itself by local support of their events rather than by increased civic taxation.

Municipal government has been less successful in some other townships in the Bay of Islands, and residents have been reluctant to come forward and offer their services. Several reasons have been suggested. One reason is that the smaller communities cannot afford to pay salaries to their councillors. Government grants have been reduced, and the economic base is small. In addition, some say that attempts to force delinquent residents to pay taxes, such as cutting off their water supply, is almost impossible because of family and friendship ties in these small communities. But the municipalities in the Humber Valley and Deer Lake have less difficulty in finding residents willing to stand for council.

Federal and provincial politicians have played an important part in our past history and will do so in the future, so a brief sketch of some of the more noteworthy post-Confederation politicians seems appropriate. Confederation brought the new federal riding of Humber, St. Barbe, Bay St. George and local representation for the two provincial ridings of Humber East and West.

The federal riding, which now includes Baie Verte instead of Bay St. George, was first represented after Confederation by William Kent, and then for the next 16 years by Herman Batten, first elected in 1952 and nicknamed "our silent member." Jack Marshall won the election in 1968 and was certainly far from silent, promoting this area's interests vigorously in the House of Commons and also after his appointment to the Senate.

Jack Marshall was born in 1919 in Glace Bay and served in World War II in the North Shore New Brunswick Regiment—landing on Juno Beach on D-Day with his regiment. After marrying an Englishwoman, Sylvia, he and his family settled in Corner Brook where he operated a drug store on Broadway. He continued to maintain an interest in the military, serving as Commanding Officer of the local company of the Newfoundland Regiment and later ending his career as Brigadier and Area Commander. He always maintained a strong community interest, spearheading the drive to raise money for the construction of Humber Gardens, opened in 1954. After he was elected to Parliament he be-

Jack Marshall, MP for Humber St. George, later
appointed Senator

came particularly noted for his easy accessibility and helpfulness to all
his constituents. He actively promoted the opening of a federal park in
the Bonne Bay area known as Gros Morne National Park and was always a strong supporter of Veteran's rights, becoming Minister for Vet-

erans Affairs during a Progressive Conservative administration. He was appointed to the Senate in 1978 and still continues to assist constituents whenever possible, even after his retirement.

In the subsequent by election after his appointment to the Senate, this riding surprised the rest of the country by electing Phonse Faour, a young lawyer and native of Corner Brook, as the first parliamentary representative of the New Democratic Party from Newfoundland. He was re-elected in 1979. But in 1980 Brian Tobin narrowly won the seat for the Liberal Party in what turned out to be a landslide majority for the Progressive Conservative party in the rest of the country. Tobin retained this seat in two future elections, and eventually became a cabinet minister in the Chrétien administration. When he resigned his seat in 1995 to enter provincial politics, a young man Gerry Byrne retained the seat for the Liberal Party and was re-elected in 1997. Brian Tobin successfully contested the provincial riding of Bay of Islands and became Premier of the province.

This area currently has three Liberal members elected in the 1997 general election for the House of Assembly, including the Premier Brian Tobin, who is the member for the Bay of Islands, and the Minister of Finance Paul Dicks, the Member for Humber West. Lynn Verge represented Humber East very effectively for 16 years. Among her many achievements was the promotion of the East Side Redevelopment Programme, which enabled roads and sewers to be redesigned and built to parallel the previous similar development of the West Side. She lost her seat in the election of 1996 to Bob Mercer by a few votes, but implemented some innovative programmes during her terms of office as Minister of Education and Minister of Justice in the Peckford administrations.

Born in Stephenville Crossing on the west coast, Clyde Wells proved a fiscally prudent premier from 1989 to 1994, having represented Humber East from 1966 to 1971. Together with John Crosbie, he broke with Smallwood in 1970 and continued as an Independent Liberal before eventually resigning. He came back to politics as member for Buchans in a by election and represented the new riding of Bay of Islands after his defeat by Lynn Verge in the Humber East riding in the 1989 election. One of the most important contributions to the development of this area occured during his Premiership, when Government funding was provided to enable Marble Mountain to be developed into a potential international ski resort. Since Confederation the Humber East and West, and the Bay of Islands, have been considered "swing ridings," as Liberal,

P.C. and N.D.P. members have all been returned to Ottawa. So Provincial politicians keep a wary watch on this electorate, and it therefore comes as no surprise that this area has elected 4 Premiers and 2 Leaders of the Opposition to the House of Assembly in the past 35 years.

CHAPTER 12
Corner Brook's Magnets
and the Lundrigan Era

As I have previously noted, while many of Corner Brooks original settlers came from Nova Scotia, the construction of the paper mill and the jobs that followed was accompanied by migration from all parts of Newfoundland, especially the east coast. Businesses were started up by Canadian immigrants as well as families from St. John's and other parts of Newfoundland. At first, commerce in the Bay of Islands remained centred on the main railway station at Curling because travel across the bay was still only possible by boat, but once roads were built around the north and south shores Corner Brook gradually attracted customers to the commercial, professional, and shopping areas from all parts of the bay.

The Ballam Bridge, the first bridge across the Humber River below Deer Lake, was opened October 31, 1955—Stewart Noseworthy drove the first vehicle to cross the new bridge. The north shore highway was then passable, after a fashion, as far as McIvers and enabled people from the communities along that shore to visit or commute to Corner Brook by road. Later the road was continued over the hills to Cox's Cove. When this road was eventually paved the work was carried out in sections. Frank Colbourne describes an incident when the residents of McIvers blocked the highway to prevent paving equipment from reaching Cox's Cove, as a decision had been made to pave Cox's Cove first. This resulted in the so called "McIvers scuffle." Eventually the RCMP cleared the road and paving proceeded as scheduled. This road has been renamed the Admiral Palliser Trail in honour of Governor Palliser, whose squadron visited the Outer Bay of Islands in 1764, the first Governor to do so. He was Governor of Newfoundland from 1764 to 1768.

The South Shore Road was built also in stages as far as Frenchman's Cove and extended to Lark Harbour in 1960. William K. Sheppard claims to be the first to motor to Corner Brook on October 10th of that year. This highway linked up with roads to small communities at Bottle Cove and Little Port. When the provincial parks were developed, one was opened at Piccadilly Beach between York and Lark Harbour. This South Shore Road was upgraded and paved in 1975 and renamed the Captain Cook Trail in 1996 in honour of James Cook's 1767 visits.

After these roads had been constructed it was possible for all communities in the Bay of Islands to drive to Corner Brook, which provided several magnets to attract visits from people living outside the city. Commuter travel to Corner Brook was now possible, driving to work and back daily. The success of the mill provided spinoff employment in service industries which grew and multiplied. Other manufacturing and construction industries such as the Lundrigan group also proved to be magnets for employment. Medicare was the magnet that attracted patients, as well as more doctors and health staff to work in the now improved facilities. The malls attracted more shoppers to the Corner Brook area. Memorial University, opening Grenfell College in 1975, provided a magnet attracting students from all over west Newfoundland and Labrador.

The influx of people to the city of Corner Brook because of these magnets forged a sense of optimism amongst citizens in the late 1950s and 1960s. New houses and subdivisions were completed and town planning was predicated on a city of about 50,000 people. This did not happen for various reasons, attributed primarily to the high property taxes in Corner Brook. Bay of Island communities did in fact increase in size and some of these residents preferred to buy a car and commute and to develop the amenities of their own homes rather than move into the city and pay city taxes. Communities in the Humber Valley, such as Steady Brook and Pasadena, also showed population increases and a fine new community known as Humber Village was founded by Lundrigans across the Humber River, with large lots of several acres and expensive housing. From a peak population of nearly 30,000 the census in 1971 showed 26,520 residents in Corner Brook.

The Lundrigan Group of Companies was one of the most important magnets attracting workers and their families to Corner Brook, second only to the paper mill company, and employing at one time some 1500 employees across the island. In 1979 the company purchased Comstock International, a mainland engineering and construction company which in itself employed more than 2000 people or workers throughout Canada. The story of the founding of the company empire is a fascinating one which is worthy of a book of its own. Its sudden collapse and bankruptcy, with international overtones associated with the loss of the Hibernia construction project and the political manoeuvring that had to be faced in trying to obtain that contract, cannot yet be told, because all the facts have not yet come to light.

William J. Lundrigan, known to many was W.J., was born in 1901 at Blaketown, Trinity Bay. He came to Corner Brook in 1922 as an unskilled worker with his wife, Naomi Dawe, who had been a Salvation Army officer. In all they had 12 children, including 5 boys, the eldest being Arthur, who eventually succeeded W.J. as manager of the organization.

W. J. started work in the Fisher sawmill as a checker and worked briefly for the paper mill construction company, Armstrong Whitworth. In 1926 he started working as an agent for the food company that later became known as Canada Packers. Shortly afterwards he opened a store by himself on Broadway, joining a small group of entrepreneurs in that area. But in the depression years his business failed and collapsed and he was forced to work in the woods as a small contractor for Bowaters. Before this he had established a friendship with the <u>Humber Herald</u> reporter and union organizer, Joseph Smallwood. This friendship continued through their lives and was to assist each other in their respective future endeavours.

After the depression W. J. opened a small sawmill on Poplar Road. By the time war broke out and the US Air Force arrived at Stephenville in 1941 to build the base there, he was able to supply them with lumber and millwork from his Corner Brook mill. Later he supplied lumber and materials for the air base at Gander and other sites, so that by the end of the war he had established a sizeable and successful building supply and construction company. With the coming of Confederation and the desire of the new government to build roads, hospitals, schools, and other infrastructures the company was able to bid successfully on major contracts. With a new head office and construction centre at Brake's Cove, Corner Brook, it became a major factor in the expansion of Corner Brook and its development into a modern city.

Besides major road building contracts for the construction of parts of the Trans Canada Highway and the road to the Northern Peninsula, the new buildings built by Lundrigan's included the Bank of Montreal on West Street, the Herald Tower, the 10-storey Sir Richard Squires building, the Royal Trust Building in St. John's, the Bank of Montreal Tower and the Sheraton Hotel in Halifax. The company built the first shopping mall—Millbrook Mall—at Corner Brook, which opened in 1964, as well as several other malls around the province.

While opening the Sir Richard Squires building, or "skyscraper" as he grandiosely termed it, Joseph Smallwood announced that Bowaters would contribute $300,000, Lundrigan's $200,000, and the Government of Canada the balance, to build the Arts and Culture Centre in Corner Brook. At the time, some people felt that Joey had pulled the numbers out of the hat and was indulging in a bit of political arm twisting, but Arthur Lundrigan assures me that he was fully aware of the project; Bowaters had agreed to contribute to the cost, and his company had agreed as well. He also says that his company built the centre and swimming pool at cost and no profit, which was also a part of their contribu-

William J. Lundrigan

tion. The federal government contribution was a part of the Canada Centennial contribution to Newfoundland in 1967.

The Lundrigan Group was a family-run business until they acquired the Comstock International Company in 1979. W.J. was a humanitarian of the old school and was a devout Salvationist who tried to improve the wellbeing of the people of Newfoundland and Bay of Islands in particular. For many years his work force was not unionized. The organization had an Industrial Council whereby the employees elected members each year and the company appointed an equal number of persons to form the Council which was to meet regularly on company time and review grievances and wage adjustments. The system apparently worked quite well until the company expanded outside Corner Brook and when unions became involved.

W.J. was Chairman of the Western Memorial Hospital for several years after its opening in 1951. He was also an active member of the School Board for many years. Arthur, the eldest of his five sons, went to work with his father at an early age, not completing high school, and proved to be an astute businessman. Together with a group of other businessmen, including Dr. Noel Murphy, they founded the radio broadcasting station, CFCB, with its community broadcast stations throughout the west coast of Newfoundland and Labrador. He retained his personal interest in the North Star Cement Company after he retired from the Lundrigan Group. He received honourary degrees from Memorial University and Technical University of Nova Scotia and in 1991 was appointed an Officer of the Order of Canada. This history of the Lundrigan organisation was recounted to me when I interviewed Arthur in 1997.

All of the brothers were at some time or other involved with the company. Harold, who succeeded Arthur as President of the company, earned a degree in engineering from Nova Scotia Technical College in Halifax and he too was appointed to the Order of Canada. Their brother, William (Bill) is active in the business community and is currently President of the local Chamber of Commerce, while Thomas operates his own business on Broadway; Maxwell is retired.

In the early 1980s the Lundrigan Group, including Comstock International, formed a partnership with a group of Norwegian companies and US companies to form North Atlantic Contractors to bid on the Hibernia oil rig construction project. Because of the federal government policy whereby all such investments in Canada came under the Foreign Investment Review Agency (FIRA), 50% of the cost of that project fell to the Lundrigan Group. The considerable expense involved in the complicated and prolonged bid submissions and promotion activities necessitated major borrowing on the part of Lundrigan's. Later the FIRA arrangement was scrapped when the change of government took place in Ottawa and the Lundrigan share of the equity in the project was reduced to 1/3 or less with the other partners picking up the difference. At last only two companies remained in the contract bidding, one being the Lundrigan Consortium, known as North Atlantic Contractors, and the other a French-controlled group called NODECO. To the surprise of many, NODECO got the contract.

The loss of the Hibernia contract was disastrous for Lundrigan's, after having put so much effort and borrowed funds into the project to promote their bid. The banks became nervous. Lundrigan's then started to divest themselves of several of their operations, but ultimately the bank forced the company into receivership and bankruptcy. Ironically, NODECO was unable to fulfil the contract at Hibernia and the Norwegian and US partners of the original Lundrigan Consortium were brought in to complete the project, which it did on time and under budget with the assistance of many Newfoundland workers.

Despite the ultimate collapse of the Lundrigan Group, the company did contribute significantly to the feeling of confidence in the future of Corner Brook which until then had been dependant on finance and expertise from outside sources. This local family-based company had become a national company in the course of a generation and has given encouragement to Bay of Islands entrepreneurs, such as the Coleman Group and Barry Group of companies and many others like Genesis Organic, who nowadays look to the rest of the country and even to the world for markets. Several other companies and executives throughout Newfoundland have also benefited from the knowledge and experience gained from the activities of the Lundrigan organization. By building roads, erecting buildings and injecting funds into many other activities, money spent on these projects remained in Newfoundland. Lundrigan's contribution to the development of Corner Brook and Bay of Islands was a major one, and should not be forgotten.

CHAPTER 13

The Pulp and Paper Mill and the Kruger Purchase

The largest magnet to attract workers and settlers from the Bay of Islands to Corner Brook was the Paper Mill. After its purchase by Eric Bowater in 1938 it made profits even during the Second World War, when the mill was still able to sell paper to the US, sometimes using the Great Lakes route. It even continued to transport pulp to the UK in the North Atlantic Convoys, although at least one paper carrier was sunk by German U-boats. After the war, profits boomed from $1,000,000 in 1945 to $8,000,000 in 1951 and production increased in 1951 to 300,000 tons a year, after No. 7 paper machine had been installed and run in.

The decision to build and install No. 7 machine was another big gamble by Eric Bowater, Sir Eric since his knighthood in 1944, and nearly led to his downfall because of opposition to his plans on the Board of Directors. And a mistake was made, and was later admitted by the general manager Monty Lewin, in trying to install the big machine, the largest of its kind at the time, by using mainly local workers. It was usual to bring in an outside specialist firm on contract to carry out this type of work. Unfortunately there was a 43% cost overrun on the project and the machine never ran properly for several years. Paper makers jokingly referred to the foundation being built on empty beer bottles. But John Manuel states that the main reason for the poor performance of No. 7 was that it was of prewar design and therefore not state of the art. According to Manuel, after extensive modernization this machine now runs smoothly and there is no trouble with its foundation.

This cost overrun resulted in the first blunt refusal Sir Eric had ever experienced. The Bank of Montreal, having already lent several million dollars to the company, refused point blank to lend any more. But such was Sir Eric's charisma that he had little difficulty in floating an issue of 4.5% cumulative participating preference shares on the market. Two years later he wrote: "yesterday I had lunch with the Bank [of Montreal]. Amusing. Two years ago we owed them 12 million dollars. Today we have 2 million to our credit and they were very polite."

The Corner Brook mill was making excellent profits in 1951 and Sir Eric had convinced a still doubting Board of Directors to agree to the construction of a pulp and mill at Calhoun, Tennessee. The Corner Brook mill provided $8,000,000 out of its profits to provide equity capital and to purchase two new ships for the Bowater fleet. In spite of this, all the funded debt of the Corner Brook mill was paid off in 1955 after the sale of Corner Brook Power for $8,628,800 to a newly formed power company, which remained a Bowaters subsidiary. In retrospect, this was the peak of Corner Brook's influence on the affairs of the Bowater Corporation. From then on this influence and investment gradually passed to the new mills in the USA in Calhoun and Catawba.

There was a devastating fire in April, 1957, which destroyed four paper machines. The remaining three machines were back in service in 2 days but the other machines took several months to return to full output. The mill manager, George Hobbs, lost his job, but again a mistake seems to have been made by the administration by not taking the opportunity to use the fire insurance to install modern paper machines, as those damaged machines were already 30 years old.

The post-war boom was soon over and there was a glut of newsprint on the North American market. Prices plummeted. There was a proposal to close the sulphite mill because of poor quality of the product. There was trouble in the woods. The International Woodworkers of America (IWA) had already organised lumber workers in British Columbia and were anxious to do so in the Maritimes. They visited this province in 1957 and must have been horrified by what they saw, as woods camps had hardly changed from the conditions that had existed when the mill opened. Low wages, now only $1.05 to $1.30 an hour instead of by the cord, were set annually at a certain level by the provincial Woods Labour board under a government-appointed chairman—a patriarchal St. John's dominated organization, liable to raise the hackles of any Bayman. Poor food and appalling camp conditions were readily apparent. The IWA was very well received by the loggers and were certified as their bargaining agent after a large majority vote. In 1958 they demanded a new contract and targeted the Anglo Newfoundland Development Company (A.N.D.) in Grand Falls, probably because they operated their own woods camps, whereas Bowaters used some 30 or so independent contractors scattered over the island. These contractors shipped wood pulp by barge from places like Hare Bay and Hawkes Bay as well as by train from Gander from their scattered woods camps.

Initial demands of the IWA were only modest. The union asked for an increase of 25¢ an hour and a reduction of the work week from 60 to 54 hours, and the provision of running water in the camps. But the A.N.D. company refused these demands and the dispute went to a conciliation board. The response of that board fell far short of these reasonable requests—it only recommended an increase of 17¢ an hour without including any shortened hours, and refused that elementary sanitary request for running water. The A.N.D. Company rejected the board's recommendation and even refused to negotiate further, and would have nothing to do with the IWA. Now it appeared that the very existence of the IWA was at stake and a strike was called, with the loggers walking out of the A.N.D. camps on January 2, 1959.

The strike was bitter and brutal. The A.N.D. Company immediately brought in workers from surrounding areas, who were anxious to work because of the depressed economic situation in the province, with unemployment running higher than at any time since before the Second World War. The walkout spilled over to many of the Bowater contractor's camps in wild cat strikes. When so called "scab" labour was employed, the strikers retaliated by all kinds of measures—stealing equipment, immobilising snowmobiles and machinery, and using aggressive picketing.

The people of Newfoundland responded with a division of opinion, predictable at that time, though hard to understand now, nearly 40 years later. Smallwood was at the height of his powers, with virtually no opposition, and people were not so much as afraid of opposing him as of "losing their vote" and therefore being left behind in the gravy train. In this dispute Smallwood had the support of the merchants of St. John's (formerly his natural opposition), the millworkers at Grand Falls, and, shamefully, some churchmen. But the mill workers in Corner Brook supported the strikers and gave generously to the strike fund. Sympathizers on the mainland of Canada also supported this fund to a then-record amount of $860,000. The Western Star attempted to give equal space in its columns to both parties in this dispute. But their owners in St. John's demanded that it cease publishing union reports which they termed propaganda, whereupon the whole senior managerial staff, to their credit, resigned. These included Ed Finn, Jr. who later stood as an NDP candidate in Humber West in 1962 and City Editor Tom Buck, as well as Tom Cahill, who joined the Canadian Broadcasting Corporation, and Alex Powell, who then began teaching at Herdman Collegiate.

On February 12, 1959, Premier Smallwood announced that he was going to revoke the certification given to the IWA by the Labour Relations Board. Like the announcement of J. F. Kennedy's assassination in 1963, I am sure many of us living in Newfoundland then and listening to this radio broadcast can remember where we were when "Joey" made this shattering announcement. His speech was given in his usual demagogic style and particularly appalled me, coming as I do from a socialist background (my grandfather stood unsuccessfully after WWI as a Labour candidate in Tamworth, UK). Smallwood even compared the IWA and its president Landon Ladd to Jimmy Hoffa and his Teamsters Union, which were then being investigated for racketeering by the US government and he referred to the IWA as "godless agitators, spreading class hatred and violence." He also made skilful political use later, on March 10th, of the death of William Moss, a Newfoundland Constabulary officer who was accidentally killed during an attempt by RCMP and police to force a way for strikebreakers to enter a woods camp.

There was no effective opposition to Smallwood in the legislature at that time and the IWA were duly decertified and sent packing. But there was eventually a happy result, because in a few years most of the terrible conditions were rectified, at least in the Bowaters woods camps. Within 3 years regular inspections were started and woods camps became properly heated, with hot and cold running water and better food. Pay was also improved and the work week was cut to 50 hours. Most of the credit for this striking improvement is probably due to Woods Manager J. D. Roberts and his assistant Max Vardy. Chain saws had now completely replaced the old bucksaws and cross saws. The outcome was to enable a much smaller work force of professional loggers to replace a previous larger force of part-time fishermen and loggers. A logging school was built and started up close to Corner Brook. Smallwood set up a puppet union, the Newfoundland Brotherhood of Woods Workers, after the decertification of the IWA, but it collapsed 2 years after the strike. The loggers were then ordered by Smallwood, without a supervised vote, to join the International Brotherhood of Carpenters and Joiners, and they obeyed. How times have changed!

Another result of this strike was seen in the next election for the House of Assembly in 1962. Ed Finn, Jr., who had resigned in 1959 from editorship of the Western Star, joined the newly formed NDP party and came within 264 votes of unseating the long time Liberal incumbent Charlie Ballam. In Humber East, the Progressive Conservative candidate Dr. Noel Murphy defeated the incumbent Jack Forsey by a similar margin but he now states, as one would expect he would, that his success was not materially improved by any pro-IWA vote.

Some Corner Brook residents had opposed the IWA, although the mill and union workers were supportive. But most disliked the premier's dictatorial abuse of democratically elected power. Smallwood must have sensed this, although the Bay of Islands electoral district had wholeheartedly supported him in his confederation campaign. To make quite sure, he parachuted himself into the Humber West district in 1966 and promoted and supported the young Liberal Clyde Wells in Humber East to defeat Noel Murphy. Dr. Murphy courageously visited the old

Orangeman's Hall in Corner Brook to congratulate Clyde Wells after the election result. There were some boos, but Smallwood told them to be quiet and he and Clyde both shook hands with Noel. With a classic Murphy ad lib, Noel said, "There, you see, it took two of them to defeat me!" In the following election Corner Brook East and West both remained in Liberal hands until 1971 and after Smallwood was finally defeated both ridings remained solidly PC until 1990.

After Sir Eric's death in 1962, the Bowater parent organization clearly lost interest in the Corner Brook mill. Profits and employment were variable in the 1960s due to the international market but when the Canadian dollar rose to near par with the US dollar there were losses at the Corner Brook mill from 1970 to 1972, as much as $4,646,000 in 1971. This prompted Martin Ritchie, who had succeeded Sir Christopher Chancellor as president of Bowaters, to propose closure of No. 7 machine with accompanying layoffs. Moreover, he publicly announced that he was seeking a purchaser for the mill. Joey Smallwood was furious and, embarrassed by an upcoming election, threatened to nationalise the mill, giving $200,000 to Bowaters as an option for 2 years to buy the mill. But Smallwood was impotent. No. 7 closed for a short period in December 1971 and Frank Moores won the election, never exercising the option.

John Manuel, a former Bowaters mill manager with employment experience in Canadian mills, returned to Corner Brook Pulp and Paper Company in 1987. According to Manuel, in 1973 the Corner Brook mill was still known by people in the newspaper industry to be for sale. Rupert Murdoch, the Australian newspaper publisher, showed interest, as he wanted a secure source of supply for his newspapers. But the sale fell through when Ben Pryde, then head of sales for Bowaters North America, informed the negotiating committee that Bowaters had long-term contracts with publishers in the US which could not be broken. And so the sale was never completed.

The Bowaters story was not over yet and in fact the mill now had its most profitable period, going into the black later in 1973 and making record profits of no less than $25,264,000 in 1978. This enabled Bowaters Newfoundland to increase dividends to the parent company to record levels, but not enough was put back to renovate the mill or the paper machines, now over 45 years old, despite promises. When some upgrades were made in 1981, thermomechanical pulping was only partially introduced to replace the older chemical sulphite pulping process.

When Wally Clark, the General Manager, announced the shutdown of No. 7 machine for good on December 1982, with the loss of 746 unionised, non-unionised, and woods workers, the effect on the community was that of shock and dismay. For in addition to the shutdown of No. 7, there were to be layoffs lasting several weeks for the remaining workers, occurring over Christmas and through the New Year. Besides this, silviculture expenditure, essential to preserving the future of the industry in Newfoundland, was to be cut from $2,000,000 a year to $600,000. One didn't need to be a Rhodes Scholar then to figure out that Bowaters had again lost interest in the Corner Brook mill and were planning to pull out completely. And sure enough, 2 years later the Corner Brook mill was again put up for sale.

George Hutchings, the mayor of Corner Brook at the time, remembers his sense of despair when Premier Brian Peckford informed him in confidence that negotiations were in progress for the sale of the mill. The government didn't want publicity of this fact to affect the negotiations, which from the early stages involved Bowaters and a privately owned Montreal-based company, Kruger Incorporated. But Hutchings felt that the people of Corner Brook deserved to be informed and he called a press conference 2 days later, much to the annoyance of Peckford and his government. City Council was subsequently shut out of the negotiations, losing the opportunity to assert its position on the paper mill municipal tax problem during the negotiations with Kruger. Nor was there any discussion with the unions, until council was asked for concessions. Lynn Verge, then the MHA for Humber East, remembers these negotiations and their successful conclusion as one of the major successes of the Peckford Administration.

Negotiations completed, the deal was signed in Corner Brook on December 21, 1984, but only after Peckford had secured the passage of Bill 37 in the House of Assembly by using closure. This strange piece of legislation, insisted on by Kruger, was an amendment to the Labour Standards Act and was designed to shorten the period required for notification of temporary layoffs to a period of 1 week and was retroactive to 1978. The province also provided $64,000,000 in loans, grants, subsidies, and guarantees. The unions agreed to some loss of benefits in return for job security and a promise to re-start No. 7 paper machine.

Kruger Incorporated, with Joseph Kruger II as chairman of the company, took over the mill. But this sale had eroded public confidence in the viability of the pulp and paper industry in Corner Brook. The public, especially those who remembered the Eric Bowater days, were shaken and confused by the lack of confidence in the mill operation which had been shown by the Bowater management. They were apprehensive and uncertain about the motives of the Kruger corporation, a private company which had an excellent record in Canada of making mills profitable that other companies had considered to be uneconomic, but whose public relations were indifferent. Nevertheless over the succeeding years confidence in the operation was gradually regained. Actions speak louder than words, and the actions of Kruger have been most impressive, and some of them should be listed for the record.

The mill operation was obviously not up to industry standards when Kruger took over ownership, nor did it come anywhere near Canadian environmental standards. In the course of the next 12 years over $350,000,000 was expended including:

- Restart of No. 7 paper machine.
- New dry debarkers, ending the pollution of bark in Humber Arm.
- The end of the Humber River Drive and booms, avoiding pollution of the river and wastage of wood.
- Complete conversion to thermomechanical pulping in 1988, eliminating unpleasant sulphurous fumes from sulphite plant, and permitting some heat recovery to increase efficiency.
- Progressive modernization of most of the paper machines to improve quality to world class (There were inevitable temporary layoffs during these shutdowns).
- New steam boilers No. 3 & 6.
- A recycling plant.
- Compliance with government orders to reduce the emission of pollutants into Humber Arm, now completed.

This is an impressive list and the mill is now one of the best in the country. The work force is now about 600, and this employment remains a most important magnet for maintaining the quality of life that has evolved in the city. In 1989, the last year for these statistics provided by Statistics Canada, the average weekly wage in Corner Brook was $532 as compared with $464 in St. John's and with $461 in Newfoundland. The high wages paid to workers in the Corner Brook Pulp and Paper mill are largely responsible for these figures.

The present relationship between management and unions appears to be fairly good, but both sides appear wary, although there have been no significant work stoppages or strikes since 1988. In fact management eventually kept their bargain with employees by paying them back a cut in wages and salaries which had been reluctantly agreed to by the unions 3 years previously, at a time of weak markets. Employment in Kruger's woods operations has been significantly reduced recently following the purchase of several mechanical harvesters. The machines cost about a million dollars each, but can cut and trim a tree and load the logs onto a pallet for transportation, replacing the work of about 12 men. These remarkable machines are directed by one person, who is able to work in comfort in a cab protected from the elements. It was hoped that the displaced loggers would be all re-employed in silviculture but this has not turned out to be as successful as was first hoped.

The Kruger Company seems much more diversified in its marketing strategy than Bowaters or the previous paper companies who had owned the mill. They seek markets worldwide and have centralised and downsized management, avoiding the policy drift and tug of war between London and New York offices which plagued the Bowater organization after the death of Sir Eric.

There was a difference of corporate culture between Bowaters and the Kruger Company which required time for workers and administration to adjust. The Kruger executives have a much more "hands on" approach without the layers of bureaucracy in New York and Montreal and London that had impeded the Bowater operations. Their senior management really try to carry out their three ideals of customer service, productivity, and cost effectiveness. These ideals are shared by other paper companies but not always implemented. From the very significant improvements to the mill operations, the Kruger Company appears to be in Corner Brook for the long haul. If this is the case it will be a continuing and essential stabilising influence on the economy of the whole area.

CHAPTER 14

Medicare and Hospitals

The location of hospitals, doctor's clinics, dental and paramedical services have been some of the principal magnets to attract people from Bay of Islands into Corner Brook. Some of these facilities were made possible by federal and provincial grants popularly known as Medicare. Before the government of Canada became involved, the provincial government passed acts to provide free dental services in 1950 and free medical and hospital care in 1957 for children under the age of 16. During the period from 1959 to 1969 the government of Canada passed acts providing equalisation payments to the provinces to try to standardise the quality of care across the country. In patient, emergency care, and all basic hospital services were to be provided at no extra charge to the patients. There was to be no charge for medical doctors' services either in or out of hospital.

These were bold and, for North America, revolutionary schemes, which were tax supported and have proved to be widely popular. Few people at the time foresaw the almost exponential increase in annual costs needed to support these programmes that have led to the present cutbacks. In the Bay of Islands these Medicare Acts not only were the means of attracting residents to visit the city for medical attention, but have also resulted in a large increase in workers and staff in the now Regional Hospital. At one time the hospital employed over 1000 persons, making it the largest single employer in the city. Most of these employees are now unionised, belonging either to CUPE or NAPE.

Now there is no living person who can remember the first physician to set up practice in the Bay of Islands. Noel Murphy, who is a fountain of knowledge on early Bay history, thinks that the first physician was a Dr. Miller. He believes Miller set up practice in 1878 in Birchy Cove but can provide no further details. In 1887 a notice, a copy of which still exists, called for a meeting to be held to consider the offer of a Dr. Carey to practice in the Bay of Islands and to reside at Birchy Cove. We do not know whether or not he practised there but we do know that Dr. Franklin Fisher, son of the owner of a sawmill in Corner Brook, established a practice in Birchy Cove from 1904 to 1934, covering an area from St. George's to Bonne Bay. At the same time, or perhaps a little earlier, George Webber practiced as an apothecary in Birchy Cove. He knew how to dispense drugs and had developed some skill in medical matters but had no formal medical training. An act had been passed by the House of Assembly in 1870 licensing certain unqualified "doctors" who were practising in larger communities on the island and who had developed skills in setting broken bones, pulling teeth, performing minor surgery, and "borning babies." One of these early "doctors" mentioned on the west coast, possibly the first, was George Preble who practiced in Bonne Bay before 1870. The successful appendectomy carried out by Charles Farnell was mentioned earlier in a previous chapter.

When the first settlers arrived in the Bay they were dependent on the periodic visits of a surgeon attached to one of the visiting Royal Naval warships. But as the settlements grew they would have a "handy woman" who would act as a midwife and several would have a "charmer," usually an older person who was believed to have the power to relieve minor aches and pains and to charm away warts. Strangely enough, these charms sometimes worked!

British naval surgeons continued to treat sick people in the Bay of Islands up until 1900 when one recorded the following comments:

"The naval surgeons report that they are visited by a great number of people from such populous centres on Sandy Point, Bay of Islands and Bonne Bay. It was never intended that these officers would attend to people living in places like these, where it was felt that a medical practitioner could make his home and find sufficient support to induce him to remain. These ship's doctors do not want in the least to take away from the practice of the local physician. The increase of cases has made it impossible for the naval doctors to keep up with the work and a halt has to be called. It has therefore been decided that naval surgeons [will] no longer attend to the sick at Sandy Point, Bay of Islands and Bonne Bay. The [ship's] doctors say that they have quite enough to do in the smaller coves and hamlets where there is no resident physician and where the people have not the advantages enjoyed by the inhabitants of the larger settlements." [37]

French naval surgeons also provided medical care on occasion and customarily did not charge for their services. In 1879 Captain Kennedy R.N. of HMS Druid sent a letter to the Governor on behalf of Dr. Louis Esnault, a French surgeon who claimed to have treated residents in the Port au Choix area for the previous 2 years all through a diphtheria epidemic. The letter requested remuneration for the Frenchman's dedicated services but payment was refused by the Governor.

Up until the discovery of insulin in 1921 and the sulphonamides in 1930s there were less than a dozen drugs of any significant value in medicine. There were Aspirin and Morphine as pain relievers, and digitalis leaf and dried extract of thyroid, sedatives such as Bromide and Chloral, and anaesthetics like ether and chloroform, among others. Doctors dispensed their own drugs from their surgeries. Many people

[37] Morris, D. Vignettes of the West.

used home remedies which varied from settlement to settlement. Some of these remedies contained ingredients that are now known to be effective; others probably had only psychological value. An effective home remedy for lacerations was to cover the wound with a cobweb and then to seal it with "myrrh" or sap from balsam fir (which also made fine chewing gum!). Other less effective "cures" included wearing a haddock's fin bone to prevent rheumatism and tying a split herring around the throat for diphtheria! Nowadays there is increasing interest in alternative medicine and some of the old folk remedies may have had some value.

Later on, the Gerald S. Doyle programme on the CBC Radio from St. John's advertised homeopathic remedies which were extensively used in this area up until recent years. These concoctions included Buckley's Mixture, Vicks Vapour Rub, Minard's Liniment, Scott's Emulsion, Cod Liver Oil and the old favourite for loss of appetite, Brick's Tasteless, which I believe contained a little strychnine. I preferred and occasionally suggested Maltlevol for loss of appetite, which had a sherry base and was especially appreciated by teetotallers! The first pharmacy in Corner Brook opened on West Street much later, after the Second World War. It was known as the Humber Pharmacy and owned by H.O. House. The first pharmacist and manager was "Pops" FitzGerald.

When the construction of the mill started, Dr. Robert H. Kerr was contracted to supply medical services to the construction workers. In 1923, a first aid station was set up at the bottom of Fisher's Hill. This building consisted of a dispensary and 6-bed ward with living quarters for the staff on the second floor. Arthur Hammond was employed as a first aid worker and when the first general hospital was opened he became the radiography technician..

Art Hammond's name is frequently mentioned in the early medical history of Corner Brook. He had served in World War I and was awarded the Military Medal. He continued to be active in the 1st Medical Company of the Canadian militia after World War II. He described himself as a medical "Jack of all trades" and was appointed as the first administrator of the new Western Memorial Hospital and afterwards, when an experienced administrator became available, he became the first radiography technician in the new hospital.

In 1924 the first aid station was moved to a site on Humber Road near the present site of the Corner Brook Hotel and its capacity was increased to 12 beds. The main hospital at that time was a 12-bed unit in Deer Lake with Dr. W. E. Weeks in charge and Miss Florence Scott the first nurse—perhaps the first registered nurse on the west coast. Anyone who required hospital care for more than one night was transferred from the Corner Brook first aid station to the Deer Lake Hospital by a railcar marked with a red cross and designated Railcar Ambulance Number 1590. After the first permanent hospital was completed in Corner Brook, the first aid station was phased out and closed in 1929.

The first General Hospital in Corner Brook was constructed on land behind the Goodhouse building now standing on West Street. At first it had only 22 beds and was inadequately heated and staffed, but soon the beds were increased to 40 and X-ray equipment and operating room facilities were acquired. Dr. W. J. Cochrane was the first medical superintendent and chief surgeon and the first matron was Mary Keegan, R.N. The staff included four nurses, an X-ray technician, an orderly, janitor, cook, registrar, and three maids. The first chairman of the hospital board was Mr. Meeberger, and six beds were reserved at all times for the use of the paper company. On August 25, 1925, the hospital was opened.

Another hospital that has now been almost forgotten was built many years later by Bowaters in George's Lake, located at the mouth of Pinchgut River on the present site of the Boy Scouts camp. It operated from 1942 until 1948 while the woods operations were in progress in that area. This hospital had 16 beds and was under the management of the Corner Brook Hospital board. It was used for nursing care and convalescent care only. The first nurse in charge was Miss Doris Sheppard and the last was Mrs. Joan Sparkes.

The facilities in the first General Hospital in Corner Brook were

The First General Hospital, Corner Brook

owned and operated by the company that owned the mill and were chiefly used by mill workers and the residents of Townsite. Maternity deliveries were still often carried out at home, with Nurse McDonald assisting as the first community nurse. Nurses in those days gave the anesthetic for surgery and caesarian sections, usually employing the "rag and bottle" method for Ether, Chloroform or Ethyl Chloride, and the mask for Nitrous Oxide. Dr. Cochrane was apparently a strict disciplinarian but a good administrator and a reasonably competent emergency surgeon. Other surgeons included Dr. Webster, who worked in Corner Brook for a short time and later became chief of surgery at the Montreal Victoria General Hospital, and a visiting surgeon Sir Henry Grey, most likely from England.

The other doctor who worked in the hospital was Dr. Frank Fisher, who had set up practice in Curling. He was well liked in the community and known to all as "Pops." Frank had intended to be a clergyman. The story goes that when his father Christopher Fisher heard him preach he sent him off to McGill Medical School in a hurry!

Dr. Baggs, who joined the hospital staff in 1940, goes down in medical folk lore as the doctor who, on entering the house on a maternity call, would first ask the mother "whether she had the $50 under the pillow." No one recalls if anyone ever said "No," so one can only imagine what his course of action—or lack thereof—might have been.

Dr. T.T. Monaghan, joined the hospital staff in 1936. He was born in Prince Edward Island and in 1938 studied surgery in Vienna, witnessing the occupation of Vienna by Nazi Germany. He was a good physician and a very good obstetrician, but was somewhat blunt and outspoken and had several rows with Dr. Cochrane, but said that he respected him as an individual. After Cochrane retired in 1944 he had a marked influence on the younger doctors, and provided much needed leadership. He was well respected in the community and had a considerable office practice almost up to the time of his death in 1982. In 1970, his name was given to Monaghan Hall, part of the Nursing School in recognition of his services.

Ken Parsons started practice in Corner Brook in 1945, having previously practiced in Howley. He had an interesting career, having been born in Harbour Grace and trained first as a teacher. He later worked in the Bank of Montreal in Curling before studying medicine. He was what you might call a good country doctor, with a small general practice which he looked after assiduously, not hesitating when asked to do a house call in the dead of the night in wintertime. He had a dry sense of humour and a fund of stories and his letters to the <u>Western Star</u> were a particular delight. He disapproved of what he felt was advertisement and self display in the career of Dr. Noel Murphy, a colleague and later a Member of the House of Assembly and Mayor of Corner Brook. I often wonder what happened to the album of newspaper clippings and photography relating to his illustrious colleague that he said he had collected!

Dr. Robert F. Dove was perhaps the most gifted surgeon on the staff of the hospital until Drs. R. Hearder Butler and R.M. Butt joined the staff in the early 1960s. Dr. Dove practiced in Bonne Bay before he came to Corner Brook in 1944, and before that he had made at least one trip to the Arctic with Captain Bob Bartlett, the captain of Commander Peary's ship, to whom he was related. He himself was a keen outdoorsman and fisherman, a generous man, and a real gentleman. After his death his name was given to the Dove Wing of the new Regional Hospital in recognition of his contribution to the planning and organization of the Western Memorial Hospital, opened in 1951.

From 1935 to 1940 doctors worked together in the Humber Clinic. After the Second World War several other doctors joined the group which used the former first aid shed on Main Street which they called the Medical Arts Building. Besides doctors offices, it included a small laboratory and an X-ray room with Miss Gregory as the X-ray technician. These new doctors included Dr. W.D. Rowe, an orthopaedic surgeon born in Newfoundland and trained in UK, Dr. J.H. King of Carbonear, specialising in ear, nose and throat problems which included eye conditions in those days, Dr. R. Bugden, and Dr. T. C. Farrell who arrived in 1956. At that time, Dr. L. Pullen had his office near Broadway, Dr. B. Murray practiced in Curling and Dr. O'Leary in Humbermouth. Dr. Charles Henderson was the first anaesthetist in the hospital, and Dr. Neil Walsh the first radiologist, arriving in 1955.

Construction of the 110-bed Western Memorial Hospital was planned by the Commission of Government and its foundation stone was laid by the Governor, Sir Gordon McDonald, in 1949. It opened in January 1951. The cost of construction was funded from several sources, the main amount collected from a public subscription campaign spearheaded by H. O. House. This was spectacularly successful, raising about $350,000 and enabling the hospital to be built as a memorial to those from the area who had fought and died for their country in the Second World War. Bowaters gave a handsome contribution and the provincial government supplied the rest to cover the cost of about a million dollars.

The first matron of the new hospital was Miss Geraldine FitzGerald, daughter of a well respected outport doctor. Mr. Stocker, an Englishman who had spent much of his life in what was then known as Southern Rhodesia, took over from Arthur Hammond as hospital administrator. The first Hospital Board was naturally chaired by H.M.S. Lewin. Other members were M. G. Basha, S. D. Cook, J. Cramm, N. Short, A. M. Dunphy, W. L. Whelan, J. C. FitzGerald, and Dr. Leonard Miller, who as Deputy Minister of Health represented the Newfoundland government. While this Board shone with worthy members of the community it suffered from an important defect in its membership which was to handicap it for the next 20 years or so. This was the absence of any representative from the health care givers in the community. Dr. L. Miller was an excellent administrator but more concerned with the operation of the General Hospital in St. John's, the Sanatoria, and the other government institutions. The lack of local medical input hampered the development of modern medical facilities in the new hospital.

Doctors Dove, Monaghan, Baggs, Rowe, King, Parsons, O'Connell, and Cant were the first medical staff. Dr. Donald Cant had previously served in the Cottage Hospital system before and after serving in the war with the Canadian Armed Forces. He was born and trained in England and after the war he did postgraduate study in thoracic surgery and was the first doctor in Corner Brook to pass the certification examination of the Canadian Royal College. (Drs. Dove, Monaghan, and King were given honorary certification when Newfoundland joined Canada in 1949.) He practiced general surgery in the hospital.

The staff of the hospital numbered less than 100. Bedside nursing was carried out by a handful of registered nurses and by pink and blue aides, the colours denoting their experience and seniority. There was always a shortage of registered nurses, particularly during summer holidays. Until the Nurses Training School was opened here on September 15, 1969, recruiting drives always had to be organized to hire nurses from other countries, particularly the UK. The first director of this sorely needed Nursing School was Katherine Wells. The 2-year programme was the first of its kind in Newfoundland but has been recently expanded to a full degree programme. Another important training programme was that for Nursing Assistants centred in the West Coast Sanatorium from 1952 until 1964. Miss Frances Cheek, now Frances Bouzanne, was its first director. A nurses training programme was then continued in the new Regional Hospital.

The West Coast Sanatorium was the only one outside St. John's except for a small unit in St. Anthony. Opened in 1951 and operated by the Newfoundland government, it had 270 beds to accommodate tuberculosis, still the major health problem in the province, and was especially prevalent in the isolated communities along the coasts, where the MV Christmas Seal visited these smaller communities to recruit patients for treatment. Dr. E. S. Peters was the Medical Superintendent. He had a small staff of physicians and appointed Donald Cant as a part-time thoracic surgeon. But at the very time that the new sanatorium was being built a newly discovered antibiotic called Streptomycin was revolutionising the treatment of tuberculosis, permitting the arrest of the disease without long periods of bedrest. In combination with other newly discovered drugs some patients began to require only a week or two of hospitalisation. Yet long periods of bedrest were still being prescribed in Corner Brook and in St. John's Sanatoria all through the 1950s, while the case load dwindled.

By 1960 this shameful state of affairs, where a large staffed facility was often only 25% occupied, was partially rationalised when the Department of Health agreed to open one of the floors in the West Coast Sanatorium to general medical patients. The unit was known as the Christopher Fisher Division after the pioneer resident of Corner Brook. Its opening made a great deal of difference to medical practice in the community, as by that time facilities for hospital care were becoming congested in the Western Memorial. Often hospital staff were having to take extreme measures to keep beds available for emergencies, even to the extent of denying admission of elderly patients who had had a stroke, as they might occupy a bed for several weeks. So it was decided to make the Western Memorial an exclusively surgical and obstetrical hospital and to admit all medical cases to the Christopher Fisher Division. In 1964 the West Coast Sanatorium closed for good, with Dr. Peters relocating to St. John's. The Out Patient Tuberculosis and Chest Unit headed by Dr. Norman Wass, with Gertrude Caines as the Nurse Supervisor, remained.

Improving hospital facilities have lead to a gradual increase of hospital personnel over the last 45 years, including doctors, nurses, and laboratory and radiological technologists. The influx of new doctors was not always welcomed by the older established doctors. When Donald Cant moved here in 1951, he founded the Cantlee Clinic on West Valley Road in partnership with Dr. Brian Lees and two others, Dr. Peter Edward and Dr. B. J. O'Brien. The result was a period of rivalry between the newcomers and the doctors in the Medical Arts Building on Humber

Road. This rivalry became somewhat childish when the Medical Arts group objected to a sign that the Cantlee Clinic erected outside their premises on West Valley Road, claiming that the sign was too big and therefore violated the Canadian Medical Associations guidelines on professional advertising. The sign came down, but the rivalry continued until the Cantlee Clinic was bought out by several doctors from both clinics who then established their offices in the Kimberley building above the City Pharmacy on West Street in 1958.

The medical profession in the city remained divided on other issues. While some were quite happy with the new hospital and had a vested interest in preserving the status quo and its associated standard of living, others realised the necessity to catch up with health standards on the mainland and were supported by some members of the hospital board. I myself arrived by invitation and set up a solo referral practice. These circumstances enabled me to be nonpartisan and noncompetitive with other established physicians. Fortunately I had had some experience in paediatrics as well as general internal medicine, as the population at that time was young and the birth rate was high. Before the Red Cross organised a nation-wide blood transfusion service we had our own donor panel which worked out quite well, but we lacked a diagnostic laboratory and pathologist. Dr. Neil Walsh, who came from the UK to practice in 1955, was the first radiologist and introduced some basic diagnostic procedures. Psychiatric care was practically nonexistent in those early days. There were no modern tranquilizers then; if a disturbed or manic patient presented there were only two alternatives—either to admit the patient to one of the two private rooms in the hospital and to sedate him or her heavily with paraldehyde, or to certify the individual as insane. In the latter case the patient became the responsibility of the RCMP, or in earlier years the Newfoundland Constabulary, who would take the person to the Waterford Hospital in St. John's as quickly as possible, usually by train and if necessary in a strait jacket! The local Constabulary records indicate that a strait jacket was delivered to the Curling detachment in July 1919.

This primitive state of affairs lasted until suitable space was made available in the Sanatorium, but a psychiatrist was not acquired until 1965 when Dr. B. J. O'Brien returned from resident training to become the first psychiatrist. The lack of a pathologist was of more concern to me than to other doctors, as I was a diagnostic physician (To some local residents I was known as the "Art Specialist;" some Newfoundlanders drop their aitches as in parts of Dorset, England!). In 1959, I interviewed a well qualified and agreeable pathologist in England and persuaded him to come to Corner Brook only to find that he had what is termed as a "minimal active tuberculous chest lesion" on his immigration chest X-ray and so was denied entry to Canada. Knowing that these cases were usually sputum negative and were now able to be treated at home with antibiotics after a week or two in hospital, I personally appealed to Dr. Miller, Deputy Minister of Health, to ask him to overrule the decision, but after consulting with Dr. Peters, the Sanatorium Superintendent, he refused. I was chagrined to get a Christmas card from Australia later that year, telling me that the doctor was in Melbourne, doing well and working there.

I cannot resist recounting an amusing sequel to this story which gave me some quiet satisfaction. The Department of Health agreed with me that a pathologist was now needed for the west coast and also agreed to provide him with a modern department located in the West Coast Sanatorium. The first doctor they hired, with no interview, was a young Scotsman who arrived in Corner Brook and was lodged in the Nurses Residence of the Sanatorium. He seemed anxious to display what was under his kilt to some nurses—I believe the legal expression is that he "exhibited his person in public!" He was soon on the plane back to Scotland. But, to be fair, a growing physician population in Corner Brook was bound to attract some strange characters and some charlatans. One newly hired Irish doctor at the Sanatorium got drunk in the Canadian Legion lounge and, producing a pistol, threatened the loyal Legionnaires present with retribution from the IRA. He too was quickly sent home. Another doctor, English this time, had a bee in his bonnet regarding smoking and cancer. Although his theory has much merit, his ethics did not, as he dispensed quack remedies including his own so called cancer-free cigarettes. He practised on the north shore in Summerside or Meadows for a short time before returning to England. I believe he then set up practice on Harley Street in London where I am quite sure he found company with a few other odd ball characters.

But the search for a clinical pathologist continued to be frustrating. The first doctor to practice in the new department in the Sanatorium was a trained pathologist who nevertheless had no clinical background and was quite unable to satisfy or even to understand the demands of the clinical staff. To our relief, he soon resigned. The community was then fortunate to acquire the services of Dr. A. Dimakalangan, who became known to all and sundry as Dr. D. He was born in the Philippines and did his training in the USA before coming to Newfoundland. Dr. D.

showed exceptional administrative ability and built up a large, well run laboratory. His friendly outgoing personality enabled him to get on well with staff as well as with the public, the RCMP, and the department of health. His presence was particularly important to myself and enabled me to attract a paediatrician, the first being Dr. A. J. Davis, now Professor of Paediatrics in St. John's, and other Internists including Dr. Donald Angus who came to work with us in 1966, followed by Dr. J.D. Graham in 1971, the first trained cardiologist who was able to set up and equip the hospital's first intensive care unit in 1972.

The completion of the paving of the Trans Canada Highway in 1965 provided the necessary infrastructure to increase the number of referrals of more complicated cases to Western Memorial Hospital, and new family doctors and specialists began to locate in Corner Brook. Prior to this I had attempted to provide some consultant advice to doctors caring for patients in Norris Point and Stephenville Crossing visiting on a monthly basis, as well as to some more distant locations. This service was greatly appreciated by the doctors at these isolated hospitals. Before 1965, cottage hospitals in Port aux Basques and Stephenville Crossing had usually used the General Hospital in St. John's as a referral centre because of the railway link to specialist care in St John's. After the completion of the highway, patients from these west coast hospitals could more easily be driven to Corner Brook.Whereas in earlier years the opening of the road system to the north and south shores of the Bay of Islands had quickly led to overcrowding in the Western Memorial, leading to opening of the Christopher Fisher Division, now the additional patients from outside the Bay of Islands led to urgent demands for a new and larger Regional Hospital. This was made possible by the health acts of the federal government in the 1950s and late 1960s and a committee was set up to draw up plans. Professional input was fortunately included and the result was a fairly successful new hospital, incorporating much of the structure of the old Sanatorium building. It was constructed in two phases, first the Dove wing to the front and then the new wing added on behind. The completed building was opened by Premier Frank Moores in 1973. The old Western Memorial was scheduled to close down at this time but as a result of public pressure remained open for geriatric care and continues to provide a very useful community function, with recent reconditioning of a Veteran's Pavilion, opened in 1996.

Some thought that the new hospital was again too small, and that a hospital of 500 beds instead of 380 was needed. This was probably true at the time, as the new hospital was overcrowded from its opening, but that opinion failed to take into consideration the future problems of the provincial government, which finances the hospital, and soon after the opening of the hospital it had to close beds, and even whole floors, in order to keep within budget. Fortunately some surgical procedures can now be carried out as an outpatient and length of stay for some conditions has been considerably shortened. A Nuclear Medicine department was opened in 1976 and incorporated in the new radiology department in 1981, which was enlarged to house a C.T. Scanner and modern diagnostic facilities in the 1990s.

The emphasis recently has been on acquiring new or upgrading old technology. A Hospital Foundation has been organised for the purpose of raising funds for the hospital, allowing clinical department to prioritise their requirements. The response to this cause, highlighted in the annual CFCB Radio Telethon, has been truly amazing, with contributions to the Foundation from not only the Bay of Islands, but the whole of the west coast as well as Labrador. Paul Seaward was the first director of this foundation, followed by Mary Ann Murphy, in 1997 by Jane Jesseau, and now again by Mary Ann Murphy.

Before leaving the subject of the hospital, the growth of which has obviously been a source of personal pride and concern to myself over the years, I should repeat that the Western Regional Hospital is still the largest employer in the community, with over a thousand employees and a medical staff of over 50 doctors. There is an emergency department and a hospital-based ambulance service covering the Bay of Islands. The major specialties are reasonably well covered, though emergency physicians and some subspecialists are still needed, and at this time the community has only one or two vacancies remaining for family physicians. Administration of the hospital has often been a source of irritation to the doctors and hospital staff, but this was markedly improved when Dr. Harry Watts became Medical Director and Administrator in 1979. Unfortunately he was forced to resign in 1997, replaced by Dr. Eric Parsons. The hospital is now under a Regional Health Board based in Stephenville.

With hospital care continuing to be funded by taxation as costs increase, the future of medical care is likely to pass back again to home-based care, but not as it was in the Bay of Islands a hundred years ago. Some steps have already been taken in this direction. The VON started in this area in 1952 and has been expanding its services outside the city, now in cooperation with the West Coast Regional Board. Public health nurses are active on both sides of the bay and a Meals on Wheels programme was started several years ago in the Corner Brook area with transport provided by the Rotary Clubs. Low cost accommodation for seniors has been provided in the city by the Interfaith Group, proving very successful, and smaller units have been built in Corner Brook to take care of the elderly, frail, and those with disabilities. Recently an elevator system in some doctors' offices has been introduced.

Fifty years ago patients still came to doctors offices to have their teeth pulled. Now there are more than a dozen dentists in the area providing the most modern dental conservation techniques, assisted by both dental hygienists and denturists. Dr. Stick was the first dentist to practice in this area. Optometrists started practicing here even later. Karl Trapnell carried out refractions but he was what one would describe as an optician. Now half a dozen optometrists practice here and ophthalmological services, including laser therapy and lens implants, are provided in the hospital under the care of Dr. Y. Wijay.

Within the same period of time other paramedical and support agencies have been started. Voluntary organisations such as the Red Cross, St. John Ambulance, and Victorian Order of Nurses were the first, providing blood procurement, first aid training, and the loan of appliances such as crutches and wheelchairs. Max Fillatre first started an ambulance service now operated from the hospital by the hospital board. He also started a funeral service, until quite recently the only one in the area. Nowadays there are private paramedical services provided by chiropractors and private physiotherapy and occupational therapy clinics. The primitive state of mental health facilities which I have described 40 years ago has been greatly improved by the presence of psychiatrists and psychologists and by the efforts of support groups like Alcoholics Anonymous, as well as by a Halfway House for battered women, better drugs, and improved facilities.

Health care improvements have indeed been remarkable in the past 50 years in the Bay of Islands. One hopes that improvements will continue under the new West Coast Regional Administration and that modernisation continues in the regional hospital. If that is the case it will continue, I am sure, to receive whole hearted support from the community.

CHAPTER 15

Memorial University, Sports and Drama, Churches and Service Clubs

The opening of the Western Regional College campus of Memorial University on September 7, 1975—later called Grenfell College— was a landmark in education in the Bay of Islands and was to prove a powerful magnet, attracting students from all over the west coast and Labrador. The campus was built on 185.3 acres of land donated by Bowaters Newfoundland and constructed by Western Realties Limited on a lease-back arrangement for 30 years at a cost of $10,000,000 and a rental agreement with the provincial government of Frank Moores. Both the Premier and Dr. Tom Farrell represented Humber West and Humber East at the time and were largely responsible for the political initiative, the object of which was to enable 1st- and 2nd-year university students to attend courses closer to their homes and to avoid overcrowding at the main Memorial campus in St. John's. Jack Marshall, Member of Parliament for Humber, St. Barbe, St. George's was also influential, as he was in so many of the initiatives on the west coast, especially Gros Morne National Park.

At the opening ceremonies Premier Frank Moores stated: "A university is much more to a community than a place of training for young people. It is a social centre, where the arts and sciences flourish, creating new awareness among the people in their surroundings." How true. It is impossible to overestimate the social effect of the university on the west coast, and especially Bay of Islands and Corner Brook. The influx of professors and teaching staff to the community was in itself important, as up to then Corner Brook had been essentially a working class community (using old fashioned terminology). Besides 366 full-time students (50% from Corner Brook) and 250 part-time students, the Extension Service started to run "off campus" credit courses. 200 people registered for these courses in the 1st year; these included a Mr. Colin Benton, who was 81 years old!

But accommodation for out of town students was a major concern at the outset. An appeal to the people of Corner Brook to provide accommodation for these students was fairly successful. By 1987 1st-year enrolment had risen to 500 students and 300 more were in 2nd year, and full degree status was sought for the college although most students more than held their own with their peers when they attended 3rd and 4th years in St. John's. The response of the university was to complete and open a Fine Arts Building in September 1988, offering the first Memorial University Bachelor of Fine Arts degree in visual arts. At the same time a new library was built, designed to hold more than 70,000 volumes and with computer access to the library in St. John's.

It was named after Ferriss Hodgett, who was the first vice principal.

The first principal of the new campus was Dr. Arthur Sullivan, a Rhodes Scholar and native of Trinity. He was a former head of the Psychology department and Dean of Junior Studies at Memorial University. In 1977 he was succeeded by Dr. Cyril Poole, born in Pilley's Island, whose dry sense of humour and administrative ability guided Grenfell College until his retirement in 1989. The late Ferriss Hodgett took over for a year on a temporary basis and was succeeded by Dr. Katie Bindon, who in turn was succeeded by Adrian Fowler in 1998. The Music department got a great start by appointing the well known Ignatius Rumboldt as Music Director for the first 2 years. Other professors and teachers contributions are too many to mention individually but one interesting milestone occurred on March 17, 1976, when the Western Regional College (as it was then called) Drama Group performed Rope Against the Sun written by Al Pittman and directed by Ian Mennie, the first full-length play written by a native of Corner Brook.

There is now a new Forestry Centre building, and degree granting courses in the Fine Arts Centre, with the theatre department headed by Dr. Roy Hostetter. This department continues the evolution of many years of development of theatre in the city of Corner Brook. Starting with Christmas nativity plays and pageants and concerts in schools and one-act plays in church halls in various communities in the bay it evolved to include two amateur drama groups in the 1950s and 1960s in Corner Brook who produced three act plays, mainly for competition in the provincial Drama Festival.

The Amateur Players was the first group, formed in the late 1940s or early 1950s with Doris Janes as director and Mary Monaghan as a talented cameo actress. The Amateur Players first entered a play in the Regional Drama Festival in 1951. Two excellent performers, Márin and Neil Walsh, joined the group in 1955 when they acted in Dangerous Corner by J. B. Priestley. The other group, the Playmakers, started in 1954 under the direction of Paul O'Neil, and later under Tom Cahill. Their first production was My Three Angels, which earned the leading actress a Best Actress Award in the Drama Festival; the only other Best Actress Award awarded to this group was given to Gillian Wass for her role in The Bad Seed. In 1956 the Playmakers started to produce Home Brew which would provide extremely popular Christmas entertainment every year for 20 years, even after director Tom Cahill had moved to St. John's to continue his illustrious career as director and playwright with CBC in St. John's. Home Brew was a mixture of skits and songs enabling citizens to laugh at themselves and to poke fun at their mayor, councillors, and city notables. Several character performances come to mind, particularly Uncle Llewellyn by Joe Mullins, Joey Smallwood by Jim Butt and the Welfare Housewife by Judith Monaghan, and the character Aunt Luce. The Amateur Players and the Playmakers joined forces in 1964, allowing more ambitious productions to be staged and culminating in a win in 1972 in the Drama Festival with a production of Live Like Pigs. This was directed by Howard Rishpan, a professional director from Montreal. The set design and construction by Hans and Ingrid Tode was, as usual, highly commended.

Playmakers productions, including Home Brew, continued until 1983, the last year the Regional Drama Festival was staged in Corner Brook. Theatre Newfoundland and Labrador (TNL) was formed in 1983, inspired by its first director, the late professional actor and producer Maxim Mazumdar. TNL is based in Corner Brook and is financed largely by private subscription from businesses and individuals. Many fine productions were performed in subsequent years and the annual Stephenville Festival is a spinoff event. TNL now produces three plays every year, a summer festival in Cow Head, travelling to many townships on the west coast with productions. TNL was the principal cause of the death of amateur theatre groups in Corner Brook. But amateur productions were already suffering from the growth of television, which came to the west coast in 1959 just in time to cover Queen Elizabeth's first visit to Corner Brook. Cable television came later in 1964, as a result of investment from a group of local entrepreneurs.

This medium also affected attendance at local hockey and baseball games, which were much more popular and better attended than they are now. In former years there was keen rivalry between the teams from the local settlements on the island and among the four Corner Brook teams, the Humber Hawks, the Town Aces, the West Side Monarchs, and the Curling Rangers. To be a member of the Royals or Barons and to represent the city in hockey or baseball meant that you were a celebrity in the community. Everyone knew Danky Dorrington, who was perhaps one of the best hockey players never to have played in the NHL but Doug Grant and Joe Lundrigan were two that did. Baseball players were equally famous, such as Frank Ryan, Gerry Basha, and Joe Rousseau, the first three baseball players from Corner Brook inducted into the Baseball Hall of Fame; more recently Frank Humber has played for an American farm club. Cliff Gorman was an outstanding president of the Corner Brook Hockey Association in the 1970s and 1980s. After several attempts, winning the Eastern Division Cup twice only to lose both times in the national finals, many were surprised when the Corner Brook Royals won the Allen Cup in 1986, a national trophy, but the financial effort put the club deeply in debt and the club was later forced to withdraw from the West Coast Senior League for a period of time.

One of the almost incredible feats in our local history was that achieved by the late Chester Lawrence in 1934 at the British Empire Games in London. Without much in the way of training facilities he obtained a Bronze Medal in the 220 yards. He later served in the Second World War, married, and settled in Corner Brook as a mill worker. Other important sports in the community are golf, where leading local golfers in recent years have included John LeDrew, three-time runner up for the Newfoundland Amateur Championship, George Dolomount, John Sears, and Bobby Hull, who have each won the men's championship, and Becky Stark who won the ladies championship. In curling, Bud Fisher's rink in the 1950s and Gary Oke's rink in the 1990s have represented the city in the Brier. Other popular sports include bowling, darts, swimming, and soccer, where Walt Lemessurier excelled and is in the Sports Hall of Fame together with Gord Grant. [38]

At the same time as Grenfell College opened in 1975, the District Vocational School in Corner Brook began to offer a 2-year programme in Secretarial Science. This vocational school had been started in 1963 by the federal government of John Diefenbaker and the project included several other vocational schools in the larger communities in this province and in Canada. The school offered a 1-year programme of training in mechanical and building trades and in business education. W. J. Howell was the first principal. But mechanical and building trades became saturated and it became clear that there was a great need for a larger technical college for the west coast. Eventually in 1985, supported by Lynn Verge, the provincial Education Minister and MHA for Humber East, the Fisher Technical College was built on O'Connell Drive in Corner Brook as one of three provincial technical colleges. The name of the college was designated to honour Christopher Fisher, whom we remember as one of the founding fathers of the Corner Brook community. The next year its title changed to the Fisher Institute of Applied Arts & Technology, offering 2- and 3-year programmes in arts and technology, including programmes not available elsewhere in the province. Max Renouf was the first principal of the Technical College, becoming vice principal of the institute 1 year later, under principal William Barker.

The institute was later called West Viking College and after yet an-

---

[38] An incomplete list of other local sportsmen elected is in an appendix.

other reorganisation and name change is now part of The College of the North Atlantic. It is a significant magnet, second only to Grenfell College in attracting students from all over the province and Labrador, but principally from the west coast and Bay of Islands. Douglas Fowlow is now the President. Over 800 students are enrolled at this time and according to librarian Marian Burnett there is even a waiting list. The continuing need for the type of training offered by the college has resulted in the growth of several smaller privately run colleges in this area including the Career Academy, Keyin Technical College, Academy Canada, and Nordeco. Academy Canada offers shorter courses leading to a diploma in various trades in four campuses including Wild Cove and Fern Street, making use of the premises of a now-closed elementary school.Unfortunately the Career Academy has been forced to close this year because of bankruptcy.

Due to the isolated geography of the Bay of Islands, the churches essentially serve local communities—there are no cathedrals or large churches covering a wider area, as in Europe. The early churches were fundamental to the start of education and religious worship in the Bay of Islands. Their influence is still local, but although a denominational school system was stipulated in the Terms of Union with Canada, it has proved to be obsolescent and expensive and is in the course of revision. One hopes that parents will in the future have more choice in the type of schooling they feel they require for their children.

The Salvation Army came late to the Bay of Islands. It was not until 1910 that Ensign Fannie James was the first officer appointed to Curling, with her first meeting held at the Orangeman's Hall, Petries. It was well attended and subsequent recruitment was very successful. Two years later a citadel was erected near Allen's Groceteria and a one-room school was converted from a house located opposite Ellsworth's Store, taking pupils from all religious denominations. Before Ensign James was transferred 3 years later there were 96 people registered as Salvationists, mostly from the Curling and Petries Point areas.

When the mill construction started in 1924 Adjutant Carter was appointed as the first officer in Corner Brook. The Orangeman's Hall in Humbermouth was used for meetings and many were held in the open air around the millsite. In 1926, two citadels were built, one at Humbermouth under Adjutant Carter and the other in Corner Brook with Commandant John Ebsary as leader. Since then the Salvation Army has flourished, and new citadels have been constructed in Corner Brook off O'Connell Drive and on Premier Drive.The Army operates the Red

Kettle at Christmas time to provide hampers for the needy.

In recent years several other religious organisations have formed congregations, not only in Corner Brook but on both sides of the Bay. Some are quite small groups, but the Pentecostal Church has had an increase in adherents in the last few years and have built their own schools. There are small congregations of other religions in Corner Brook including the Bahai, Seventh Day Adventists, Mormons, and Jehovah's Witnesses and Baptists. Presbyterians now number only a few hundred and those of the Jewish faith less than a dozen, so different from their numbers in the early days of Corner Brook. In the early 1960s, Rev. Montgomerie built a church on the upper end of what is now Montgomerie Street and attempted to revive the Presbyterian church. But his attempts were shortlived and he himself was in poor health. After his death the church was sold to the Church of Latter Day Saints or Mormons. The numbers professing the Protestant faith have probably slightly increased from the 1971 figures, when they were about twice as numerous as the Catholic population in Corner Brook.

Service organisations have been formed in several of the larger communities in the Bay, but chiefly in Corner Brook. According to Arthur Alcock, a Masonic Lodge was started in 1926. The Lodge building is now situated next to the Bank of Montreal on West Street and there are several other lodges. The Knights of Columbus built their centre at the bottom of Reid Street and the Bentley Club was in existence before the Second World War, but appears to have disbanded. Some important contributions of service clubs to the social life of the community include Branch 13 of the Royal Canadian Legion, which was instrumental in the development of a Veteran's Division in the old Western Memorial Hospital, the Lions Club who were the first service club in Corner Brook and who built the recreation centre on Wellington Street, the Kinsmen, chartered in 1953 who spearheaded the construction of the Kinsmen Arena and other recreational facilities, the Royal Purple Elks Club, and a branch of the Shriners. The Corner Brook Rotary Club was formed in 1956, whose major contribution to the cultural life is the Music Festival. This was the brain child of the late Hayward Matthews and is, according to the adjudicators, one of the best in Canada. It was started in 1963 and is supported by a group of brilliant music teachers such as Gary Graham and Katie Anderson, to name just two. The Festival has seen several promising young people gain maturity, including the operatic singers Joanne Hounsell and Brenda Dawe.

The churches and the service clubs support the Food Bank Network which helps needy families and was founded by the Bay of Islands Ministerial Association in 1992. It may be surprising to some readers that in 1996 there were 1896 requests for food hampers, this area containing a city where the weekly average wage in 1989, the last available estimate, was $532.01, over $70.00 higher than the Newfoundland average,and the requests will be even higher this year. The main cause of this social tragedy is unemployment, which may in 1997 have been as high as 70% outside the city. There are other factors such as gambling, lotteries, drugs and alcohol, but frank malnutrition and vitamin deficiencies are now very rare. Still, a surprising number of children even now come to school without having eaten breakfast, and there is still an appreciable difference between the economic status of residents of the Inner and Outer Bay of Islands.

CHAPTER 16

The Malls, Merchants, Banks and Lawyers

If you visit one of the three shopping malls in Corner Brook, especially at Christmas time, you cannot fail to notice the large number of shoppers there who come from out of town, emphasizing the fact that these malls have become one of the most powerful magnets for attracting visitors to the city. Some former residents now find it just as convenient to live outside the city rather than pay the higher city taxes. All the other communities in the Bay have noted slight increases in population in the last 20 or 30 years, new communities in Humber Village, Little Rapids and Steady Brook have grown, and others in the Humber Valley have flourished, especially Pasadena-Midland, while the population of Corner Brook itself has declined to 22,410 in 1991. Recent efforts by the provincial Department of Municipal Affairs to consolidate the smaller communities closest to Corner Brook, such as Massey Drive and Mount Moriah, into a single city structure have met with no success. This is a pity, as some federal and provincial grants and services are dependant on the size of population. For instance, it was touch and go whether we could attract the Canadian Winter Games in 1999 to Corner Brook, and it was the visible and determined support of its citizens that determined the outcome.

The first development was the Millbrook Mall, built, owned, and opened by Lundrigan's Limited in 1964, who constructed all three malls. The Corner Brook Plaza opened in 1972 and the Valley Mall in 1984. These malls enabled mainland firms like Sobeys, Dominion Stores, K-Mart, Sears, and Hudson's Bay to open stores in the city and people quickly noticed the difference in prices and quality. Soon shoppers were coming into Corner Brook not only from Bay of Islands, but from Deer Lake, White Bay, and Bonne Bay areas. Inevitably the result was financial disaster for some established stores, particularly on West Street and Broadway including Goodyear and House, Eatons, and Woolworths. Even the Coop Store could not declare a dividend. Some of the new mall stores found that their goods did not sell well in this area, such as Hudson's Bay, which was replaced by Zellers. Privately owned pharmacies were threatened by chain stores such as Shoppers and Lawtons and some, including the pioneer store Humber Pharmacy on West Street, were forced to close.

But one family-owned store group weathered the storm, and has actually expanded outside Corner Brook. This is the Coleman Group of Companies, founded by A. J. Coleman in 1936. Mr. Coleman came from Nova Scotia in 1934 and established a retail store, moving to Caribou Road close to Broadway in 1946. He had six sons and one daughter and members of this large family and their children eventually found employment with the Coleman group of companies as it expanded to open other stores in Corner Brook, Deer Lake, Port aux Basques, and now in St. John's and Harbour Grace. The company also bought out some of their competition, such as Hann Brothers Furniture Store and the Food Centre on Broadway. Their staff are non-unionised but obtain benefits comparable to unionised workers in similar stores.

It is not easy to determine what made Coleman Stores successful while other stores failed. Perhaps management were more conservative than others in the boom days of Corner Brook, or perhaps it was the old fashioned combination of able and loyal employees and good customer service. At any rate, they remain one of the successful stores in both Humber West and Humber East, where so many stores have closed, and where vacant store windows are now frequently noted. Other survivors of competition with the malls are the Alteen Brothers' jewellery store on Broadway and long-time resident Elias Tuma's jewellery store. A former landmark on Broadway was the curious triangular shaped 2-story building built by Louis Rumbolt in 1956, originally used as a barber shop. It was torn down in 1997 to make way for road improvements. According to Elias Tuma, most of the stores on Broadway were rebuilt after the disastrous fire on November 29, 1952. This fire started in a radio repair shop next door to Tuma's Jewellery Store and destroyed all the business premises from Caribou Road to Rumbolt Avenue.

One of the advantages of Corner Brook as compared with other cities is that some of the former townships' central cores have been preserved. Its true that it has no central shopping area, with Broadway on the West Side and Humber Road on the East Side separated from the Townsite Shopping Centre of West Street by more than 2 kilometres. But two of the malls and Corner Brook Garage (the first garage in Corner Brook but now out of business) and the Canadian Tire Store, Herald Tower and the new federal building occupy some of the middle ground, as well as the large commercial area behind Corner Brook Garage. A problem has recently developed in the central area of the city behind Corner Brook Garage. As can be seen from the early photography, this land was originally a swamp or marsh and was developed into a commercial area. But there is a source of oil pollution somewhere, and until this is dealt with it is unlikely that any permits will be given for further construction there.Curling, the largest community at the start of the century, has now lost Water Street, where most of the merchants' stores were located, as this street was closed and the buildings demolished when Marine Drive was constructed.

The Corner Brook Plaza on Confederation Drive is on its own, but not outside the city, as many malls are. All these malls have begun to be appreciated by the senior citizens, who gather to gossip and pass the time in warm conditions with enough space there to walk and complete a walking exercise programme if need be! In wintertime this social activity takes the place of, in other countries, a stroll along the promenade or a walk to the local pub or post office. Since the Civic Centre was completed in 1997 many citizens use it's walkways for exercise.

Main Street and West Street in Corner Brook have been completely transformed. In the original development of Townsite, these streets were mostly occupied by houses built by the paper company but have now been changed into boutiques, stores, and office buildings. Some of the original structure has often been incorporated in these new buildings, for tax purposes. The results are a strange collection of buildings along both streets with the Holiday Inn, one of the few totally new constructions, now occupying the site of the old school building. So Corner Brook has thus far escaped the inner city blight which has affected so many other larger cities. Broadway was always a street with small stores and only a few of the original stores have survived, although ownerships often changed hands and the Wild West atmosphere of boardwalks and muddy streets and shop facades has been tidied up. Drugs and drunkenness are still problems, but the latter much less so than in earlier years. Drugs used now are mostly cannabis, with so called "hard" drugs more infrequent, so they say.

While the malls have been the biggest magnets to attract people to Corner Brook, other services are important, some of them since the early days of the township. Perhaps the most important have been the banks. Three Canadian banks were invited to open business in Newfoundland following the collapse of its banking system on Dec. 10, 1894. For many years the Bank of Montreal was the only bank on the west coast, with the Curling branch opening in 1902. It suffered three times from fires, the last in 1960. Two branches were built in Corner Brook, the main branch on West Street in 1925 (where Shoppers Drug Store parking lot is now located) in a building owned by Peter Daniels with Morgan A. Johns as the first Manager, and the Caribou Road branch in 1938. The West Street branch was relocated to its present site in 1939 in the upper end of West Street and Mr. C. McKay took over as manager in 1940. The building was enlarged by Lundrigan's in 1958 but a fire on December 22, 1963, destroyed the building, though most of the records were preserved. The Bank took advantage of this calamity to rebuild an even larger building using the Masonic Lodge building next door to carry on business during construction. Other banks followed, the Royal Bank opening on West Street and the Canadian Imperial Bank of Commerce in the new Herald Tower Building, but the Bank of Nova Scotia on the corner of Herald Avenue and Broadway was opened as long ago as 1948. More recently a branch of the Newfoundland Credit Union has opened on Main Street.

The legal profession arrived late in Corner Brook. Judge P. Lloyd Soper says that George Bernard Summers was the first lawyer to practice in Corner Brook in 1929, probably practising as a local extension of a St. John's firm. He later went on to become Secretary for Justice in the Commission of Government. In the early days, justice was administered by British naval captains in a summary fashion. When magistrates were later appointed they handled petty crimes in much the same fashion—in fact the first stipendiary magistrate in the Bay of Islands, Commander William Howorth, was a retired naval officer, appointed in 1877. One head constable and two others arrived in 1878, when the first court house was opened in Birchy Cove where the War Memorial is now located. In the same year the first session of the Supreme Court on circuit was held on August 9th. Probably two or more lawyers from St. John's accompanied the judge on these occasions to represent clients in this area.

The Curling jail was located below the court house and incarceration there must have been particularly unpleasant. When Augustus Mallow was jailed because he had been accused of stealing over three hundred dollars from Captain Joseph Hackett's cabin on his schooner, he was twice found unconscious, and had to be resuscitated possibly due to hypothermia (the month was December). Thankfully, a day or two later a supply of coal from Public Works, and utensils supplied from friends in Lark Harbour helped him to survive.

After the construction of Townsite, the Court House and jail in Curling was torn down and a new building constructed in what is now called Remembrance Square, which remained in service until the provincial building was opened in 1968. The nearby jail was always full every night in those early days, usually with drunks and vagrants, according to Walter Mugford, a former constable. Next morning they would be hauled before the magistrate and in most cases treated fairly leniently. Magistrate Andrew Vatcher transferred his office to Corner Brook from Curling in 1926. He was succeeded by Nehemiah Short, then

Howard Strong after World War II, followed by Art Cramm. The Newfoundland Constabulary policed the Bay of Islands until Confederation,when the Royal Canadian Mounted Police took over all duties outside of the capital. In this city the R.C.M.P. operated a city and a rural detachment. In 1986 the constabulary took back the duties of the city detachment,and are located in a new building near O'Connell Drive.

Residents in Townsite obtained their land title deeds from the company running the paper mill through the company lawyer. They were not allowed to sell property without the company's permission, and, regrettable though it may seem to us nowadays, those of non-Anglo Saxon origin were excluded from ownership. Those millworkers and others that had to live outside Townsite obtained their grants of land from the Crown, through the Registration office in St. John's. Mr. William Verge was the first surveyor. The resale of houses was difficult, as many owners transferred their property with a signed document rather than going to the trouble of re-registering in St. John's with search of title. City resident Edna Osmond recalls that her father bought property from a previous owner who subsequently died and he was only able to prove title by the affidavit of one of the witnesses to the transaction, who happened to be still alive.

One of the first lawyers to practice in Bay of Islands was Leonard Hawco, a Rhodes Scholar. Others included Loyola Whalen, who helped organize Humber East township in 1944, and Bill Smith and Kevin Barry, who helped with the incorporation of the City of Corner Brook. The first district court judge was William R. Kent in 1953, having served as the first member of Parliament for Humber, St. George's, St. Barbe in 1949. Judge P. Lloyd Soper followed him as district court judge in 1964. In 1986 the District Court merged with the Supreme Court of Newfoundland and is now staffed by three resident judges, who also go on circuit in the west coast region. Today a score or more of lawyers practice in Corner Brook, independently or in firms.

Barry's Fishery is another of the success stories of the Bay of Islands. Jim Barry, of Irish descent and originally from Placentia Bay, settled in the Bay of Islands some time in the early years of the century. He started out as a fishing captain working for Gorthon Pew of Woods Island. At that time the so called bloater trade in herring was an important trade with the US. After Scotch Cure was phased out, several small fish plants started up in the bay and in Birchy Cove in 1948 there were at least six. Net fishing was carried out locally until 1952 when the herring left the bay, possibly because of increasing pollution or because their spawning grounds had been spoiled. Fortunately technology became available at that time to continue looking for herring schools outside the Bay of Islands using sonar and seines. Now mackerel and caplin are also seined in season.

Gradually the other fish plants in Curling closed or were taken over by Barry's, including most recently Dunphy Fisheries and Humber Cold Storage. Allen's Fisheries in Benoits Cove remains active and independent. Sixteen seining licences are now held in the Bay, some owned by Barry's but most held by independent fishermen in Benoits Cove and Frenchman's Cove who sell to the fish plants. The owner of the boat usually takes 44% of the value of the catch, and the crew get the remainder divided amongst themselves. Herring catches are now limited by government quota; there is a quota for fixed gear fishing and if this quota is not used up it can be reallocated to the seine fishery. Eli Payne of Cox's Cove says that herring were also plentiful in Middle and North Arm and that several firms prosecuted the fishery from Cox's Cove. He is convinced that the subsequent failure of the herring fishery in the Bay of Islands was caused by seine fishing in the herring spawning time in springtime.

The success of Barry Fisheries can be largely attributed to their realization that there is a global fishery and market for fish products. This market demands a quality product which in turn can only be achieved by modernisation and mechanisation. The processing of herring by machine now involves skinning the fish as well as beheading and gutting. The product is exported to the mainland markets by the Midland trucking company in specially chilled trailer trucks.

The Barry company, now called Seafreeze, also purchases redfish and North or Barents sea cod from the Russians who catch and process it on giant factory ships. Recently they have brought in small shrimp from China and Iceland which undergoes secondary processing in the plant to add value to the finished product. When production of the whole plant is at its maximum, 200 employees from all over the Bay find work and earn pretty good wages; machine tenders get $400 a week. The Barry brothers have become two of the most successful Bay of Islands entrepreneurs.

The modern Seafreeze plant and fishery is completely different from the largely inshore bay fishery noted by the Rev. Moses Harvey in the Maritime Monthly in 1873 after a visit to the Bay of Islands. The main reason for his article was to show that west Newfoundland was a promising area for migration from Great Britain. Besides condemning the current (and still current) opinion that Newfoundland was regarded as "a barren rock, shrouded in chilling fogs" based on another writer's stay of a few days in St. John's in 1843, Harvey stated that land on the west coast could be purchased for 50¢ an acre with a gratuity of $8 for the first acre cleared and $6 for each succeeding acre up to 6 acres, at which point the settler was entitled to a free grant. As far as the fishery was concerned he claimed that a man should be able to take a barrel of herring out of the water each day, fetching $4 in the US market (but far less for the fisherman). A boat containing a crew of seven might bring 2000 barrels on shore during the season. At this point in time, however, such days seem but a distant memory. It now seems unlikely that an inshore fishery will ever regain its former importance to the economy of the Bay of Islands.

CHAPTER 17

Marble Mountain and Other Sports

One of the potential magnets for attracting tourist business to Corner Brook is Marble Mountain. The history of the development of this ski hill, only 5 kilometres from Corner Brook, is full of tales of hard work and enthusiasm by a group of citizens. I am grateful to Kevin St. George for some details, whose own involvement with the Corner Brook Ski Club dates back to 1950, when he was employed with Bowaters.

(Above) Above the ski lodge at Marble Mountain—
Doug Cook photo
(Below) The view from the top of the slopes—
K. Nichol photo

Kevin says that it all started on a small hill (not the steep cliff) behind the old Woolworth's building on West Street. The Corner Brook ski club was later formed in 1937 and the International Power and Paper Company built a log cabin for the club on Massey Drive. At that time there were three types of skiing—Alpine, jumping, and cross country, but they only used one type of ski, which was made of wood and had a leather harness into which was inserted a leather boot with a square toe. On its initial formation the club had about 100 members but membership dwindled during WWII, reviving afterwards only to fall again in the face of some winters with little snow. In 1959 Ernie Langins, who had emigrated from Latvia to work as an industrial chemist in the paper mill, held a meeting in his cabin to reactivate the club and it was decided to abandon Massey Drive and to ask Bowaters for permission to use Marble Mountain. Knut Fosnaes, another experienced European skier, Haakon Wick and others were convinced that the slopes of Marble Mountain, facing in a northerly direction with 1500 feet of vertical drop, offered great potential for Alpine skiing. But the initial development of the hill relied not only on the generosity of Bowaters, who provided loggers to cut the first slopes and a generator for the rope tow and a base hut, but on the hard work and enthusiasm of the members of the club. We were all young in those days, and challenged the moguls and blue ice with no benefit of mechanical grooming. "Grooming" was carried out by experienced skiers carving the slopes and challenging us neophytes to follow, and later by snowmobiles. Its a wonder we survived!

In 1966 the club borrowed $5,700 as a down payment to install a T Bar. The provincial government must have been impressed by this show of confidence and provided a grant to cover the cost, on condition that the club encouraged tourism. This condition was accepted but it started a divergence of emphasis between the ski club on the one hand, comprising mostly local skiers, and the provincial government. The club's emphasis was threefold—to promote skiing in the local area, to develop a modern ski base chalet, and to develop a racing programme for young skiers. The provincial government's aim (and it was Liberal and PC governments) was to try to maximize the tourist potential. In 1971 a firm of consultants were hired by the government for a feasibility study and concluded that the area could be developed as a four season resort.

After this, Marble Mountain obtained a double chair lift in 1976 and in 1977 a grant of $15,000 to cover the cost of operating 7 days a week, but this project was financially unsuccessful because of the lack of modern facilities, such as wide ski trails, snow making, and snow grooming in the uncertain Newfoundland weather. Progress languished until 1986 when a second study, initiated during the Premiership of Clyde Wells, a former resident of Corner Brook and member of the ski club, confirmed the previous recommendation for the construction of a four season resort but advised that in order to achieve this a Crown Corporation would have to take over the facilities. All parties involved, including the province, the ski club and the town of Steady Brook, accepted the proposal and in March 1988 the Marble Mountain Development Corporation was established, with the ski club's remaining assets transferred to the Corporation. Two quad lifts were later installed as well as snow making equipment. Now up to 30 ski trails are well groomed and a magnificent base lodge has been built, opening in February, 1995.

The Corner Brook Winter Carnival's inaugural year was 1962. The object was to have some fun and to introduce new skiers and visitors to the facility, with races for young skiers and veterans. The selection of a mascot for the Carnival was an inspired one, with the late Scotty Robson and Bob McLeod claiming some responsibility. The mascot was "Leif the Lucky," whom they believed landed at L'Anse aux Meadows—Leif's Vinland—1000 years ago. This selection was based on the premise that, as Leif was a Scandinavian, he must have been an avid skier and would surely have brought his skis with him to Vinland to try out the slopes, and would therefore qualify as our first downhill skier. Scotty Robson was the first Leif in the Carnival Procession, which started off Carnival week with a route through Corner Brook.

Marble has undoubted potential as a tourist centre. But much further development needs to be done for an all season operation, and there are plans for walking and snowmobile trails and a golf course on the other side of the Humber River. Recently additional plans have been put forward for a winter trail from Marble to Harbour Deep. The provincial government has announced that it will not put any further money into the ski area, and wants the facility to be taken over and operated by a private operator instead of the Marble Mountain Corporation. One hopes that this operator will have deep pockets and a long-term outlook. Another doubt has been raised by the warm temperatures and relative absence of heavy snowfall in Eastern Canada in the winter of 1996. A global warming trend of increased magnitude would put the whole project in doubt, but if the Winter Games can be carried out here in 1999 successfully it will put Marble, Bay of Islands, and the whole west coast on the national map and will be an incredible boost to the economy.

Marble Mountain may not be the only showpiece, and downhill skiing is not the only sport in the winter games. The new Civic Centre in Corner Brook has opened its doors to the public in the fall of 1997 and will enable Humber Gardens and Kinsmen Arena to be closed down or adapted for purposes other than hockey and skating. The Silver Blades organization has been prominent in encouraging figure skating in the community and of course hockey and broomball and other sports will be able to use the new facility. But the other sport which has expanded in the area in recent years is cross country skiing. The club, now called the Blow-Me-Down Cross Country Ski Club, started off in 1974 with about 50 members as a part of the Corner Brook ski club, using whatever slopes in the area they could for cross country, including Massey Drive and the Blomidon Golf Club. The club became fully independent when it acquired a suitable area off the Ring Road in Corner Brook and began to develop the land for cross country skiing in 1986. Since then the club has expanded to 600 members with some former club facilities acquired from Marble Mountain and many kilometres of groomed ski trails of varying difficulty.

The development of the Blow-Me-Down Club's cross country trails near the ring road has literally avoided collision with another growing sport, that of snowmobiling. Prior to the construction of trails dedicated to cross country skiing, skiers on woods roads near the city such as Twelve Mile Dam and Lady Slipper Road were often confronted with visored and helmeted riders capable of striking in skiers as much fear for life and safety as would the medieval knights of old. Snowmobiling is an expensive sport, a new machine costing from $4500 to $12,000, but many like the sense of freedom and speed, and "going on a randy" is a popular outing for many during winter (This term is not to be confused with the British meaning, i.e. Randy Andy, the nickname for Prince Andrew!). Snowmobile trails are found all over the west coast, using woods roads like the popular Loggers School Road and the old railway bed as well as winding moose trails through the woods and over frozen bogs and lakes. Many men use their snowmobiles to haul sleighs in winter to gather wood. Day excursions or safaris are becoming popular and plans are being explored to organize a wilderness safari down the Northern Peninsula from St. Anthony to Corner Brook every winter, which could prove a tourist attraction.

Marble Mountain Development Corporation will have to develop summer activities such as golfing to become an all seasons resort. At present the only course in the city is one managed by the Blomidon Club. Before 1951, the Blomidon Club used the Glynmill Inn as its headquarters, and in that year a new club house to be known as the Blomidon Golf and Country Club was completed and a new 9-hole golf course opened on land leased from Bowaters. The clubhouse was a handsome building of log construction but burned down in 1973 together with the curling rink and the old pro shop. After rebuilding with a prefabricated wooden building and using an Atlantic Design home as a pro shop, the golf course was expanded to an 18-hole course with help from Bowaters. The late H. O. House was chiefly responsible for organising this expansion. Membership of the golf club is now about 500 men, women, and juniors who avail of the junior golf programme. An ambitious redevelopment programme has been started in 1998 to lengthen and improve the golf course and to bring it up to modern standards. Gary Oke is the golf professional but has recently resigned as the club manager, having succeeded the late George Daniels. The genial and well loved Leander Gosse was the first manager and the present one is Gerry LeDrew.

Golf was first played in 1924, when a 9-hole course was built near the Petries hotel. The first professional was John Stevenson and the course remained open until 1937. Many fine golfers who subsequently played at the Blomidon Club in later years learned to play at Petries Point, including John's son Dave Stevenson, Sandy Candow, and Ron Dunphy, to name a few. There was no golf course from 1937 to 1951 in the Bay of Islands but Gar Elliott, a retired mill worker, says that when he was a boy, he and Dave "Vinegar" Smith and others used tree roots shaped into wooden clubs to play a crude type of golf game on the farmland at the top of West Valley Road.

The first tennis court was located in the grounds of the Petries Hotel where there was also a croquet lawn and bowling green. The hotel building was apparently quite luxurious and included a fine ballroom. It was popular with American sports fishermen and tourists, but was destroyed by fire in 1929. Tennis has never really caught on in this region, probably because summers are short and the weather is uncertain and often breezy. There was a tennis court behind the Glynmill Inn at one time, and Monty Lewin built a grass court at Corner Brook House. Two dry surface courts were available until recent times at the Blomidon Club but saw little use. Asphalt surface courts are now used and there are several of these. Badminton started with a club on Main Street, but it seems strange that squash has never become popular, as it is an indoor sport requiring fairly basic facilities. The new Civic Centre now boasts squash facilities and the popularity of this sport may soon rise.

Curling started in Corner Brook before World War 2 using a disused wood shed as an ice rink. John Stevenson, the Petries golf professional, used to travel to Corner Brook to make the ice in winter. Later the club used a rink on Main Street where Gullage's store is now located. After the war the Blomidon Club rink was built, again serviced by the golf professional. But after a fire destroyed the Blomidon Club in 1973 the Rec Plex was built close to the Arts and Culture Centre with 4 lanes. This has proved to be a financial mistake as the facility is unable to make a profit and is fortunate to be presently subsidised by the city. There have been many prominent curlers who have represented the city at a provincial and national level including Skips Bud Fisher and Gary Oke with their local teams.

Organised baseball first started in the province in Corner Brook in the 1930s, long before it was played elsewhere on the island. This was probably due to the presence of the American International Pulp and Paper Company. Jubilee Field was donated to the city by Bowaters in 1935, but other baseball fields are now found in several locations in the city and in other communities in the Bay. The Corner Brook Barons have won the Provincial Championship several times, and several past players have been admitted to the Hall of Fame. Soon after the first indoor swimming pool was opened in Corner Brook, a swimming club for young swimmers was formed, known by the strange title of the ANC Swim Club. The first coach was Betty Dean. Later the name was changed to the Western Whales Swim Club. Some of the club members represented the club in national swim meets, including Robby Dean, Margaret Ann McLeod, Nancy Sweetland, Brent Staeben, and Skylar Pike. Anna Krizan, who represented her native country Czechoslovakia before coming to Newfoundland, has provided invaluable coaching.

Social and sporting activities have changed considerably in the past century. Better communications have enabled schools and amateur groups to compete in a wide variety of sporting activities. More leisure time and the increasingly realization that exercise is an important health factor have encouraged men and women to take part in a number of indoor and outdoor activities. Fishing and hunting still play a large part in most men's and an increasing number of women's sporting pursuits, but salmon fishing is no longer carried out for food. The bag limit for grilse is now limited , and now this season only barbless hooks are permitted, as in some other North American rivers, in order to permit better catch and release. Concern for the west coast Atlantic salmon stock is nothing new. It was noted as far back as the 1870s when Commander

Knowles of the Naval Fisheries patrol made this statement:

"The salmon fishery on this [West] Coast, both in the rivers and bays and creeks of this island is very severely becoming exterminated. In the bays, fleets of nets are frequently laid down, sometimes 20, 40 and 50 at a time, and every inlet stopped; and the rivers are so obstructed by weirs, traps, dams and nets that it is a wonder that the fishery has not long since come to an end."

Eventually the first river wardens were appointed in 1891, and a system of licensing was introduced. Commercial fishing, however, was not stopped until 1992 on the island part of the province, and is still allowed in Labrador, despite an offer by the government to buy out the remaining commercial salmon licenses. Sports fishing now requires a licence, and a licenced guide is compulsory for salmon fishing with a visitor's licence. But there has been a marked drop in the numbers of salmon returning to spawn in our rivers. The reasons are multiple— some blame commercial fishing in Greenland, some blame the rising seal population, others clear cutting of the paper companies at the headwaters of salmon rivers, and still more blame continuing poaching and illicit netting, which is a problem in some areas.

Trout stocks are also becoming depleted, but moose and caribou populations seem to be fairly stable as a result of the limitation of licences. Snow shoe hares, known as rabbits, ptarmigan, grouse, and ducks are still hunted but again their numbers seem to be diminishing. We can only hope that conservation measures, better policing, and a change of attitude to hunting and poaching by the public will gradually improve matters.

Not until Humber Gardens was opened on September 22, 1955, did Corner Brook possess a proper indoor skating rink. Half of the cost of construction was raised by public subscription, organised by a local committee headed by Jack Marshall and Carl Hansen. Before that the building recently owned by Stan Dawe Limited and torn down in 1997, behind the Anglican church, was used as an indoor rink—standing room only for spectators. But the very first indoor rink in Corner Brook was located in No. 1 paper shed, by company permission, and three hockey teams competed there in the winter of 1925. A skating rink had been originally planned for Townsite but the company could not afford to build one. Instead, they brought a large shed which was no longer in use from Deer Lake, erecting it on a site next to the Anglican church. This structure was used up until 1953. Various local team competitions were organised over the years—a school hockey programme was started in

1928 and the Herder Competition in 1935. Austin Taylor remembers playing in the first game in Humber Gardens, against St Bonaventure College, popularly known as St. Bon's. Much later the Kinsmen arena was built near Humber Gardens, but the planned outdoor track and soccer field were never completed. During the Bowater years, the Glynmill Pond was cleared as a skating arena, with public skating under lights while recorded music played. Few Corner Brook hockey teams could beat Grand Falls until the team was able to train on an indoor rink, like Grand Falls. The Corner Brook Royals went on to win the Herder Trophy for the first time in 1935. They won again in 1962, 1964, 1966, 1968, 1977, and again in 1985, 1986, and 1988. The greatest feat of all, the Allen Cup, was realized in 1986. Now several communities around the Bay have their own indoor rinks and Corner Brook has a new Civic Centre and arena. These rinks have fostered figure skating in the area, beginning with Angie Dorrington's Silver Blades club in the 1950s. The new Civic Centre is expected to host visiting figure skaters and ice shows and may eventually be the home of a professional hockey team if sufficient local support is forthcoming.

CHAPTER 18

The Future

While it is impossible for anyone to predict the future, it is possible to try to record the present hopes and aspirations of some of the people living now in the Bay of Islands and to compare these hopes with those of previous generations. Of course, those earliest settlers were chiefly concerned about whether they would be able to receive sufficient supplies from the merchant or supply vessel, in return for their fish and furs, to enable them to last through the next winter. Lawlessness and drunkenness were apparently widespread in following years and those early churchmen looked forward to the days when these vices were no more and when children had some religious instruction and schooling, and all were baptised, preferably in their own particular religious sect of course. Monsignor Thomas Sears was an exception. He had a broad vision, looking forward to a future agricultural economy assisted by a good road communication system, but he could not have imagined industrial development and a paper mill at that time, even in his wildest dreams.

Following his leadership and those of other churchmen, the following generation continued to press for better communications with the outside world, and the Colonial Government eventually responded with a railway system, from St. John's to Port aux Basques.

The 30 year period between the railway construction and that of the paper mill in Corner Brook seems to have been characterised by a quiet and fairly comfortable existence for most families, provided, of course,

The Glynmill Inn after the fire in 1929

that they all remained healthy. The Great Depression meant great hardship for some, but not all.

After construction started on the paper mill a radical change occurred. Although some workers had been employed previously in saw mills, men and a few women could now receive regular wages. Some of their comments on working conditions have been recorded in previous chapters, but not their hopes for the future. One man, who was probably an expatriate working in a managerial position for the construction company produced a little book called "The Ballads of Corner Brook" in 1925. He apparently resided in the company staff house, known now as the Glynmill Inn. His name was R.G. Ogden and he thus qualifies as Corner Brook's first poet. One of his poems is entitled "A Dream of the Future" and I quote:

"To deal in prophecy now I'm stirred—
One night as I slept a dream occurred,
I think it was due to hope deferred
And indigestion blended;
The form that this flight of fancy took
Was all related to Corner Brook—
A vision of how the town will look,
Construction being ended.

The Mill was finished and working fast—
And permanent roads were paved at last,
So mud belonged to a period past—
That mud so deep and sticky!
And night in the town was bright as day,
For lights were lit in a grand array,
No longer you had to grope your way
In corners dark and tricky.

And shops devoted to every trade
A wide selection of goods had made,
While plate glass windows these wares displayed
And people thronged the portals.
The Liquor Commission possessed a store,
So trains no longer those parcels bore,
For which had waited a week or more—
A crowd of thirsty mortals!

Another enjoyable boon would be,
That Saturday afternoons were free,
For strenuous sport or social spree
At Corner Brook or Curling.
And then regarding the Railway run—
A first class service had just begun,
And people no more were poking fun
Or rude remarks were hurling.

And houses with well found frames supplied,
Embellished the landscape far and wide;
Their watertight cellars a thaw defied,
And fears of flooding banished.
A dearth of houses no longer rife,
And dwellings on hand for man and wife,
That bar to a bachelor's change in life
Had altogether vanished.

But here the end of the story lies—
What further visions I can't surmise
Might then have come as a grand surprise
To greet this earthly heaven!
Although I should like to tell you more—
Fate on the wings of the morning bore—
And a plaintive voice at my bedroom door
Proclaimed the hour of seven!"

Today our hopes would be somewhat different from those of that previous generation! And there would be a marked difference between the hopes of those living in the Outer Bay, and those living in Corner Brook and the Humber Valley.

Some men and women in the communities of the Outer Bay of Islands look forward to the return of the old inshore fishery, providing employment for themselves, and their children without the need to relocate to the mainland of Canada. This would preserve their traditional way of life, but their hopes are unlikely to be fulfilled in the near future, as I have previously explained.

Most of those older persons and pensioners in Corner Brook and the Humber Valley would like to preserve and improve the old peoples homes and health care facilities in the area; there are a growing number of senior citizens. Our younger people probably look forward to increasing their opportunities for education and job training to enable them to obtain employment in this area, without having to emigrate to the mainland.

Controversially, I would assert that the inshore cod fishery using motor dories, will never return to be a profitable occupation. It seems ludicrous to try to glorify this former industry by preserving the image of "Kissing the Cod" in inauguration ceremonies so often promoted by Newfoundland Tourist Groups. In this part of Newfoundland it would be more appropriate to kiss a herring or a salmon or, heaven forbid, a lobster! The State of Wyoming in the USA, has a similar historical image, perpetuated by Hollywood, where the rugged cowboy is immortalised, never mind that he was usually indentured to his boss. Now dude ranchers and city slickers occupy most of the old properties. I wonder how many city slickers will buy up our scenic property in the next millennium.

Another way of guessing how the future may unfold can be obtained by analyzing some of the present day concerns regarding the environment and the economy which today are being discussed, in this era of falling birthrates and increasing numbers of pensioners. Fewer workers are now needed in such industries as logging and papermaking and our young people have had to leave in increasing numbers to find work. In the outer bay area, inshore cod fishery is under a moratorium and there are certainly no longer the "mounds of lobsters" that were remarked on by M. Gobineau in 1857—in fact, these crustaceans appear to be smaller and less plentiful. Nor are there "thousands of barrels of herring" to be processed, as was remarked on by Thomas Sears, as these fish are now schooling outside the bay and catches are limited.

Service industries are growing, but have been unable to fill the employment gap. The collapse of the Lundrigan organization has been keenly felt in the area, not only because of the loss of employment, but also because of the loss of a local entrepreneur big enough and bold enough to build and finance local developments. One result has been a lack of condominiums and one level dwellings suitable for the elderly or residents with disabilities to live independently. Fortunately, Corner Brook has had some seniors' residences built in previous years, such as the Interfaith homes on Elizabeth Street. But there is still a need for low cost accommodations for out of town students attending the Grenfell College campus and also for students enrolled at the College of the North

City of Corner Brook —1998

Atlantic and the private colleges, all of which have increasing enrolment of students from all parts of the west coast.

The hope and necessity of employment versus the desirability of maintaining a natural and healthy environment is likely to prove increasingly controversial in the future. Unemployment amongst fishermen in the Outer Bay of Islands was as great as 70% in 1997; these numbers make it difficult for political leaders to turn down any project that might

Photo courtesy of Douglas Cook

reduce this unemployment figure, even if it is only of a temporary nature. A recent decision not to bid for the Voisey's Bay smelter to be located in the Bay of Islands was generally supported by public opinion.

At the present time there is concern over a plan by Kruger to construct a dam and hydro development project near Silver Mountain on the Upper Humber River. Construction of this project could employ 200 workers over a 2- or 3-year period. Concerns have centred on the change in the flow pattern of the Humber River that could result from the presence of this dam, possibly affecting the breeding sites of salmon and of wild life. People remember that in 1923 the construction of Main Dam at Junction Brook deprived salmon in the Humber River of half their spawning grounds by flooding 290 square miles. Residents of Steady Brook also have unpleasant memories of spring flooding of their properties when the Deer Lake Power Company allowed runoff from Grand Lake to exceed 28,000 cubic feet per second. The Power Company's attitude to the Steady Brook flooding was initially somewhat callous, claiming that they were in the business of making electricity, and that flooding in the Steady Brook area was an unfortunate side effect, and therefore none of their concern. Fortunately the two sides were eventually able to come to some agreement, and flooding has been much less severe in recent years as spillage from Main Dam can now only occur with governmental permission.

The projected development of the Upper Humber project at Silver Mountain now depends on the results of an environmental study but it is good to see that individuals like Gene Mannion of Steady Brook are voicing the concerns of the general public. At the present time it appears likely that the Provincial Government has responded to public opinion by cancelling all potential small hydro developments and is relying on the future development of the Lower Churchill river as a source of power for the province.

Since further large industrial developments in this area appear unlikely on environmental grounds, what about the future expansion or survival of our four magnets? Many people in Corner Brook and in the rest of the island believe that the survival of the economy of the Bay of Islands depends entirely on the future of the paper mill, now owned by Kruger Incorporated, a privately owned Montreal-based company who own several other successful mills in Canada. Residents living in Townsite are daily reminded of the presence of the mill in their lives by the mill whistles at 7:45 and 8:00 in the morning, 12 noon, and 4:00 in the afternoon. Indeed, in 1986 Harold Horwood subtitled his book Corner Brook, the history of a paper town. For many years in the early days Corner Brook was just that. Now, however, it is much more than just that. Nevertheless, it is quite true that any closure of the paper mill and woods operations would have very serious effects on the economy, including the loss of many hundreds of jobs and the loss of "new" money coming into the economy coupled with "recycled" money generated from shopping sales and services.

Fortunately there seems to be no imminent prospect of any closure or significant downtime at the mill, which presently runs smoothly with steady production, good markets, and a reasonably contented work force. In addition the mill has met or even exceeded all federal pollution controls and regulations. There might even be some chance of increased production in the future as the Corner Brook Pulp and Paper Company has a proposal to produce at the mill site up to 15 Megawatts of power to supply Newfoundland Hydro with additional power to sell to the International Nickel Company's proposed smelter at Argentia. A new boiler has already been installed to burn bark to produce extra electrical power for the mill, but in order to produce enough bark for export of this power, paper production might have to be increased from 1050 tons a day to 1200 tons.

The woods operations and the supply of pulpwood to the mill have been a recent cause of concern and may hamper any expansion of output at the mill unless recycling can somehow be increased, as the mill does not yet have de-inking capability. In earlier days people assumed unlimited resources of wood for the mills of Grand Falls and Corner Brook, relying on natural regeneration of the forest in a cycle of about 70 years. However, natural regeneration produces clumping of the growth of small trees, particularly balsam fir, thus rendering them more susceptible to the predation of defoliating insects, such as the Wooly aphid, the Spruce budworm and the Hemlock looper, and this year the Balsam saw fly. Chemical spray programmes were introduced to combat these pests, using aircraft, but these were met with public opposition because of possible interference with water supply. More recently a spray programme using a biological agent B.T. has met with some success and less public opposition to its operation.

Forest fires could wreak havoc on the mill's operations, destroying its timber supply. In earlier days only fire fighters on the ground were employed to control the blaze, not without personal risk. Nowadays water bombers, such as the Canso, filled with water tanks and scoops to enable the aircraft to pick up water from local ponds, have proved most effective. There have been no major forest fires on the island for the past few years.

In recognizing the concern for a future groundwood supply a real effort has been made in recent years to introduce silviculture methods, such as planting young trees and thinning thick stands, and the provincial government is cooperating in these efforts with the paper companies. Kruger officials acknowledge that the wood supply will be tight for the next 20 years, but they expect that silviculture will shorten the growth cycle of industrial pulpwood from 70 to 40 or so years. They have also emphasized the use of recycled paper in the mill operations since 1993, as Kruger buys waste paper from Nova Recycling and imports waste paper from the US, carried on the returning voyages of the paper carriers.

As far as another of our other magnets—the malls and manufacturing—are concerned, there seems no present likelihood of any large future manufacturing or industrial development that will result in attracting income and population growth in the city of Corner Brook. There has been talk of a WalMart coming to the area, sending shivers down the backs of all retail businesses in the city, great or small. The major impediment to this company seems to be the lack of any large area of flat land close to the city suitable for a business or store like WalMart. Moreover, a WalMart store in Stephenville is only an hour's drive distance.

In the outer bay area future development is still considered to be dependent on the fishing industry. Barry's fisheries has led the way here with some innovative secondary processing but there seems to be little room for any similar processing plants, although Allen's Fisheries in Benoits Cove have recently started to process crab successfully. At the time of writing, the groundfish moratorium is in effect, but its ending would not make a great deal of difference to the local economies. Even if an inshore fishery is revived, it will now be of decreasing importance as the quality of the product is often not up to the standards required by the export market. Because of ice conditions codfish or salmon aquaculture seems unlikely to be successful in this bay, although it may be an industry worth pursuing for other species, such as scallops and mussels.

Mining and oil exploration and development would seem to offer the best chances of industrial growth. There has recently been some interest in oil exploration in the Deer Lake area and knowledgeable experts assert that the area of the island between St. George's Bay and Roddickton has similar geological features to some of the oilfields already found to the west of the Appalachian Range in the USA. Development of a large oilfield or mine anywhere on the west coast would have an effect on Corner Brook and also on Deer Lake and Stephenville because of their airports.

At this time it seems likely that another of our magnets, the Western Regional Hospital, will not expand further, but will endeavour to keep up to date by upgrading equipment and facilities. It is not outside the realms of possibility, however, that a new hospital-based treatment for cancer or another common disease or disorder will require further expansion. But Medicare would appear to be able to survive for the immediate future only if further financial resources become available from the federal or provincial governments. Any Government, right or left wing, must accept by now that more money for the programme cannot now be raised by increased borrowing, or by an increase in corporate or personal taxation. The institution of user fees, such as payment for room and board in hospital, would not be popular but would provide money for additional services and maintenance. My personal preference at present is a designated and separate "Health Tax", with a comparable reduction in income tax, so that one could at least know that our tax dollars were being spent on health and not on perks for our honourable members.

The Great White Hope of the tourist industry in the Bay of Islands is Marble Mountain and its future development as an all season resort. And a white hope it is, as its development as a downhill ski facility of national or international class is largely dependent on abundant winter snowfall. According to long-time residents and confirmed by weather statistics, this has been much less than it was before World War II. Marble typically receives over 200 centimetres a year. Snowfall has been quite light in the past 2 years, and one season in the past 20 years recorded so little snow that only 1 week's skiing was possible. The acquisition of state-of-the-art snow making equipment is a type of insurance against a poor snowfall, but snow can only be made when temperatures are below zero and in the last 2 years there have been several above-zero warm spells. In fact global warming has apparently become a reality and makes one question whether Marble can generate enough reliable snowfall to make a profit when the facility is turned over to a private operator, who one hopes will have enough financial resources to develop it into a three season facility (Newfoundland has no Spring!) We really hope that the Canada Winter Games will be such a success that it puts Corner Brook and Marble Mountain on the national map for winter sports.

On both sides of Bonne Bay, Gros Morne is developing as a tourist attraction and this park, along with the opening of the Viking Trail to L'Anse aux Meadows, has greatly helped the growth of Deer Lake. Tourism has certainly grown in the area over the years. Since Leonard Earle, a pioneer farmer in Pasadena, showed that the Humber Valley, was capable of growing excellent strawberries many years ago, people have grown strawberries in the region. More recently, several growers have also cultivated strawberry crops and U-picks in the Humber Valley and the Strawberry Festival, centred in Pasadena during the month of July, attracts people from all over the province.

The lower Humber River was well known to international sports fisherman 100 years ago, but bag limits and the diminished run of big salmon led to declining interest. Due to the efforts of the Salmon Preservation Association for Western Newfoundland (SPAWN) and of sports fishermen such as the late Art Barnes, Ches Loughlin, Don Clarke, Tom Farrell and Tom Humphrey, salmon runs have been slowly improving and there would seem to be a chance of more tourists returning to fish the Lower Humber as they used to do a hundred years ago, especially as there are now several good bed & breakfast accomodations close to the river. In 1997, an American tourist landed a 36.5 pound salmon on the river. Strawberry Hill, formerly the private resort of Sir Eric Bowater, is now a tourist lodge with a magnificent view over the Humber River. It is possible to fish some pools by using chest waders, but the river is deep, the current is strong, and most pools are more readily accessed by boat. It is possible to hire local boats and guides.

Fall colours and pleasant autumn weather have started to attract bus tours from the mainland. The Elder Hostel project also helped to introduce visitors to the culture and history of this area. I have often wondered why more cruise ships do not include Corner Brook in their itinerary, as the Bay of Islands and Bonne Bay are quite deep enough to allow the largest liners to visit, and accessibility has been improved by the Corner Brook Harbour Development Plan. The Queen Elizabeth II visited the port in 1983 and an even larger liner, the Enchantment of the Seas, visited twice in 1997. In discussing the subject with Pat Pye, the present Tourist Development Coordinator for the city, she feels that Corner Brook should become a port of entry to Newfoundland in addition to Port aux Basques, presumably on a route from a port on the mainland and run by a private company. Visitors to Newfoundland travelling to the island by Marine Atlantic are unhappy with the North Sydney—Port aux Basques service, particularly the bus tour operators. Privatisation of Marine Atlantic could be a solution, though the political difficulties are formidable. MP Gerry Byrne's idea of making it an essential service could also be a help if he can get an act passed in Ottawa. There is also a small marina at Allen's Cove which needs financial support to improve facilities and attract yachts and motor cruisers from the mainland. Another much needed addition to infrastructure is now completed with the extension of Marine Drive to Humbermouth, which was actually a part of the original city plan.

There has been a slight decline in the number of visitors to the Provincial Parks. Some of these parks have been privatised, and most of them offer facilities for camping, trailers, and motor homes. One of the more exciting possibilities for future tourism is a projected extension of the Appalachian trail from Port aux Basques to St. Anthony. Back packing and hiking is becoming very popular in North America and Europe and the trail is well used and maintained in the United States, currently terminating in the Gaspé region of Quebec. Plans are in progress for a survey of a route between Port aux Basques to the Humber Valley as the first stage but much further work and money needs to be expended to make this project a reality. Hopefully some development may be possible through the extension of the Trans Canada Trail project.

The fourth magnet, Memorial University campus in Corner Brook known as Grenfell College, is in my opinion one of the keys to the future success and prosperity of the entire west coast. Of course this magnet includes the highly successful College of the North Atlantic with its West Viking campus and the private colleges. Grenfell College campus now has the new Forestry Centre completed and is considering a centre for applied research to link the university's professors and teaching programmes to the needs of industry and society. Most students still go to the Memorial campus in St John's to complete their courses, but Grenfell now offers a nine degree programme.

Unfortunately Newfoundland has been slow to recognize the increasingly important requirements for education in modern society, enmeshed as it has been in its sectarian religious roots in elementary and high school education. The grade system is in need of reorganization as progression through this system is not always on the basis of merit, and compares unfavourably with other provinces. This sometimes causes discouragement to students in their 1st year of university, when they find that they have to think for themselves and have to learn good study habits. I remember one of my children complaining to me after her 1st year at university "no one seems to care what I do here"—in other words, students have to learn in their 1st year at university self-reliance, a sense of personal commitment, and competition, values which should ideally be developed at an earlier age. Moreover, it strikes me as a strange contradiction that, of the pupils in Corner Brook, part of a professed bilingual country, only 6% learn French as a working language. Failure to become proficient will inevitably handicap our students from employment in a federal organization.

I have to admire the Republic of Ireland's Educational system, a predominantly Catholic country, but which escaped the Church's control when it became a republic. It is now considered to have one of the best educated work forces in the world, with post-secondary education that is largely free. This has now resulted in an increasingly successful economy and a reversal of out migration. In this province we still have only a third of our students going on to higher education, though admittedly this number has been increasing. But even those obtaining higher education sometimes find themselves without suitable employment. For instance, in 1 year over 60% of the graduating class in medicine moved to the mainland or to the United States to find work, although there were many posts unfilled for doctors in rural Newfoundland. Money was one of the reasons given, but not the only one.

Some of these posts in Newfoundland have been filled by immigrant medical doctors, and we must not forget that the Bay of Islands in particular has grown and prospered because of the influx of immigrants of all types. As we have previously noted the early immigrants were fishermen mostly from other parts of Newfoundland and originally most of the men, and some of the women, came from Europe. But we must also remember that many Mic Mac native Indians originally from Nova Scotia settled here. They were followed by saw mill workers from Nova Scotia, railway workers, lumberjacks, and mill workers, and Lebanese, Jewish, and Chinese businessmen and shopowners. In the post-war period there was immigration from cement and gypsum workers from Eastern Europe and health professionals from the British Isles and Ireland, and latterly from the Indian subcontinent and South Africa. More recently there was immigration of professors and teachers from many foreign countries and other Canadian provinces when Grenfell College was founded. All these new residents gave a boost to commercial and cultural growth, particularly in Corner Brook. Fortunately the earlier residents are tolerant of newcomers and there seems to be less xenophobia in this community than in some others.

There is no denying that important contributions to the welfare of this area have been initiated since confederation by governments, both federal and provincial. These include the Trans Canada Highway, and two of our four magnets, Memorial University and Medicare. Unemployment Insurance has been a mixed blessing in Eastern Canada, resulting in a quest for enough stamps to earn the benefits rather than acquiring the skills for a permanent job. Nevertheless, entrepreneurs and pioneers have had a great deal to do with the economic and social progress in this area. It is disturbing therefore to hear one of our teachers describing a sense of dependency that he has encountered in some of our young people, especially, so he says, among the communities in the Outer Bay of Islands. One can understand this in some respects, as their ancestors were dependent on merchants, or on government handouts such as the dole or welfare payments. This has created a mental attitude of "waiting for the Government to create some jobs" (How I hate that use of the word create, almost blasphemous), or "waiting for the fishery to come back" (It never will, not as it was in earlier days). Unfortunately, so many of the ambitious young people find it necessary to leave for employment on the mainland. One object of the education system in this province should be to train these young people in skills that would be of benefit to them in finding work here and remaining in this area.

Computer literacy is now becoming as essential as were the "three R's" in earlier days. Some entrepreneurs, working at home with their computers, fax machines, and cheap long distance telephone calls, have successfully built up businesses and there is no reason why they cannot do this anywhere in the Bay of Islands. Maybe some of our young migrants, after learning the economic facts of life on the mainland, will return with skills to open businesses here. I already know some who have already done so.

Small businesses need start up or "seed" money; government efforts such as ACOA to provide this money have not proved very successful so far. The large banks have been helpful, but require full collateral in many cases, rather than agreeing to share the risk by taking an equity position. One partial success story is the incubator mall in Pasadena, a brainchild of a previous mayor which has enabled small businesses to start up for an initial period without heavy overhead expenses. I feel that our government should closely study the results of the Republic of Ireland's initiatives, allowing businesses a tax-free period after start up and encouraging writers and artists to settle in this beautiful part of the world with income tax relief on their royalties,(there is no personal reason for this suggestion, I can assure you!).

I have attempted to show in earlier chapters that the Bay of Islands has had a completely different history of settlement and development from the east coast of Newfoundland and from St. John's, and also from other parts of the west coast. Would we in this part of the island have been better off in seceding from the rest of the colony and joining Nova

Scotia in the 1870s as part of Canada? Later, in the post-WWII referendum would we in this part of the island, with the U.S. base in Stephenville, have been better off joining the U.S. instead of confederating with Canada? I leave it to readers to form their own opinion.

In 1949 the west coast provided the majority vote to confederate with Canada in the final referendum. Since then, the Bay of Islands has undoubtedly prospered and few would now want to return to Responsible Government, although I have heard some old timers on talk shows praising the Commission for their impartiality, and incorruptibility. The provincial government now has responsibility for several areas of government, including the ones that our people seem to feel are most important, namely health care and education. We must all be vigilant in improving our hospitals, schools, and colleges by electing representatives ready to stand up for our rights, whether it be in Parliament in Ottawa, in the House of Assembly, or in our city and local town councils.

I hope that this account of the social and economic development of a unique part of Newfoundland will inspire greater interest among visitors to the beautiful West Coast of the Island, and that it provides encouragement for future generations to develop its full potential.

APPENDICES

Roll of Honour—1914-1918
Gilbert BALDWIN
Arthur G. BALLAM
Stewert BELLOWS
George E. BRAKE
James M. BROWN
Edward BUTT
John T. CURLEY
George R. CURNEW
Hubert DIAMOND
George W. HARRIS
George A. MADORE
Hugh W. MCWHIRTER
William H. MURRIN
Campbell NICHOLS
Duncan G. NICHOLS
Augustus P. PARK
John T. PARSONS
Charles PENNELL
William C. PENNELL
George R. SAMS
Walter STRICKLAND

Roll of Honour—1939-1945
ARMY
George E. BURCHELL
Raymond DINGWELL
Albert E. HYNES
Raymond R.W. JOHNSON
Derek A.W. LODER
Percy MAYNARD
Alphonsus NOAH
Ingwald A. OSMOND
Augustine PUMPHREY
Llewellyn SNOOKS
Willis WHEELER
William J. MOORE
Frederick NOFTALL
Bert NASH

George RANDELL
Frederick ROBERTSON
AIR FORCE
John Hamilton BARRETT
John A. BUCKINGHAM
Eric T. BUGDEN
Reginald C. CARTER
Keith R. COOKE
John L. COOKE
Granville M. EASON
Gerard F. FRENCH
Douglas M. GRANT
John J. GRIFFIN
Edwin A. HOUSE
Fowlow KING
Kevin F. NEVILLE
Ralph O'KEEFE
Gerald PUMPHREY
John W. SHARPE
Selby TULK
ROYAL NAVY
Andrew BAKER
Stanley BENNETT
Warren R. BLANCHARD
Gordon BRINSTON
John CULL
Patrick J. DELANEY
Milton E. DWYER
Edward FEWER
Ralph FOSTER
Albert GABRIEL
George P. GILLETT
Howard GALLIOTT
Frederick GULLAGE
Wilfred GUY
Samuel HUTCHINGS
Frederick JESSO
Ronald PELLEY
Joseph LAVIS

Everett LAWRENCE
Reginald WHEELER
George LAWRENCE
Francis LODER
George MESSERVEY
Frank MORRISON
Arthur O'CONNELL
Henry O'NEILL
Raymond PEARCEY
Wilfred G. POOLE
William H. SNOOKS
Matthew SPENCER
MERCHANT NAVY
Charles M. BABSTOCK
Lloyd BISHOP
Michael CAREW
Maurice CARBERRY
Cecil CLARKE
William J. WHITEWAY
Ezekiel CLARKE
George CROCKER
Beaton CUNNING
Chesley FIFIELD
Melburn FOOTE
Hubert FRY
Walter MADORE
John O. NICHOLS
Ronald O'BRIEN
Charles PIEROWAY
Ignatius WOODS

Military Decorations WW II
BURSEY, Frank M.M.
59 Nfld. Heavy Regiment R.A.
CHAFFEY, Lionel M.M.
166 Nfld. Field Regiment
R.A.CROSS, Harold M.C.
Canadian Army R.C.A.
DOLOMOUNT, Percy M.I.D.
59 Nfld. Heavy Regiment R.A.

GILES, William M.M.
166 Nfld. Field Regiment R.A.
GOODRIDGE, Alan M.C.
166 Nfld. Field Regiment R.A.
GRACE, Martin (Tony) D.F.C.
R.C.A.F.
GUY, Wilfred D.F.M.
R.A.F.
HUTCHINGS, Gerald M.I.D.
166 Nfld. Field Regiment R.A.
QUIGLEY, John P. D.S.M.
R.C.N.V.R.
SCOTT, A.K. M.I.D.
166 Nfld. Field Regiment R.A.
SWEET, Murdock
Croix De Guerre
166 Nfld. Field Regiment R.A.
STRATTON, John A.F.M.
R.A.F.
YOUNG, Wilfred D.F.C.
R.C.A.F.

— — — — — — — — — —

Corner Brook residents Inducted Into Newfoundland and Labrador Sports Hall of Fame— 1973-1988
Bud FISHER
Albert MARTIN
Carl HANSEN
Chester LAWRENCE
Mike SHALLOW
Arthur HAMMOND
Frank DORRINGTON
Doug GRANT
Walt LEMESSURIER
Frank RYAN
Gerry BASHA
Joe ROUSSEAU

MALE RESIDENTS OF BAY OF ISLANDS
From Lovell's **Province of Newfoundland Directory**, 1871

Bay of Islands—A large bay on the western coast of the island, forming part of what is called the French Shore. The resources of this portion of the island are quite sufficient to support a much larger population than at present reside here. Indeed, both in the way of agriculture and the fisheries, no section of the country offers greater inducements to settlers than does this section. The herring fishery forms the staple industry of the people, and is prosecuted with great success. Herrings are taken during the months of January, February, March, May, June, October, and November. In the winter months nets are used, which are let through holes and channels cut in the ice, but in summer the herrings are mostly hauled in seines. The average quantity of herring annually taken may be stated in 30,000 barrels, most of which find a market in the adjacent provinces. On the banks of the Humber River, which flows into this bay, large quantities of fine lumbering which is however, as yet availed of but to a small extent, together with large beds of limestone, and marbles of beautiful varieties, and masses of gypsum almost exhaustless in quantity. The land around is level and is capable of easy cultivation, but is availed of merely as an accessory to the herring and cod fishery. The bay is studded with islands and the scenery remarkably fine. Distant from the north head of St. George's Bay 55 miles. Population 947.

Allen, John; fisherman
Antle, Barney; fisherman
Antell, George; fisherman
Bailey, John; fisherman
Balem, John; fisherman
Balem, Joseph; fisherman
Barrett, John; fisherman
Barry, John; planter
Bashvoan, John; fisherman
Batien, James; fisherman
Bego, William; fisherman
Bennett, Stephen; fisherman
Bennett, David; fisherman
Bennett, Simeon; fisherman
Black, William; fisherman
Black, Ambrose; fisherman
Blanchard, John; fisherman
Blanchard, Thomas; fisherman
Blandford, Joseph; fisherman
Bolan, Edward; fisherman
Bolan, Moses; fisherman
Brake, Abraham; fisherman
Brake, Benjamin; fisherman
Brake, Edward; fisherman
Brake, Edward; fisherman
Brake, Joseph; fisherman
Brake, William; fisherman
Brake, William; fisherman
Brine, Thomas; fisherman
Brooking, Augustus; fisherman
Brown, John; fisherman
Bute, John; planter

Callahan, Patrick; fisherman
Calm, John; fisherman
Clarke, Frederick; fisherman
Cleary, William; planter
Cheeld, Michael; fisherman
Chiles, Silomon; fisherman
Christopher, Patrick; fisherman
Christopher, William; fisherman
Cole, James; fisherman
Coles, James; fisherman
Condon, Aaron; fisherman
Connell, Moses; fisherman
Conway, Thomas; fisherman
Cook, John; fisherman
Dargan, Maurice; fisherman
Delaney, Alen; fisherman
Dennis, Burridge; fisherman
Dunn, Joseph; fisherman
Doodey, John; fisherman
Dorroty, Edward; fisherman
Drake, John; fisherman
Duggan, Patrick; fisherman
Durke, James; fisherman
Evans, John; fisherman
Farrell, Charles; fisherman
Foran, James; fisherman
French, Thomas; fisherman
Gallivan, Richard; fisherman
Garry, William; fisherman
George, Stephen; fisherman
Giles, Joseph; fisherman
Gosher, Michael; fisherman
Gregory, Thomas; fisherman
Gregory, William; planter
Green, John; planter
Haines, William; planter
Hallahan, Joseph; fisherman
Hallahan, Joseph; fisherman
Hand, James; fisherman
Hayes, John; fisherman

House, William; fisherman
Hurley, Joseph; fisherman
Jayers, John; fisherman
Jesso, Daniel; fisherman
Jesso, William; fisherman
Johnston, George; planter
Kelly, Michael; planter
Kennedy, Jeremiah; fisherman
Kenney, William; fisherman
Keough, James; fisherman
Keough, James; fisherman
Keough, James; fisherman
Keough, William; fisherman
Leader, William; planter
Lewis, John; fisherman
Ligo, Robert; planter
Londer, John; planter
Lovell, Thomas; fisherman
McCarthy, John; planter
McCarthy, William; planter
McCasell, James; fisherman
McCoysh, John; fisherman
McDonald, Alexander; fisherman
McDonald, Alexander; fisherman
McDonald, Alexander; fisherman
McGinnon, Robert; fisherman
Mareson, John; fisherman
Marshall, Joseph; fisherman
Marshall, William; fisherman
Martin, William; fisherman
Matthews, Samuel; fisherman
Mean, James; fisherman
Mearns, Edward; fisherman
Michall, James; fisherman
Moran, Edward; fisherman
Moren, Joseph; fisherman
Murphy, Michael; fisherman
Nocks, James; fisherman
Norget, William; fisherman
Pales, John; fisherman

Pane, George; fisherman
Paresay, Patrick; fisherman
Parritts, Nathaniel; planter
Parritts, William; planter
Park, James; fisherman
Park, Robert; fisherman
Park, Thomas; fisherman
Park, Thomas; fisherman
Parke, Samuel; fisherman
Parker, William; fisherman
Parry, John; fisherman
Parry, Thomas; fisherman
Parsons, Charles; planter
Parsons, John; fisherman
Parsons, Richard; fisherman
Penny, Samuel; fisherman
Power, Henry; fisherman
Power, Michael; planter
Prosper, James; fisherman
Quinning, James; fisherman
Quissen, Jean; fisherman
Rier, Reuben; fisherman
Robie, Jean; fisherman
Rose, Alexander; fisherman
Rose, William; planter
Rude, William; fisherman
Rule, Rev. U.Z.; Church of Eng.
Sears, Rev.; Roman Catholic
Silver, James; merchant
Sivier, Alexander; fisherman
Waller, John; fisherman
Weir, Richard; planter
Whelan, Thomas; fisherman
Wills, James; fisherman
Wills, James; fisherman
Wills, Richard; fisherman
Wills, Richard; fisherman
Wills, William; fisherman
Snook, John; fisherman
Sterling, James; fisherman

Stricklin, James; fisherman
Stricklin, William; fisherman
Sweet, George; fisherman
Thistle, Thomas; fisherman
Verge, George; fisherman

BIBLIOGRAPHY

Beaglehole, J. C. (1974). Life of Captain James Cook. London.

Begg, C., & Begg, N. (1970). James Cook and New Zealand. Wellington: A. R. Shearer, Government Printer.

Briere, J.F. (1990). Le Pêche Francaise en Amerique du Nord au XVIII² Siècle. St. Laurent, Quebec; Fides.

Brosnan, M. (1948). Pioneer History of St. Georges Diocese, Newfoundland. Toronto: Mission Press.

Brown, H. (1972). A Study of Curling 1860-1920. Unpublished manuscript. Queen Elizabeth II Library, Memorial University of Newfoundland.

Campbell, Captain R.N. The Lobster Fisheries on the West Coast. Report to Captain Hamond R.N. Oct. 10th 1888. Enclosure 8 in No. 126 appendix to Chapter XVII. Prowse, D.W. A History of Newfoundland, 1st edition.

Cartier, J. (1953). La Grosse Maladie. Montreal: XIX Congress Internationale de Physiologie.

Carpenter, K. J. (1986). History of Scurvy and Vitamin C. Cambridge: Cambridge UP.

Cell, G. T. (1982). Newfoundland Discovered. London. Hakluyt Society.

Chadwick, St. J. (1967). Newfoundland Island Into Province. Cambridge: Cambridge UP.

Churchill, W. S. (1956). History of the English Speaking Peoples. London: Cassell and Co. Ltd.

Cook, R. (1993) The Voyages of J. Cartier. Tor.: U. of Toronto P.

Crellin, J. K. (1994). Home Medicine: The Newfoundland Experience. Montreal: McGill-Queen's UP.

Cuppage, F. E. (1994). James Cook and His Conquest of Scurvy. Greenwood Press.

Descottes, Edouard. (1919). Contribution à l'Histoire de la Medicine sur les Bancs de Terre Neuve. Paris: Libraire le Francois.

Downer, D. (1997). Turbulent Tides. Portugal Cove, NF: E. S. Press.

Feild, E. (1850). Journal of a Voyage of Visitation in the Hawk Church Ship in the Year 1849. London: F. Clay, printer, Bread St. Hill.

Gobineau, A. de. (1861). Voyage à Terre Neuve. Paris: Hackette.

Hackett, J. B. (1992). Heartbeat. Author.

Harris, M. (1992). Rare ambition: The Crosbies of Newfoundland. Toronto: Penguin.

Harvey, Rev. M. (1873). Western Newfoundland: A New Home for Emigrants. Maritime Monthly, 1(2), 97-125.

Harvey, S. L. (1996). The Forgotten Bay. Author.

Hiller, J. K. (1971). A History of Newfoundland 1874-1901. Doctoral thesis, Cambridge University, U.K.

Horwood, H., & Butts, E. (1984). Pirates and Outlaws of Canada. Toronto: Doubleday.

Horwood, H. (1986). Corner Brook, a Social History of a Paper Town. St. John's, NF: Breakwater Books.

Hough, R. (1994). Captain James Cook. New York: W. W. Norton.

Innis, H. A. (1954). The Cod Fisheries. Toronto: U. of Toronto P.

Janes, P. (1970). House of Hate. Toronto: McLelland & Stewart.

Janzen, O. A. (1987).Une Grande Liason : French Settlement, Coast of South West Newfoundland 1714-66. Newfoundland Studies, 3(2).

Janzen, O. A. (1997, July 28). Western Star.

Janzen, O. A. (1993). "Showing the flag": Hugh Palliser in Western Newfoundland. Northern Mariner, 3(3).

Jelks, R. H. (1910). Life of James Curling. Oxford: Fox, Jones & Co.

Jukes, J. B. (1842). Excursions in and about Newfoundland During the Years 1839 and 1840. (Vol. II). London: John Murrary, Aldermarle Street.

Kelland, O. (1997). Strange and Curious. (2nd ed.). St. John's, NF: Creative Publishers.

Lind, J. A Treatise on the Scurvy. London: Original edition in Royal College of Physicians Library. London, U.K.

Loewus, F. A., & Loewus, M. W. (1987). Biosynthesis and metabolism of ascorbic acid in plants. CRC: Critical Reviews in Plant Synthesis, 1(5), 101.

Lysaght, A. M. (1971). Joseph Banks in Newfoundland and Labrador 1766. Faber & Faber.

Mannion, J. (1990). The Peopling of Newfoundland. Toronto: U. of Toronto P.

Martin, W. (1983). Once Upon a Mine. St. Anne de Bellevue, P.Q.: Harpell's Press Cooperative.

McDevitt, R., Dove, M. A., Dove, R. F., & Wright, I. S. (1944). Vitamin status of the population of the West Coast of Newfoundland. Annals of Internal Medicine, 20(1), 1-11.

McGrath, P. T. (1911). Newfoundland in 1911. London: Whitehead, Morris and Co. Ltd.

Muir, J. R. (1939). Life and Achievements of James Cook. London: Blackie.

Murphy, N. An Outline of the History of West Newfoundland. Unpublished manuscript, Grenfell College Library.

Neary, P. F. (1961). The French Shore Question 1865-1878. Master's thesis, Memorial University of Newfoundland.

Nicholson, G. W. L. (1964). The Fighting Newfoundlander. Newfoundland Government Publication.

Nishikimi, M., Noguchi, E., & Yagi, K. (1978). Occurrence in yeast of L-Galactonolactone oxidase. Archives of Biochemistry Biophysics, 191, 479.

Ogden, W. H. (1925). Ballads of Corner Brook. St. John's, NF: Dicks & Co. Ltd.

Penney, A. R. (1986). History of the Newfoundland Railway. Newfoundland Government Publication.

Prowse, D. W. (1986). A History of Newfoundland. Eyre and Spottiswoode, London.

Reader, W. J. (1981). The Bowater Story. Cambridge: Cambridge U. Press.

Rule, U. Z. (1927). Reminiscences of My Life. St. John's, NF: Dicks & Co. Ltd.

Smallwood, J. R. (1931). The New Newfoundland. New York: Macmillan.

Thompson, F. F. (1961). The French Shore Problem in Newfoundland. Toronto: U. of Toronto Press

Wharton,W.(1893).James Cook's Journal. London.

Whitehead, R. H. (1991). The Old Man Told Us. Halifax, N.S.: Nimbus Publishing Ltd.

Wix, E. (1836). Six Months of a Newfoundland Missionary's Journal (2nd ed.). London: Smith, Elder & Co.

Wonders, W. C. (1951). Settlement in Western Newfoundland. Ottawa: Dept. Of Mines and Technical Services, Programme of Research on Canadian Geography.

ADMIRALTY DOCUMENTS

-located at National Archives Library, Kew, U.K.

H.M.S. Grenville Log and Journal

7 parts

Signed, but not written, by James Cook ADM 52/1263

Minutes of Admiralty Board ADM 3/76 5/04/68

MICROFICHE
CIHM-ICMH Microfiche Series No 32371
The Humble Memorial of Thomas Bridge to the Commissioners of the Admiralty. Ottawa: National Library of Canada.
PROVINCIAL ARCHIVES OFFICE
-Colonial Building St. John's
FA 1879 13 Reference to Louis Esnault, French physician treating a diphtheria epidemic, Port au Choix.
FA 1877   May 10 Petition of Benjamin Brake to Governor Sir John Oliver.
FA 1881/34 Petition from West Coast, headed by Rev. Joseph Curling.
Historical Chronicle of the Gentleman's Magazine. Nov. 17, 1763.
-letter from an officer on board HMS Lark
-"To the Cocoa Tree" 33, 1763, p. 614.
-reference to one of the articles of impeachment against the Earl of Oxford

OTHER REFERENCES
The Encyclopedia of Newfoundland
Western Star
Humber Log
Daily News
Evening Telegraph
City of Corner Brook 25th Anniversary Commemoration Issue: 1981.
Memories: An oral history of the Outer Bay of Islands compiled by several contributors. Unpublished.
The Curling Station Occurence Diary 1916 to 1923. Royal Newfoundland Constabulary Museum, Corner Brook.
Bowater Oral History Project 1980.
Taped and typed copies in Grenfell College Library, Corner Book.
Contributors included Mona Collins; Phyllis O'Leary; Edith Dawe; Ches Randell; Ted LeDrew; Fred Ginn; Clayton Loughlin; Arch Lawrence; Ethel Rowsell; Arthur Lundrigan; W. J. Lundrigan; Raymond Hunt; George Tipple; George Basha; Bob Penney; H. O. House; Joe Chaulk; Frank Milley; Winifred Cook; Elizabeth Corbin; Eugene Clark; Frank Colbourne; Clayton Jones; Calvin Normore; Dr. T. T. Monaghan; Emily Watson; Frank Webber; M. S. Leggo; Willis Goulding; Andrew Barrett; Ralph Tulk.